KING JOHN

Anthem Perspectives in History

Titles in the **Anthem Perspectives in History** series combine a thematic overview with analyses of key areas, topics or personalities in history. The series is targeted at high-achieving pupils taking A-Level, International Baccalaureate and Advanced Placement examinations, first year undergraduates, and an intellectually curious audience.

Series Editors

Helen Pike – Director of Studies at the Royal Grammar School, Guildford, UK
Suzanne Mackenzie – Teacher of History at St Paul's School, London, UK

Other Titles in the Series

Britain in India, 1858–1947
Lionel Knight

Disraeli and the Art of Victorian Politics
Ian St John

Gladstone and the Logic of Victorian Politics
Ian St John

KING JOHN

AN UNDERRATED KING

Graham E. Seel

ANTHEM PRESS
LONDON · NEW YORK · DELHI

Anthem Press
An imprint of Wimbledon Publishing Company
www.anthempress.com

This edition first published in UK and USA 2012
by ANTHEM PRESS
75-76 Blackfriars Road, London SE1 8HA, UK
or PO Box 9779, London SW19 7ZG, UK
and
244 Madison Ave. #116, New York, NY 10016, USA

Cover image 'Portrait of King John of England' © Getty Images
Credit: Photos.com

British Library Cataloguing-in-Publication Data
A catalogue record for this book is available from the British Library.

Library of Congress Cataloging-in-Publication Data
King John : an underrated king / Graham E. Seel.
p. cm.
Includes bibliographical references and index.
ISBN 978-0-85728-518-8 (pbk. : alk. paper)
1. John, King of England, 1167–1216. 2. Great Britain–History–John, 1199–1216.
3. Great Britain–Kings and rulers–Biography. I. Title.
DA208.S44 2012
942.03'3092–dc23
[B]
2012015547

ISBN-13: 978 0 85728 518 8 (Pbk)
ISBN-10: 0 85728 518 1 (Pbk)

This title is also available as an eBook.

For my sixth form classes at the Grammar School at Leeds, 2006–2012

CONTENTS

ACKNOWLEDGEMENTS

A book of this nature is necessarily a collaborative effort. It has been a pleasure to work with Helen Pike, Janka Romero and Rob Reddick at Anthem Press. As the bibliography makes clear, this book rests upon the work of many scholars. I am especially grateful to the following, all of whom either responded to questions of technical detail or read the work and made valuable suggestions as to how it might be strengthened – or both: Matthew Strickland; Robert Bartlett; Emilia Jamroziak; David Kirby and Mike Dickenson. David Smith read the book at all its stages, sometimes several times, and his felicitous eye for detail has saved me from many errors of that nature. I owe a particular debt of gratitude to Mark Bailey for introducing me to this project and thereafter, despite his busy schedule, finding time consistently to provide me with support, advice and warm encouragement. He has made me feel like a true medievalist even though the truth may be otherwise. Finally, thanks are due to the sixth form historians at the Grammar School at Leeds for suffering patiently, though not uncritically, my enthusiasm for King John and who, by means of their questions and ideas, have given me much food-for-thought. It is as an attempt to redress the balance and give them something in return that I therefore happily dedicate this work to them.

As is usual with a work of this nature, I acknowledge that I am entirely responsible for any errors that might be found within.

Graham E. Seel, Snape, Lower Wensleydale
May 2012

LIST OF FIGURES

Every effort has been made to trace holders of copyright material. The author would be grateful to hear from any such holders who have not been contacted.

Chapter 1

OUTLINE OF THE REIGN

A) An Outline of the Reign of King John, 1199–1216

> Foul as it is, Hell itself is defouled by the foulness of John.
> —Matthew Paris, *Chronica Majora*, composed 1235–59[1]

Born in Oxford on Christmas Eve in 1167, John was the youngest son of Henry II and Eleanor of Aquitaine. With three significantly older brothers, John's prospects of becoming king were remote (see Figure 1, page 2). Indeed, for a time it seemed he would be denied any meaningful inheritance, thereby earning the epithet John Lackland. Nonetheless, chance events meant that gradually the path to the Crown became shorter and straighter: John's eldest brother Henry died in 1183, followed by Geoffrey in 1186; then, upon the demise of his remaining brother, Richard the Lionheart in 1199, John became king.

John's inheritance as king was substantial. His father and Richard had governed not only England, but also Normandy and, in addition – though sometimes in name more than in reality – territory covering in total roughly one third of the area of modern France, from Poitou in the north to Gascony in the south. Some historians have referred to this cross-Channel dominion as the Angevin 'empire' (see Figure 2, page 3; and page 27).[2]

John's reign had a number of phases, each shaped and defined in particular by foreign policy. The initial phase can be perceived as existing from 1199 to 1203, years in which John fought to secure his inheritance. Arthur, son of Geoffrey and his wife Constance of Brittany, contested John's claim to the Angevin 'empire'. Born in 1187 and designated by Richard in the Treaty of Messina in 1191 as heir to all the Angevin lands, 'Arthur was one of the many kings England almost but never had'.[3] Having gained the backing of the French king, Philip Augustus, Arthur put himself at the head of a rebellion directed against the claims of his uncle. He disappears from the pages of

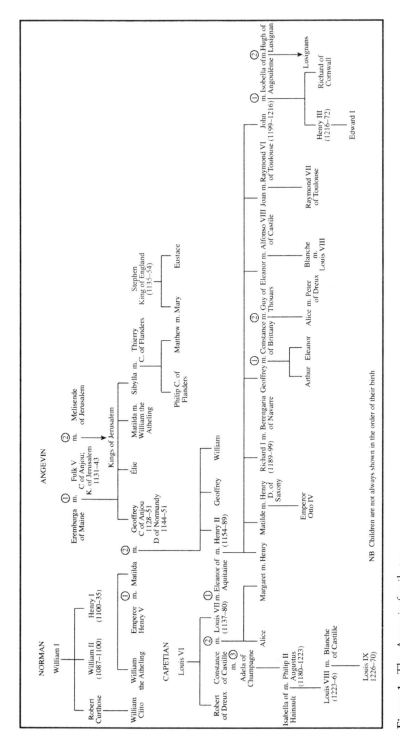

Figure 1. The Angevin family tree
(The dates in brackets refer to the dates of the reign. John's eldest brother, William (d. 1156) is not shown.)

Figure 2. Map of the Angevin 'empire' at the time of John's accession

history in 1203, some chroniclers asserting that John killed him with his bare hands. A second phase can be delineated from 1203 to 1204, the period in which Normandy and other substantial Angevin territories were lost. Unable successfully to relieve important castles, above all Chateau-Gaillard in Normandy, John returned to England. A third phase covers the years from 1205 to 1214, a period in which John, now residing in England, sought to regain the lost territories. Several proposed expeditions (1205, 1212 and 1213) were aborted, significantly because of baronial recalcitrance, though an expedition of 1206 enjoyed some success. The final military campaign set forth in 1214. This met with defeat at the Battle of Bouvines in July of that year. The failure of reconquest led directly to the final phase of John's reign, 1215 to 1216. These last years were characterized by civil war and French invasion. John's plans to regain the lost territories had necessitated the implementation of a fiscally harsh regime in England, the objection to which is articulated loud and clear in Magna Carta. Having lost control of London in 1215 to the rebel barons, John was obliged to accept their demands in the form of Magna Carta, to which royal assent was given in the field at Runnymede in 1215. However, the extreme nature of some of the terms of Magna Carta meant that John gained sufficient support to restart civil war, during which the rebel barons invited Prince Louis, the son of Philip Augustus, to rule in place of John. It was during this stage of the war that John died of natural causes in 1216. His nine-year-old son Henry, who ruled as Henry III until his death in 1272, succeeded him.

A key feature of John's reign was his often fraught relationship with the church. The origin of what was to become a bitter and protracted struggle lay in the question of who was to succeed Hubert Walter, archbishop of Canterbury. Walter's death in 1205 made available the most important church office in England, to which John was determined that his nominee, John de Gray, should accede instead of the candidate sponsored by the papacy, Stephen Langton. The stalemate that ensued became progressively acrimonious, with Pope Innocent III pronouncing an interdict in 1208 and then proceeding to excommunicate the king in the following year. John finally submitted to Innocent in 1213.

B) A Maligned King

By the early thirteenth century, literacy existed almost exclusively amongst members of the church, the clergy. Some of these men produced chronicles. The production of chronicles – a record or register of events under the years in which they happened – had by this time become part of the routine business of some religious houses. The authors of these chronicles recorded a mixture of local and national affairs, frequently including important documents in their accounts. John's relations with the clergy were antagonistic from an early stage in his reign, his demands for money creating a difficult relationship with the Cistercians (see Appendix, Documents 4 and 16). Tensions mounted when the papacy pronounced an interdict (1208) and excommunication (1209) (see Chapter 7). Thus, chronicle material is naturally predisposed to be antagonistic to John. It is where his alleged ill-repute is most loudly articulated.

There are few strictly contemporary chroniclers of John. Among the most important for the early years of John are Richard of Devizes, who ended his chronicle in 1192, and William of Newburgh who ceased writing and died in 1198. Roger of Howden and Ralph of Diceto end their chronicles in 1201 and 1202 respectively. These writers provide evidence that John's reputation was suffering even before he became king. William of Newburgh, for example, commenting upon John's treachery towards his brother whilst Richard was absent on crusade, concluded that John was 'Nature's Enemy'.[4] Richard of Devizes also presented John as intent upon seizing the throne from Richard I and attributed to him a fearsome temper (see Appendix, Documents 1, 3, 4, 10, 16, 18 and 24). Among the most significant authorities writing while John was king were Ralph of Coggeshall (d. 1218), Gervase of Canterbury (d. 1210) and Gerald of Wales (d. 1223). Until about 1203 Ralph evinces a reasonably balanced opinion of John, but thereafter accuses him, amongst other things, of indecisiveness, duplicity and cowardice – on seeing Louis' army in 1216, Ralph says that John 'fled in terror, weeping and lamenting'.[5] Gervase agrees with these judgements, ultimately awarding John the famous epithet of 'Softsword'.[6] Gerald of Wales believed that John was a 'tyrannous whelp, who issued from the most bloody tyrants and was the most tyrannous of them all'[7] (see Appendix, Document 3).

The relative dearth of strictly contemporary chronicles has encouraged historians to rely upon writers who recorded what they knew of John after his death. Of these, *The History of William the Marshal* is of particular note because it is penned by a secular authority, an unknown poet called John. This biography of William the Marshal, Earl of Pembroke and Striguil, (1146?–1219) emphasizes the chivalric values of its subject, 'England's greatest knight' and a key figure throughout the reign of John and beyond. Assuming the form of 19,214 lines in rhyming couplets, it was composed between 1225 and 1226 and provides the historian with incidental criticisms of King John. In her summary of *The History*, A. Gransden tells us that 'the author says that John was blinded by pride and already in 1202 had lost the support of the barons who were disgusted by his cruelty to prisoners. He regards him as faithless, unwarlike and unwise, and gives instances of his meanness, nasty temper and suspicious nature. He remarks that he acted on his own, without taking counsel, and kept the barons at a distance.'[8] In contrast to the author of *The History*, the Barnwell chronicler, perhaps writing shortly after the reign, has provided by far the most fair and balanced account of John. Although ultimately judging John as 'a robber of his people', the Barnwell chronicler also believed that John was 'indeed a great prince, but rather an unhappy one, and, like Marius, experienced both good and bad fortune'.[9] However, the measured assessment of the Barnwell chronicler has been out-gunned by the voluminous chronicle material produced by monks at St Albans Abbey, notably by Roger of Wendover and Matthew Paris.

Some ten years after John's death in 1216, Wendover began his account of the reign. Across the pages of Wendover's main work, *Flowers of History*, strides Bad King John – the king who, for example, ordered the crushing to death of Archdeacon Geoffrey under a cope of lead (see Appendix, Document 13); who threatened to slit the noses and to pluck out the eyes of papal emissaries (see Appendix, Document 10); who lost Normandy because he was enjoying the pleasures of his teenage wife (see Appendix, Document 8). In short, here is John as cowardly, cruel, lecherous, tyrannical, duplicitous and irreligious. When Wendover died in 1235, Paris succeeded him in his role as historiographer, not only continuing the chronicle from 1235 but also reworking Wendover's account. Frequently writing with a style and flourish that had eluded Wendover, including readily inserting speeches into the mouths of historical figures who had hitherto remained silent, 'the portrait of King John that emerges is…even further removed from reality than that in Wendover, but it is eminently more readable'.[10] Despite enjoying something of a rehabilitation in the sixteenth century, when Tudor historians sought to portray John's defiance of the papacy as a sort of dry run for Henry VIII, the improved royal reputation proved short lived. Too vivid to forget, it is the John as portrayed by Wendover and Paris that has entered national consciousness.

For historians writing in the nineteenth century, even if some doubts about the accuracy of Wendover and Paris remained, they were brushed aside. After all, it remained the case that many of those who authored a chronicle were likely to have been well informed about events of national importance. For example, Gerald of Wales accompanied John on his expedition to Ireland in 1185; Roger of Wendover and Matthew Paris were monks in the St Albans Abbey and therefore, residing on a key artery into London, their abbot was likely to have hosted the great and the good from whom Wendover and Paris will have learned much. Scholars working in the nineteenth century, alongside their ongoing reliance upon a revived and reworked Wendover and Paris, articulated views on John that seem to have been conditioned by the suffocating morality espoused by the Victorians. Thus, for the great historian of the day, William Stubbs, John had no redeeming features whatsoever: the king 'was a mean reproduction of all the vices and of the few pettinesses of his family…[a king for whom] we have no word of pity as we have had none of sympathy' (see Appendix, Document 36).[11] In a book first published in 1874 and which went on to become a long-term best seller, finding itself carried to the loneliest places of the Empire, J. R. Green concluded that 'John was the worst outcome of the Angevins' (see Appendix, Document 37).[12]

This nineteenth-century representation of John, standing firmly on the shoulders of the chroniclers, continued to manifest itself in the twentieth century. Kate Norgate, in her biography of John published in 1902, referred to the king's 'almost superhuman wickedness'; and Sir James Ramsey, writing in 1903, considered John 'a selfish cruel tyrant of the worst type'.[13] In his book called *The Plantagenets* published in 1948, John Harvey described thus the tomb effigy of John in Worcester Cathedral: 'The face has a sly wolfish cast, with slanting eyes faintly amused at the righteousness of better men, and a sensual mouth slightly drawn into the doglike grin distinctive of the cynic born.'[14]

The image of King John as an evil tyrant has been perpetuated in twentieth-century popular culture also, such as Marriott Edgar's rhyme *Magna Carta* and A. A. Milne's poem *King John's Christmas*, in which nearly every verse begins with the refrain 'King John was not a good man.' The 1968 film *The Lion in Winter*, starring Peter O'Toole as Henry II and Katherine Hepburn as Eleanor of Aquitaine, won three Oscars. In the words of one reviewer, it portrays John as 'a rumpled, drooling, inane man-child impossibly spoiled as the King's favorite, played to pathetic amusement by a terrific Nigel Terry'.[15] Meanwhile, scores of Robin Hood films produced over the course of the past one hundred years have frequently presented John either as the principal villain or an effeminate coward, the latter tendency assuming an extreme form in Disney's 1973 animated film in which the king is portrayed as a thumb-sucking lion. In the 1990s Channel 4 made a series of documentaries called *The Most Evil Men in History* in which John took his place alongside the likes of Attila the Hun, Vlad the Impaler and Adolf Hitler. John found himself once again rubbing shoulders with history's most evil men and women in Simon Sebag Montefiore's book entitled *Monsters*, produced in 2008.[16] In June 2010 the *BBC History Magazine* carried on its front cover the headline 'Bad King John – how he saved England from a French invasion…by dying'.[17]

The vilification of John thus not only has deep roots but also has grown vigorously. Nonetheless, the systematic and extensive maligning of John has induced a reaction, encouraging representations of John as able but flawed.

For instance, C. Warren Hollister, echoing the Barnwell chronicler, concluded his research by proclaiming that 'despite a certain amount of rehabilitation on the part of recent historians, John remains a curiously twisted and enigmatic figure, a man who possessed great talents in certain areas but was afflicted with fatal shortcomings in others'.[18] W. L. Warren, in his biography first published in 1961, argued that John 'had the mental abilities of a great king but the inclinations of a petty tyrant'.[19] John's most recent biographer, R. V. Turner, concluded that the king 'appears not as a monster of superhuman evil, but merely as a twisted and complex personality, yet a man with ability and potential for greatness whose own flaws prevented him from living up to the reputations of his brother, Richard I, or his rival, Philip Augustus'.[20]

These more positive interpretations of John have been obtained in three main ways. First, those researching into John have applied a more critical approach to the contemporary and near-contemporary source material and thereby, in effect, catching up with the vicious representations of John that 'have gone echoing down the long corridors of History'.[21] Of course, historians have always been cognizant of the fact that John's antagonistic relationship with the church resulted in prejudiced comment in chronicle sources, but it would not be going too far to say that some recent work has been newly critical. V. H. Galbraith spearheaded this approach in an important lecture given in 1944. He told his listeners that 'there can be little doubt that the picture [Wendover] gives us of John is already something of a legend [i.e. unreal]. For if we look closely – and I don't think historians have – we shall find that the picture he gives us is a very savage one, so savage as to be suspect.' In the same lecture Galbraith also observed that whereas 'Wendover gives us an impossible shadow, Paris converts it into a living portrait – though the portrait is not one of John…I conclude that Paris' additions to Wendover for this reign are not merely worthless, but very misleading.'[22] Similarly, to those making use of *The History of William the Marshal*, D. Crouch reminds us that 'we must treat it carefully. Apart from its obvious bias towards its subject [who had a number of protracted arguments with John], it is written in a literary tradition that must have distorted its truth.'[23] Facilitating this more critical approach to the sources, historians have also become better aware of the fact that the start of John's reign appears to be the moment from which the secretariat of government – Chancery – begins to keep a systematic record of its business, thus providing an administrative footprint of John's governance (see Chapter 8). This so-called record evidence suggests that John was a dedicated and energetic ruler and, since these documents were attested by John, they have allowed historians to create an itinerary showing the king's movements throughout his reign (see Appendix, Document 35). From this material it is 'almost impossible to doubt that the king was actually present at the place where he expressly states himself to have been on a particular day', throwing into question the veracity of some chronicle material which asserts that John was elsewhere (see Chapter 8).[24] This is the broad context in which V. H. Galbraith judges the whole of Wendover's *Flowers of History* to be 'full of errors and inaccuracies' and in which Warren laments that 'it is a pity that [Wendover's] blooms turn out to be artificial'.[25] Second, some historians – controversially – have tried to rehabilitate John by viewing his actions against the backcloth of their own time. Thus, R. V. Turner notes that when John is viewed from the perspective of the twentieth century, 'compared to Hitler, Stalin or Pol Pot, he seems quite tame'.[26] Similarly, J. T. Appelby cautions that 'we in these present days have seen such depths of human depravity that we cannot consider [John] as the unrelieved villain that he once appeared to be. It is faint praise to say that he was not so bad as he might have been, yet when we consider what men with absolute power have done in later days we are forced almost to admire John's restraint.'[27] Such methodology is perhaps questionable and can, of course, produce the opposite outcome – after all, as seen in the writing of Stubbs, John's reputation does not benefit when measured against nineteenth century morality. Arguably, however, a robust rehabilitation is achieved when John's actions are evaluated against the context and expectations of his own day (for instance, see Chapters 4 and 6 for a discussion of the morality of John's second marriage and his habit of taking hostages; and see Chapter 9 for an assessment of how John's reputation has suffered because of the inappropriate totemic status achieved by Magna Carta of 1215). More broadly still, John's reputation benefits from an appreciation of the fact that his reign coincided with what most historians agree were two peculiarly resilient and clever adversaries in the form of Philip Augustus and Innocent III, and from a sense amongst some historians that popular estimates of the reign of Richard I are overblown. Third, judgements about John's achievement become more positive once the nature of his inheritance has been evaluated. Some economic historians, for example, have pointed out that John's reign coincided with 'an especially rapid, substantial and, as far as we can tell, fairly general rise in prices', a development which justified many of John's money-raising expedients described in Chapter 8.[28] Other historians have suggested that there were structural forces at work which meant that the Angevin 'empire' – the cross-Channel territories inherited by John in 1199 shown in Figure 2 – was on the point of collapse in 1199 (see Chapter 3). Echoing the opinion of the Barnwell chronicler, who regarded the loss of Normandy as an inevitable necessity, W. L. Warren, asserts that 'It is difficult to see how John could have averted disaster.'[29]

The purpose of this book is to further develop this sympathetic treatment of John. Most of the chapters are composed of a narrative section, in which the theme of that chapter is outlined, followed by an interpretative, analytical account that is frequently more positive towards John than existing interpretations. Where appropriate there is a sharply critical approach to the chronicle material. Space is also given to an assessment of John's reign as suggested by the record evidence and to an evaluation of John's actions in the context of the medieval period, rather than against latter-day standards. Document material is included within the body of the book but more substantive extracts are included in the Appendix. Ultimately, the king that emerges is associated more with greatness and less with tyranny; and the palpable absurdity of the famous remark by Matthew Paris with which this chapter opened is clearly demonstrated.

Chapter 2

JOHN IN THE SHADOWS, 1167–1199

Timeline

1167	John was born, last of eight children of Henry II and Eleanor of Aquitaine
1168–c.1173	John resident at the abbey of Fontevrault
1171–1172	Henry II in Ireland
1173–1174	Rebellion of Henry the Young King, Richard and Geoffrey
c.1173–1182	John resident in household of Henry the Young King
1177	John designated as king of Ireland
1183	Death of Henry the Young King
1183–1185	John resident in household of Ranulph de Glanville, justiciar of Henry II
1185	John given the title of lord of Ireland; sent to Ireland by Henry II
1186	Death of Geoffrey
1189	Death of Henry II; accession of Richard; John marries Isabella of Gloucester
1189–1193	Richard away from his inheritance: on crusade 1189–92; 1192–3 held as a prisoner in Germany
1191	Philip returns from crusade
1193	January to June: John raises rebellion in England, supported by Philip
1193–1194	John in Normandy. In alliance with Philip, John and the French king invade Normandy intent upon driving out Richard's supporters
1194	Richard returns to England; John returns to the allegiance of Richard
1195–1199	John fights in France for the interests of Richard
1199	Death of Richard

A) Narrative: Prince John, 1167–1199

John was born in Oxford on Christmas Eve in 1167, the youngest, and last, of eight children from the marriage of Henry II and Eleanor of Aquitaine. The eldest of his siblings, William, died in 1156, leaving John with three elder brothers (Henry the Young King, 1155–1183; Richard, 1157–1199; and Geoffrey, 1158–1186) and three sisters (Matilda, 1156–1189; Eleanor, 1161–1214; and Joan, 1165–1199) (see the Angevin family tree on page 2).

Very little is known about John's early years, the chroniclers understandably expressing scant interest in a royal son unlikely to succeed to the throne. At the age of one he was entrusted to the abbey of Fontevrault near Chinon in Anjou, where he remained until he was six years old.[1] From 1173 until 1182 John seems to have spent time in the household of his eldest brother, Henry the Young King, where he no doubt learned the skills of hunting and the chase, activities that John continued to prosecute with relish as an adult. Thereafter, until 1185, John was a member of the household of Ranulph de Glanville, Henry II's remarkable justiciar – Richard of Devizes called him the 'eye of the kingdom and the king' – who seems to have been charged with the education of John and was probably responsible for having developed in the young man a growing interest in administration.

In terms of his cleverness and acuity, John was very much akin to his father, in whose court one chronicler recorded that 'there is school every day, constant conversation of the best scholars and discussion of questions'.[2] The young John acquired a taste for books and later, as king, travelled with a library composed of French and Latin works. During these years John met his parents infrequently. He probably met his father probably only on great feast days and his mother even less often, especially after her imprisonment 1174–89 by her husband, who charged her with involvement in sponsoring the rebellion of Henry the Young King (see below).[3]

Before the early 1170s Henry II let it be known that he intended that the Angevin 'empire' should be partitioned, most certainly upon his death, and if his sons had demonstrated capacity to govern in the meantime, then before that eventuality. Thus, according to the terms of the Treaty of Montmirail in 1169, Henry II stipulated that when he died his eldest son, Henry, was to govern Normandy and Greater Anjou (see page 32) in addition to England. Richard was proclaimed heir to the Duchy of Aquitaine and Geoffrey, through marriage to Constance of Brittany, heir to that lordship.[4] Then in 1170, shaken by a serious illness and perhaps fearful that upon his death his succession scheme would be swept aside by baronial interests, Henry II sought to make his plans for succession more robust. Thus, in 1170, following French example, he arranged for his eldest son to be crowned king of England during his own lifetime (henceforth he was known as Henry the Young King) and in the first part of 1172 Richard was formally installed as Duke of Aquitaine. In this scheme, there was no place for John, whom Henry II referred to as John 'Lackland'.[5]

In the meantime, Henry II remained intent upon territorial expansion and now sought control of the passes through the western Alps. For this reason in 1172 John was betrothed to Alice, eldest daughter and heir of Count Humbert of Maurienne, in whose lands the passes lay. The arrangement was finalized on the basis that Henry bestow upon John the castle of Chinon in Touraine, as well as the castles at Loudon and Mirebeau, each of which were in Poitou. The granting of these important castles to John infuriated Henry the Young King. Approaching his eighteenth birthday and frustrated at having as yet no more than a title, the Young King now demanded that his father hand over any one of his inheritances. When Henry II refused, the Young King, supported by his mother, brothers Richard and Geoffrey, and backed by their overlord, the king of France, exploded in rebellion.

The Great Rebellion of 1173–4 was fought out on both sides of the Channel and, with the involvement of the French King Louis VII, was of such severity that it seriously threatened the authority of Henry II. Perhaps partly as an act of vengeance and partly in order to try and stabilize the succession, Henry II now became determined to provide an inheritance for his youngest son. Thus, in 1174 a scheme was devised whereby John was to obtain an annual income of £1,000 from royal territories in England, 1,000 livres from each of Normandy and Anjou, and the castle and county of Nottingham as well as castles in Normandy, Anjou, Touraine and Maine. Then, in 1175, Henry added to this inheritance by reserving for John the Earldom of Cornwall, it having reverted to the Crown upon the death of Reginald de Dunstanville, Earl of Cornwall. In 1176, John's prospects improved further when Earl William of Gloucester, having fallen out of favour with Henry in a dispute over Bristol, bought his peace by making John heir to all his lands in return for John marrying his youngest daughter, Isabella. Finally, in 1177 Henry designated John as king of Ireland and asked the pope to send a crown.

In defeat, Henry the Young King's resentment became yet more pronounced. The settlement he was forced to accept in 1174 'looks almost as if planned purposely to give John a foothold in every part of his eldest brother's future dominions – a strip, so to say, in every one of young Henry's fields'.[6] Renewed rebellion was only prevented by the timely death of Henry the Young King in 1183. We can only speculate as to the impact upon John of a realization that his father's schemes to include him in the succession so excited the jealousies of his brothers that the whole Angevin inheritance was placed in jeopardy.

Upon the death of the Young King, Henry moved again to reorganize the succession. He resolved to bestow upon Richard, his eldest surviving son, England, Normandy and Greater Anjou, in return for which he insisted that Richard surrender Aquitaine to John. However, Richard, having fought for eight years to impose his authority upon Aquitaine, would not surrender it for the uncertain authority proposed by Henry's scheme. Therefore, John was charged by his father to lead an army into Richard's territories. Aged only fifteen, John was no match for Richard, even having joined forces with their brother Geoffrey of Brittany. Thus, in late 1184 Henry called all three sons to a meeting at Windsor and established some sort of reconciliation, in which Richard remained as Duke of Aquitaine. Thus thwarted, in 1185 the king knighted John and resolved to send him off to Ireland with a force of three hundred knights. Since the current pope did not approve of the title of King of Ireland, John bore instead the title of Lord of Ireland.

A century after the Battle of Hastings, Ireland remained as yet untouched by the Normans. Unlike Scotland it had not achieved political unity under a single king and was populated by a bewildering array of tribes and petty kings, sometimes referred to by historians as the native Irish. The tribal divisions amongst the native Irish meant that Ireland was vulnerable to conquest and for this reason it had caught the eye of Anglo-Norman nobles, especially those of the southern Welsh Marches, such as Hugh de Lacy the elder and Richard de Clare, Earl of Striguil and Pembroke, commonly known as 'Strongbow'. Within a short period of time huge areas of Ireland had been conquered by these Anglo-Norman adventurers, and fearing the establishment of a rival Norman state, Henry II resolved to impose his authority in person. In 1171 he became the first king of England to set foot in Ireland.

It seems that most of the native Irish kings quickly submitted to Henry, probably because they saw him as their protector against the Anglo-Normans, whose ambitions the king curbed. However, with his campaign ongoing, Henry was obliged to leave Ireland in May 1172 in order to deal in England with fallout from the murder of Becket, archbishop of Canterbury, in 1170. In the king's absence, Anglo-Norman expansion into Ireland resumed. In particular, it seems that Hugh de Lacy, to whom Henry II had entrusted the task of keeping order, was in the process of weaving a 'web of influence designed to establish himself as the predominant power in Ireland'.[7] This necessarily posed a threat to the reassertion of royal authority. This is the context in which John was sent to Ireland in 1185, charged with completing the task that his father had begun.

The usual interpretation of John in Ireland in 1185 is entirely damning. When John arrived in Waterford on 25 April 1185, Gerald of Wales, who accompanied the expedition, relates that 'the Irish of those parts…greeted him as their lord and received him with the kiss of peace'.[8] In an infamous scene, John and his companions then pulled the beards of the Irish, to which, in consequence, the kings and princes of Munster and Connaught not only refused to attend John's court, but also agreed among themselves to oppose him by force. We are then informed that the eighteen-year-old John and his young companions, having spent in 'riotous living' the monies intended for the pay of the soldiers, were unable to put up effective resistance.[9] 'John lost most of his army in numerous conflicts with the Irish', reported another contemporary chronicler.[10] K. Norgate, writing in 1902, concluded that all this amounted to 'criminal folly'.[11] S. Duffy regards the 1185 campaign as 'an unmitigated disaster'.[12] 'Men could point out', laments Warren, 'that in an age when Richard had cowed and crushed the proud barons of southern France, John had shown himself nothing more than a feckless waster.'[13] After recuperating in England, John was awaiting a favourable wind to enable his return to Ireland when, in August 1186, news of the death of Geoffrey caused Henry to recall him.

Richard, meanwhile, about to embark on the Third Crusade (1189–1192) and still with no heir of his own, felt threatened by the new circumstances of 1186. When he failed to secure a clear pledge from his father that John would not supplant his place in the succession, Richard colluded in November 1188 with the French King, Philip Augustus. Hostilities ensued, in which John initially fought alongside his father against his brother and Philip. Unhappily, the sources do not allow us to estimate the military worth of John in this war. Increasingly ill and outmaneuvered, Henry finally submitted on 4 July 1189. Calling for the names of those who had transferred their allegiance to Philip to be read out, Henry was informed that 'the first that is written down here is your Lord John, your son'.[14] Gerald of Wales records that, upon hearing this, Henry 'sank back on his bed and, turning his face to the wall and groaning aloud, cried, "Now let all things go as they will, I care no longer for myself or for anything else in the world."' Two days later Henry died, prompting Gerald of Wales to conclude that 'nothing hastened [Henry's] death more than the sudden and unexpected news [about John's change of sides]'.[15]

Richard was crowned on 3 September 1189 and, impatient to set off on crusade, arranged his affairs so as to facilitate his adventure.[16] The new king allowed a regency government to develop in England so that William Longchamp became simultaneously Lord Chancellor and Chief Justiciar, and also, from 5 June 1190, papal legate. Richard endowed John with what he believed was sufficient largesse to blunt the ambitions of his younger brother. Thus, John was created Count of Mortain (a lordship in Normandy) and was also confirmed as Lord of Ireland. He received approval of his acquisition of the Lordship of Gloucester by way of his marriage on 29 August 1189 to

Isabella, to whom he had been betrothed since 1176. John also gained castles at Peverel, Lancaster, Marlborough, Luggershall and Nottingham. He was granted the profits from Sherwood Forest and that of Andover in Wiltshire. Perhaps most remarkably, he was assigned the entire royal revenues of six counties: Cornwall; Devon; Somerset; Dorset; Derby and Nottinghamshire, 'and ruled them at his will, the Crown claiming from him no account for them whatever'.[17] A glance at the map shows that John had thus been granted two great blocs of territory, each of which had an integrity that bestowed upon him significant territorial and political power. Belatedly, Richard seemed to realize that he had created an arrangement which would induce instability, particularly during his absence on crusade. Thus, Richard insisted that the initial agreement was for John to remain out of England for three years – after which time, no doubt, the king expected to be back from the crusade. However, as a consequence of Queen Eleanor's bidding, John returned to England before the end of 1190.

Rather than appeasing the ambitions of John, the settlement shaped by his brother provided John with the possibility of revolt. Indeed, circumstances now developed in a way which made such an eventuality probable. As a fiercely effective administrator, Longchamp was bound to provoke resentment, but disaffection grew yet more extensive and substantial because of Longchamp's lowborn Norman status, pluralism and ostentatious nepotism.[18] 'The laity', said William of Newburgh, 'found him more than king, the clergy more than pope, and both an intolerable tyrant'; others believed him to be as 'Caesar and more than Caesar'.[19] It was only natural that John should become the focal point of resistance to Longchamp, and many of the justiciar's detractors made their way to John's court at Marlborough.

At the same time, John's ambitions for the succession must have been sharpened by the fact that there was every probability that Richard would not return from the crusade – indeed, the emperor Frederick Barbarossa lost his life on the very same expedition – and moreover, because Richard had yet to produce an heir.[20] Although Richard had declared his nephew, Arthur, son of Geoffrey of Brittany, as his successor according to the terms of the Treaty of Messina in 1191, the young Arthur was only four years old. John was in his mid-twenties. Above all, since custom and the law had not yet pronounced definitively between rival claims made by a brother and nephew of a deceased king, John perhaps calculated that possession amounted to nine-tenths of the law (see pages 39–40 for a fuller discussion of issues relating to the succession).

This was the background against which John took advantage of the growing resentment against Longchamp, a resentment so great that it induced civil war. When the sheriff of Lincolnshire renounced Longchamp's authority and paid homage to John as heir presumptive, Longchamp laid siege to Lincoln. John took advantage of Longchamp's distraction by seizing the castles of Tickhill and Nottingham. Then, when John's half brother, Geoffrey, entered the country (September 1191) having been confirmed in his election as archbishop of York, and was duly mistreated by supporters of Longchamp, John and his adherents marched on London.[21] Though they were successful in forcing the resignation of Longchamp, they were obliged to accept Walter de Coutances, archbishop of Rouen, as Chief Justiciar – the man sent to England to restore order by Richard in the autumn of 1191.[22]

Two developments now occurred which prevented de Coutances from establishing a lasting peace: Philip Augustus returned from the crusade just before Christmas in 1191; and news broke that Richard, having been captured as he returned from the same crusade, was being held prisoner by the Emperor Henry VI, who was demanding a huge ransom of 150,000 silver marks for his release. The first of these meant that the French king was once again in a position to be able to divide and rule the Angevins, as he had done in the past, and the second was that John now acted as though his brother were dead. Thus, John travelled to Paris and by the end of January 1193 had made an arrangement with Philip whereby, in return for ceding the Vexin in Normandy, setting aside his own wife and marrying Philip's sister, Alice, and paying homage to the French king, Philip would deprive Richard of his continental possessions. John returned to England and set about overturning the government of de Coutances, loyal to Richard, by attempting to mobilize the Scots and Welsh against his brother. However, perhaps because few could steel themselves to rebel against a king who had taken the cross (and thereby acquired the persona of a crusader), and perhaps also because the removal of Longchamp had taken away resentments from which he and his supporters benefitted, John could raise only a troop of Welsh. Moreover, behind the scenes, Eleanor worked tirelessly to maintain the resolve of the de Coutances government. Nonetheless, governance was seriously disturbed and with a French fleet hovering in the Channel the prospect of renewed civil war remained very real. Then, upon hearing from Philip in July 1193 that Richard was to obtain his freedom – 'Look to yourself for the Devil is loosed' wrote Philip – John immediately fled to France.[23]

In March 1194 Richard returned to England and ordered John to appear before his Court within forty days. When the brothers eventually met – seemingly by chance, at Lisieux in Normandy in May – John prostrated himself before Richard: 'John, have no fear. You are a child, and you had bad men looking after you', said Richard[24] (see Appendix, Document 2). John in fact was twenty-seven years old and, if the author of *The History of William the Marshal* is to be believed, must have been deeply humiliated by being thus addressed. Richard stripped his brother of all his possessions and titles, except Lord of Ireland. John was, once again, Lackland.

For the next five years, 1194–9, John supported his brother loyally and demonstrated some military ability. For instance, when conducting the siege of Évreux he secured the castle within a day. John demonstrated strategic insight when he countered Philip's seizure of Nonancourt by taking Gamanches. He showed personal bravery when he led a party of mercenaries on a raid deep into French territory, capturing a number of prisoners including the warrior bishop, Philip of Dreux, cousin to Philip, and razing the castle of Milli. In fact, historians have generally failed to recognize the important role that John played in regaining most of the territories in Normandy lost to Philip during Richard's captivity. Consequently, John thus gradually found his condition restored: in 1195 he was reinstated as Count of Mortain and Earl of Gloucester, though the castles and six shires he had previously held were denied him. Nonetheless, by 1197 John had redeemed himself sufficiently to be recognized by Richard as his heir, albeit tacitly.

B) Interpretations

i) John in the Psychiatrist's Chair

We can only speculate as to the effect upon John of any realisation that, through the ambitions of his father, he was the cause of much of the internal strife afflicting his family. Nonetheless, 'insecurity about his future,' asserts R. V. Turner, 'rivalry with his brothers and awareness of their resentment over his father's schemes to find land for him must have influenced John's character. No youth growing up in such an atmosphere of suspicion and treachery could fail to absorb some poisons.'[25] Absence of evidence relating to the early years of John has encouraged some historians to offer a sustained speculative psychoanalysis of their subject, a sort of 'John in the psychiatrist's chair' approach to history. Thus, Turner further asserts that 'John's position as lastborn son with uncertain prospects for land or power must have contributed to a negative estimate of his own worth... Perhaps John's childhood insecurity contributed to his adult personality, his jealousy, insensitivity to slights, thirsts for revenge, and delight in humbling others.'[26] Speculation about John's experiences at the court of Henry the Young King has led to the suggestion that the atmosphere of jealousy, deceit and intrigue found there provides an explanation for the actions of the adult John, particularly what many see as his main trait: chronic untrustworthiness. Indeed, some have seen this tendency as so extreme that Charles Petit-Dutaillis declared, 'It is our opinion that John Lackland was subject to a mental disease well known

today and described by modern psychiatrists as the periodical psychosis…
All the symptoms we have enumerated are those of the periodic psychosis or
cyclothymia. Philip Augustus had a madman as his rival.'[27]

Psychohistory of this sort has not been accepted uncritically. Relying
overmuch upon speculation and assuming a consistency of response across
periods and personalities, it has been labelled as 'psycho-babble and pseudo-
history'.[28] There is also a sense that, having been exposed to such influences,
John simply must have been negatively affected. But this interpretation rests
upon applying early twenty-first century theory to a much earlier age whereas
in reality the two are of course very different times. John is by no means
the only monarch to have experienced what the modern world would regard
as a dysfunctional upbringing. Indeed, some of those who suffered the most
bizarre backgrounds – Elizabeth I; James VI and I (at least, after his revisionist
makeover) come to mind – emerged as the most accomplished rulers. Lastly,
politics, at least on occasion, demands dissimulation and John seems likely to
have learned this from the circumstances in which he grew up.

ii) A Prince Ill-Equipped to Govern?

As alluded to in the narrative section of this chapter it has become
commonplace to assert that John's actions even before he became king provide
evidence that he was ill-equipped to govern. In this respect historians have
pointed to three episodes in particular: the Irish campaign of 1185; John's
actions in 1189 (allegedly hastening the death of his father); and John's
attempts to usurp the authority of Richard whilst the latter was absent on
crusade. How far do these episodes actually support this interpretation?

a) The Irish Campaign, 1185

The most recent scholarship agrees with the older interpretation about
John's Irish campaign of 1185. John's visit, concludes S. Duffy, 'became in
the end a real embarrassment. For the rest of the Middle Ages, the bulk of the
Irish remained beyond the law, denied access to justice or participation in
government, and this policy began with John's lordship in 1185.'[29] Yet such
an interpretation ignores some important evidence and, so it seems, rests
upon a misunderstanding of what John was seeking to achieve in Ireland.
Thus, Warren points out that 'to complain of military "inactivity" is hardly
to the point if the main purpose of the enterprise were to establish law and
order', as it seems may have been the case; and, moreover, seems to have been
an area in which John achieved success.[30] As Warren says, 'when records
which illuminate the administration of Ireland become available from 1199

there are the clearest signs of a well established central and local government machinery, including the operation of the civil law procedures common in England, and it is difficult not to believe that the fundamental initiatives were taken in 1185'.[31] In any case, John was not indolent during his time in Ireland. He ordered castles to be built at Lismore and at two places on the Suir – Ardfinnan and Tibberaghny – suggesting strategic nous (Warren talks of the creation of the beginning of 'an arc of royal influence').[32] Moreover, it seems likely that he was hindered in his ambitions by Hugh de Lacy, Constable of Dublin and Lord of Meath, who persuaded the native Irish not to comply with John's expectations that they tender fealty and hostages. Probably at least twenty years senior to John, it is reasonable to speculate that Hugh de Lacy looked upon the young John as an upstart, and duly became emboldened to resist in the same way that the Earl of Newcastle resisted the strictures of Prince Rupert on the eve of the Battle of Marston Moor in 1644. Certainly, John himself blamed his failures in Ireland on the hostility and intrigues of Hugh de Lacy. The Irish annals record that John 'returned to his father complaining of Hugh de Lacy, who controlled Ireland for the King of England before his arrival, and did not allow the Irish kings to send him tribute or hostages'.[33] Both Roger of Howden and William of Newburgh claim that news of Hugh de Lacy's death in 1186 was welcomed by Henry II.[34] It is also worthy of note that it was not under John's personal leadership that his mercenaries had fought their losing fight with the Irish in Munster. In any case, John's was only the first of many well-equipped expeditions to Ireland to suffer defeat. Unable to deal with guerilla-style resistance, John did not 'crawl back home to his father'.[35] Rather, 'he retired in frustration' with the intention of fighting another day.[36]

There are also serious concerns about the veracity of Gerald of Wales' account, upon which critical interpretations of John rely. A writer of mixed Norman and Welsh ancestry, he had pronounced Celtic sympathies and prejudices and evidently resented John's intrusion of newcomers into Ireland in 1185. Married to this is the fact that he was critical of Henry II for not going on crusade and, on a personal level, grew to resent him for refusing to confirm his election to the see of St David's. Thus, in his work *De principis instructione* [*Concerning the Instruction of Princes*] 'it was the Angevin kings who were the targets of Gerald's vitriol, as he created an image of damned and violent rulers whose replacement by the serene Capetians of France would be a blessing for England'.[37] Interestingly, Wendover – never usually one to miss an opportunity to be critical of John – makes no mention in his chronicle to events in Ireland in 1185. All in all then, although Gerald of Wales accompanied John on the Irish expedition, there are serious reasons for doubting his account of what occurred.

b) 1189–1194: 'Nature's Enemy'?

John's detractors insist that the years 1189–1194 reveal in stark relief an increasingly disloyal brother whose unfettered ambition prevented the delivery of good governance. According to this school of thought, John's duplicity and aspiration encouraged him to betray his father (and thereby send him to an early grave), to lead England to the brink of civil war (in late 1191 and again in the spring of 1193) and to collude with the king of France whilst his brother rotted in jail. This was the context in which William of Newburgh judged John to be of such inconstancy that he amounted to 'Nature's Enemy'.[38] William the Breton (1165c.–1225c.) asserts that John deliberately hid the fact that he had been reconciled to his brother and thus the French troops at Évreux in 1194 were caught off guard so completely that John was able to perpetrate a massacre as they sat down at a banquet.[39] For all these reasons Warren concluded that John thus 'stood in 1194 as a traitor and a fool. Such a reputation long clung to him, and in some quarters was perhaps never entirely displaced.'[40]

There are reasons for questioning the validity of the judgement that pronounces John as a turncoat who betrayed his father at his moment of greatest need, not least because William the Breton's opinion must be treated carefully. Although he had personal knowledge of many of the facts he narrates, his overriding purpose was to write of Philip Augustus in laudatory terms. More broadly, historians have not been able to discern categorically whether Henry did intend to disinherit Richard in favour of John, but all are agreed that the military efforts of Henry II in the last two years of his reign met with little success against Richard and Philip. Against this background, John's action in 1189 appears less that of a turncoat and more that of a trimmer moving to back the winner. In this sense perhaps we can see John as an individual attuned to the realpolitik of the time and the shifting sands of the moment.

Moreover, a careful examination of Richard's management of English affairs at the start of his reign goes some way in explaining the actions of John at this time. J. T. Appleby believes that in four months in 1189 Richard 'did almost everything possible to break up the firm and orderly government that his father had imposed on the country'.[41] In support of this judgement, D. A. Carpenter concludes simply that the arrangements made by Richard in 1189 were 'shambolic'.[42] Richard's determination to raise money for the crusade through venality of office on a grand scale served to thwart good governance. Howden describes how 'everything was put up for sale: offices, lordships, earldoms, sheriffdoms, castles, towns, lands – the lot'.[43] Although Gillingham asserts that 'Richard may well have been indulging in some sharp practice but it was not abandoning royal rights', it is difficult to avoid the conclusion that Richard's actions undoubtedly introduced grit into the system.[44]

By any standards Richard was a man in a rush. Impatient to be away on crusade, he bestowed upon his brother in 1189 a settlement so generous that it empowered and emboldened John. Writing at the time, William of Newburgh lamented that Richard's scheme led to many evils since it encouraged John's ambition and led him into treachery.[45] Although the fact that John was denied control of the most important castles in his counties suggests at least an attempt to restrain his ambition, it is hardly indicative of a well thought-out scheme. In defence of Richard's settlement, Gillingham states that 'Richard probably had little choice in 1189'.[46] Yet, one alternative would have been to grant John much more; another, much less. Either of these may well have resulted in more stable government, particularly if Richard's choice of chancellor had not been the authoritarian Longchamp.

John's reputation for disloyalty traditionally reaches its nadir when he is seen to be colluding with Philip during Richard's imprisonment. However, we should not forget that prior to his accession, Richard had frequently allied with Philip against Henry II in order to achieve his own ambitions. In any case, it was by no means clear when – if ever – Richard would be released. Precedent suggested ongoing incarceration. For instance, had Henry I not kept his elder brother, Robert Curthose, in prison (1106–34) until his death? With the succession as yet ill-defined, perhaps there is something to be said for John making what was in effect a pre-emptive strike against any claim that might have been asserted by Arthur and his adherents.

Finally, historians should also be alert to the fact that John's reputation is further coloured by estimations of the reign of Richard I. Already known as Coeur de Lion by his contemporaries, Richard remained as Lionheart for the next four centuries. The popular perception of Richard for the Victorians was as a dramatically successful and flamboyant king, an image perpetuated in particular by the writing of Walter Scott (*Ivanhoe*, 1819 and *The Talisman*, 1825) and made real by the remarkable statue of Richard astride his horse with sword raised in triumph, financed by public subscription and placed outside the Houses of Parliament in 1860. A best-selling Victorian author believed him to be 'at heart a statesman, cool and patient in the execution of his plans as he was bold in their conception'.[47] Against this assessment of his brother, John's achievements appear necessarily diminished. Equally, it follows that when Richard's reputation came to be questioned – he has been accused of absentee kingship; of bleeding England dry; of maintaining the Angevin 'empire' by force alone; of massacring Muslims at the siege of Acre – John's reign consequently appears generally more positive.

Chapter 3

AN 'IMPERIAL' INHERITANCE?

Timeline

1066	Battle of Hastings; formation of Anglo-Norman regnum
1087	Death of William the Conqueror; Robert Curthose becomes Duke of Normandy, William Rufus becomes king of England
1100	Death of William Rufus; accession of Henry I
1106	Henry I defeats his eldest brother, Robert Curthose, at the Battle of Tinchebrai; henceforth Henry rules as king/duke
1109	Formation of Greater Anjou through a combination of Anjou, Maine and Touraine
1120	Death of William, son and heir of Henry I
1128	Matilda, daughter of Henry I, marries Geoffrey of Anjou
1133	Birth of Henry of Anjou (future Henry II) to Matilda and Geoffrey
1135	Death of Henry I
1144	Geoffrey conquers Normandy and assumes title of duke
1150	Geoffrey resigns as duke; title is bequeathed to Henry of Anjou
1151	Death of Geoffrey
1152	Henry governs as Duke of Normandy and Count of Anjou; Henry marries Eleanor of Aquitaine
1153	Henry invades England; Treaty of Winchester
1154	Death of King Stephen; Henry adds King of England to his other titles
1156	Henry overcomes claims made by his younger brother, Geoffrey
1171–1172	Henry invades Ireland
1180	Death of King Louis VII; accession of Philip Augustus as king of France

A) Narrative: An 'Imperial' Inheritance?

King John (r. 1199–1216), his brother, King Richard the Lionheart
(r. 1189–1199), and their father, King Henry II (r. 1154–1189), are known as
the Angevin kings because of their association with the county of Anjou in
France (see Figure 3).

Figure 3. The continental territories of the Angevins at the time of John's birth
(courtesy of Yale University Press)

Effective leadership by a series of counts of Anjou, particularly the father of Henry II, Count Geoffrey (r. 1129–1151), combined with episodic weakness exhibited by the kings of France prior to the reign of Philip Augustus, resulted in the emergence by the early twelfth century of Greater Anjou – that is, the county of Anjou combined with Touraine (acquired by conquest, 1044) and Maine (acquired by marriage alliance, 1109). Partly because of its geographical position and partly because its rulers had long coveted Normandy, its northern neighbour, Greater Anjou necessarily represented a threat to the Anglo-Norman realm established by the successful conquest of England by Duke William of Normandy in 1066. In order to counter this threat, King/Duke Henry I (r. 1100–1135) sought a marriage alliance with Greater Anjou. Initially this was to be achieved by the marriage of his son, William, to the daughter of Count Fulk of Anjou (r. 1106–1129). However, when William drowned in the Channel in 1120 – an event known to historians as the White Ship Disaster – arrangements were made instead for Henry's daughter and designated heir, Matilda, to marry in 1128 Geoffrey of Anjou, son of Count Fulk of Anjou and shortly to become Count in his own right. As it transpired, this was to amount to a 'brilliant success'.[1]

In the short term, however, when Henry I died in 1135 many of the Anglo-Norman baronage, uncertain of female rule and unhappy at the prospect of Geoffrey, refused to accept Matilda. These were the circumstances in which Stephen, son of Adela, William the Conqueror's daughter, successfully seized the kingdom/dukedom from Matilda. This instigated eighteen years of civil war during which Matilda fought for her inheritance, latterly with assistance from her son, Henry – the future Henry II, born in 1133. Taking advantage of the civil war in England, Geoffrey was able successfully to conquer Normandy by 1144 and thereafter assumed the title of duke until he resigned it in favour of his son Henry in 1150. One year later Geoffrey died suddenly and thus Henry inherited the title and lands of Count of Anjou to place alongside his status as duke.

Already powerful as Count of Anjou and Duke of Normandy, Henry also argued that he had a strong claim upon England via his mother. This put him in a very strong position to be able to make a powerful match in marriage. Therefore, when Eleanor, the then wife of the French King Louis VII (r. 1137–1180), became available to remarry after Pope Eugenius granted an annulment of her marriage existing on the grounds of consanguinity, Henry and Eleanor married in 1152. Since Eleanor was Duchess of Aquitaine in her own right, her territories came to Henry as prince consort. The core of the duchy consisted of Poitou and Gascony, with a large number of other lordships over which the dukes of Aquitaine claimed suzerainty.

Emboldened by his marriage, Henry was now determined to acquire what he believed to be his rightful inheritance. In 1153 he thus invaded England and sought battle with King Stephen. In the first instance, however, this invasion resulted in nothing better than a military stalemate. It was therefore fortunate when Stephen's son Eustace conveniently died, thereby opening the way for a negotiated settlement in favour of Henry.[2] By the Treaty of Winchester, agreed in November 1153, Stephen made Henry his heir and successor whilst Henry accepted Stephen as king for the rest of the monarch's life. Henry had only to wait a few months. When Stephen died in October 1154, Henry was able to add King of England to his other titles.

As king of England, Duke of Normandy and Duke of Aquitaine, Henry had inherited claims to lordship over neighbouring territories. These claims led to expeditions into Wales (1157, 1163 and 1165), into Brittany (1166) and Toulouse (1159).[3] Though not always successful, by these actions Henry consolidated the notion of Angevin pre-eminence. In the meantime Ireland was successfully oppressed in 1171–3 and Scotland was brought to heel by diplomatic pressure in 1174. Gerald of Wales, as we have seen (see page 5), by no means an uncritical observer of the Angevins, addressed this eulogy to Henry II: 'Your victories swamp frontiers. You, our western Alexander, have stretched out your arm from the Pyrénées to the western shores of the northern Ocean.'[4]

Against this backcloth, as J. Gillingham notes, 'the Angevins [should be seen as] French princes who numbered England among their possessions'.[5] As such, and considering the extent of these accumulated territories, it is not surprising that the Angevin rulers were infrequently resident in England before the loss of many of the French lands in 1203–4. During the course of his thirty-five year reign, Henry II spent a total of less than thirteen years in England, Wales and Ireland; fourteen-and-a-half years in Normandy; and a total of only seven years in his French lands outside Normandy. After his return in 1194 from the Third Crusade, Richard spent three of the next five years in Normandy and only two months in England. In total, he visited England for only five months in nine-and-a-half years. Until December 1203, John spent most of his time in his continental territories. In this world, London was less important to the Angevins than either Angers or Rouen, the capitals of Anjou and Normandy respectively. The obstacles to governance created by the frequent absence of the king were overcome in England by the appointment of a justiciar, a chief minister with viceregal powers who also had overall charge of the law courts and was head of the Exchequer. Aside from the justiciars appointed to Ireland, King John had three justiciars who governed consecutively in England – Geoffrey Fitz Peter (1198–1213), Peter des Roches (1213–1215) and Hubert de Burgh (1215–1232).

During the first half of the twentieth-century historians have generally referred to this conglomeration of territories over which the Angevins presided as the Angevin 'empire', a phrase coined by K. Norgate in 1902 but which is now frequently regarded as inappropriate by modern scholars who therefore dress it in inverted commas (see pages 31–3). What is indisputable is that this 'empire' was truly vast – stretching from Northumberland in the north to the Pyrénées in the south, and from the County of Toulouse in the east to tracts of Ireland in the west. These were the lands that John inherited in 1199.

i) France at the Time of John

If the vast Angevin 'empire' occupied much of the western part of modern France, it follows that France at the time of John was much smaller than it was to become in later centuries. The medieval kingdom of France had emerged out of the western part of the so-called Carolingian Empire – founded by Charlemagne (d. 814) – which had disintegrated under assaults from the Vikings in the ninth and tenth centuries. In 987 a royal dynasty was founded by Hugh Capet, the descendents of whom are known as Capetians. They based their authority on Paris and its close environs, collectively known as the royal domain and latterly referred to as the Île-de-France (see Figure 3, page 24). Meanwhile, elsewhere in France political units had formed by an accumulation of lordships, viscounties and counties. In this way emerged Normandy, Brittany, Anjou, Blois and Flanders, for example. The Capetians successfully laid claim to being the suzerain (feudal overlord) of the rulers of these territories. For the best part of two hundred years Capetian overlordship remained ineffective and episodic. It began to assume a meaningful form in the reign of Louis VII (r. 1137–1180) and more especially under the capable leadership of his son, Philip Augustus (r. 1180–1223). Thus, the emergence of the Angevin 'empire' brought with it a tangled web of overlapping jurisdictions, established and formalized by the rendering of homage by the Angevin rulers to the king of France. In turn, this provided disaffected French vassals of the Angevins with the potential means of protesting against Angevin rule by appealing to their ultimate overlord, the king of France.

Unsurprisingly, the very extent of the Angevin 'empire' excited the enmity of others, most especially the capable and deft Philip Augustus. Geography meant that the Angevin 'empire' was especially vulnerable to probing assaults by Philip along the rivers Seine and Loire, giving access to the important Angevin towns of Rouen and Angers respectively. For this reason the Angevin kings studded their landscapes with castles in order to bite and hold their territory. Large areas of eastern Normandy, especially the Vexin, became highly militarized in this way. By far the most important and impressive of these fortifications was Chateau-Gaillard, built at Les Andelys on the Seine at enormous cost by Richard the Lionheart. In the same way that Berlin came to epitomize the ambitions of the respective superpowers during the Cold War, Chateau-Gaillard became a 'must have' for Philip and a 'must-not-let-go' for the Angevins. (Richard was so delighted by Chateau-Gaillard that he called it his 'saucy castle' and boasted that its design was so effective that he would hold it even if the walls were made of butter!) The key tactic of the episodic wars that raged between the Angevins and the Capetians was thus the besieging of castles. Large-scale battles such as Bouvines in 1214 (see pages 72–3) were very rare indeed.

B) Interpretations

Scholars have studied carefully the essential character of the 'empire' in order better to understand the suddenness of its collapse in 1203–4. Some have suggested that there were structural forces at work which meant that the Angevin 'empire' would have collapsed whoever was king at the time.[6] 'Angevin rule in Normandy was, indeed, already a guttering candle when John came to the throne', says W. L. Warren.[7] It follows that if the 'empire' is understood as being the product of unforeseen developments and opportunism, and therefore inherently partible, then the events of 1203/4 are indeed explicable as the inevitable outcome of underlying structural weaknesses. Alternatively, if it is concluded that that the 'empire' was robust, then its collapse in 1204 is significantly the responsibility of John. Historians John Le Patourel and John Gillingham are exponents of this view. Gillingham, for instance, argues that 'the root of John's problems lay not in any underlying structural weaknesses but in the realms of policy and diplomacy'.[8]

i) The Nature of the Anglo-Norman Regnum

The most ancient part of the 'empire' was the Anglo-Norman regnum, established as a result of the Norman conquest of England in 1066. An assessment of its condition one hundred years after its formation is clearly an important aspect of any evaluation of the Angevin 'empire' as a whole.

Older historiography, defined by the writing of John Le Patourel, assumed that the first Norman king/dukes welded their Anglo-Norman realm into a single regnum, facilitated and encouraged by a political elite whose interests were best served when the titles of king and duke were held by the same person. In 1976 Le Patourel asserted that 'the upper levels of society in

England and Normandy were completely assimilated, indeed merged into one community'.[9] Certainly, in the aftermath of the Battle of Hastings almost all of the great families had estates in both England and Normandy. For instance, the earls of Chester were simultaneously vicomtes of Avranches; and the earls of Leicester were lords of the great estate of Breteuil. To families like these the political separation of Normandy and England posed a major political difficulty – if they supported the duke then they risked confiscation of their estates in England by the king; but if they supported the king then they risked confiscation of their estates in Normandy by the duke. Thus, when William the Conqueror bequeathed Normandy to his eldest son Robert Curthose and England to William Rufus in 1087, the barons lamented that 'If we serve Robert, Duke of Normandy as we ought, we will offend his brother William, who will then strip us of our great revenues and mighty honours in England. Again, if we obey King William dutifully, Duke Robert will confiscate our inherited estates in Normandy.'[10] It was therefore in the interests of the landowning class for duchy and kingdom to be governed by the same person. Partly for this reason, Henry I (William Rufus' successor as king of England from 1100) was able to mobilize sufficient support to defeat his brother in battle at Tinchebrai in 1106 and thereafter imprison him until his death in 1134. William Clito, Curthose' son, remained at large until his death in 1128 and on a number of occasions destabilized the Anglo-Norman realm. That he failed to achieve more is arguably because of the natural disposition of the Anglo-Norman elite of that time to exert itself to ensure that England and Normandy remained united under a single ruler. In 1135, upon the death of Henry I, the Normans immediately offered the Duchy to Count Theobald, the eldest son of Henry's sister, Adela. However, when they learned that Theobald's brother Stephen had already successfully seized the English throne, they withdrew their support for Theobald because, in the words of Ordericus Vitalis, they sought 'to serve one lord on account of the honours which they held in both lands'.[11] In this way the prevailing political sentiment operated to maintain the Anglo-Norman regnum.

However, Le Patourel has been accused of 'fashioning generalities out of a few examples' and his notion of one unified Anglo-Norman 'community' existing throughout the twelfth century is now no longer generally accepted.[12] A probable decline in Norman colonization of England from the 1130s, combined with an ongoing process whereby (particularly knightly class) families partitioned their estates at the Channel, meant that a clear orientation to one realm or the other was developing from even before the mid-twelfth century.[13] D. Crouch asserts that 'the great majority of the knightly families of the shires, even if of French extraction, would [by this time] have become exclusively "English" in attachment. Those of English extraction...may never have considered themselves Anglo-Norman at all.'[14] This development provides a valuable structural explanation for why John found it so difficult to mobilize support in England for a defence of Normandy (1200–1203) and thereafter a proposed military reconquest. Put simply, for an increasing number of the political nation who were resident in England, Normandy amounted to a far away country about which they knew little and cared even less. Indeed, tellingly, King Richard I had encountered recalcitrance when he demanded that his ecclesiastical tenants-in-chief, residing in England, provide him with knights for fighting in Normandy. To prove the point, Crouch argues that the same process was underway in reverse for families resident in Normandy with some territorial interest in England. His study of such families that held land in the central Midlands led him to conclude that 'the possession of one or two manors in England was simply not enough to encourage such men as the lords of Gisors or Évreux to regard themselves as Anglo-Normans as opposed to Normans pure and simple'.[15]

Research into the frontier societies in Normandy and England has further diminished the credibility of the Le Patourel thesis. J. A. Green has demonstrated that border magnates in the Vexin region of Normandy, who had lands that spread into France, tended to offer their allegiance first and foremost to their local lord – Philip Augustus.[16] Elements such as these had every reason to see themselves as Franco-Normans rather than Anglo-Normans, especially because of the growing authority and status of Philip Augustus. Green's research also shows that the border aristocracy of Northumbria behaved in the same way – this element elicited the support of the king of Scotland to counterbalance the local interference perpetrated by the king of England.

All in all, it is difficult to avoid the conclusion that for at least fifty years prior to 1204 the vast Anglo-Norman domains had been drifting apart. The ongoing process of dividing lands at the Channel incrementally diminished the centrifugal force binding together the Anglo-Norman bloc; simultaneously, the existence of increasingly impressive rival monarchies in some territories contingent to the Norman and English borders established a centripetal force that, in the frontier territories in Normandy at least, was ever-growing in strength. The effect of these two forces meant that it was only a matter of time before Normandy and England suffered a separation. The Montforts, Tourvilles and Curlis families divided their estates at the end of the twelfth century and, as Crouch observes, 'it could be suggested that they did so foreseeing the end of the Anglo-Norman regnum'.[17] 'By 1236', concludes Crouch 'Henry III might well have been alone in England in sincerely wanting to regain Normandy. What little Anglo-Norman feeling there ever had been around the king was quite gone.'[18]

ii) The Nature of the Angevin 'Empire'

The weight of recent scholarship has baulked at the use of the phrase 'Angevin empire', a term of reference which Henry II and his sons would not have recognized. 'The facts speak for themselves; the ephemeral nature of [the 'empire'] proves that the Plantagenet Empire was not an empire of the nineteenth century sort', asserts M. Aurell.[19] C. Warren Hollister has insisted that the notion of an 'Angevin Empire' is 'nothing more than a convenient invention of modern historians'.[20] Instead it is argued that the Angevin possessions should be viewed as a bundle of territories 'which did not automatically belong together' and had come about 'as an unholy combination of princely greed and genealogical accident'. The 'Angevin lands before 1204 need to be seen, not as one united territorial empire, but as a conglomeration of lordships brought into existence through time and chance'. The whole edifice amounts to 'a rickety, ramshackle affair, kept together by the military prowess of Henry and Richard'.[21] Warren asserts that even Henry II's ambition to refashion the 'empire' into a 'dynastic federation…was almost certain to be ephemeral for it ran counter to the political reorientation of France which was to make the court of the Capetians the focus of power within the kingdom'. Moreover, many of Henry II's subjects were coming to see the aggregation of Plantagenet territories as 'a curious anachronism'.[22] R. V. Turner supports this interpretation, pointing out that most 'historians tend to reject the possibility of the Plantagenets' collection of lands achieving permanence and political stability, seeing them merely 'as the lucky acquisition of a quarrelsome family and not as an institution'.[23] Even Gillingham, pondering whether Henry II had an overriding purpose, concludes that 'it is most unlikely to have been "empire-building" in the sense of consciously putting together a political structure which was intended to survive its creator's death'.[24]

Historians have pointed out that Angevin rule ran very thinly indeed in some places. Maps showing the 'Angevin empire' are often inadequate in that they tend to fail to represent the variety of authority wielded by the Angevin rulers. This ranged from what has been called 'the intensive and authoritative' in England and the Norman Duchy to 'the diffused and occasional' in the Duchy of Aquitaine.[25] Indeed, in Poitou and Gascony – territories populated by turbulent and undisciplined vassals – allegiance to the Angevin governor was consistently tenuous and difficult to enforce. (It is worth recalling that Richard the Lionheart had been killed by a rebellious vassal in the Limousin region.)

It is also now understood that the Angevin rulers probably perceived the future of the Angevin dominions not as an empire but as a federation.

Examination of the various succession schemes devised by the Angevins demonstrates that both Geoffrey of Anjou and his son, Henry II, sought to provide for their heirs by dividing their lands, perhaps recognizing the naturally fissiparous nature of the 'empire'. Thus, it seems that the territories that Geoffrey had acquired by marriage to Matilda were destined to be inherited by his eldest son Henry whilst Anjou and Maine were to be inherited by his younger son Geoffrey – scarcely the actions of an empire builder. The fact that Henry inherited Anjou and Maine as well as the Anglo-Norman regnum was only because Geoffrey happened to die at a particular moment in time.[26] Similarly, as we have seen (see page 12), Henry II's scheme of 1169 stipulated that Richard would have inherited only Aquitaine if his elder brother had not died. In 1170, when Henry II gave his daughter Eleanor in marriage to Alfonso VIII of Castile, he apparently granted her Gascony (though this was only to become operative after the death of Eleanor of Aquitaine).[27] Henry II's will, drawn up in 1170, led J. C. Holt to conclude that

> any reasonable prediction of the state of these [i.e. Henry II's] dominions in 1170 would have been that they would descend in three collateral lines: England, Normandy, Main and Anjou through Henry the Young King; Aquitaine through Richard and Brittany through Geoffrey. Upon the death of the Young King in 1183, any prediction would have been that Richard would step into the Young King's shoes and John into Richard's.

Holt concludes that 'these schemes for division will not allow any but the most elementary conception of an Angevin Empire. It was adventitious. At any moment the accident of death might lead to divisions or the revision of a division.'[28] Thus, Henry's designs to provide for his sons further encourage the conclusion that he did not perceive himself to be presiding over an 'empire'; and, moreover, that he probably did not expect the collection of territories over which he nominally governed to exist beyond his own lifespan.

From another perspective it seems likely that the Angevin 'empire' was destined to be short lived because of what the Angevin rulers did not do. For instance, none of the Angevins imposed a common coinage bearing their portraits. Henry issued only four 'imperial acts' binding throughout his lands. Above all, they did not 'create a cosmopolitan ruling class, drawn from all their possessions, united in loyalty to the dynasty and committed to preservation of the "empire"'.[29] It is true that in the northern territories the employment of men from both the duchy and kingdom in the services of the king/duke had created a community of interest, in that it was in those servants' interests to enforce their ruler's prerogatives and uphold his status in order to enrich themselves. However, as the 'empire' grew older, a distinct trend emerged whereby the number of Normans serving in administrative posts in England declined. Ominously, those who did, such as William Longchamp, found that they aroused bitter resentment (see pages 15–17). More damaging perhaps was the fact that no symbiotic relationship had ever been established between the Angevins and the political elite in the Duchy of Aquitaine. Of the men who attended Richard's household it seems that 'hardly any Angevin or Poitevin names occur'.[30] The significance of this becomes greater still when it is realized that 'only a handful' of marriages took place between Anglo-Norman noble families and their counterparts in Greater Anjou and Aquitaine.[31]

In the absence of a political elite bound together with a common ambition to preserve the 'empire', and in the face of a natural and growing disposition to split apart, the territories that John inherited could only really be held together by military force. But military force came at the price of negative political and economic ramifications. In particular, since the cost of mercenaries was met by mobilizing resources in the better-administered Anglo-Norman part of the 'empire', this created another reason why few leading families on either side of the Channel would regret their separation in 1204. R. V. Turner and R. Heiser conclude that 'by the end of the twelfth century, many Normans, both lay and clerical, were longing for peace, even at the price of annexation by the French king'.[32] When this eventually occurred in 1203–4 it carried legitimacy because of a long established Capetian suzerainty over the Angevin rulers.

Indeed it is asserted that the Angevins did not possess sovereign 'imperial' authority because, as lords of French territories, they were vassals of the overlord [suzerain] of those territories, the French king. This issue is examined in the next section.

iii) Capetian Suzerainty and Philip Augustus

Henry II and his sons rendered homage to the king of France for their continental territories on a number of occasions: Henry II in 1156 and 1183, Richard the Lionheart in 1188 and 1189 and John in 1200 as part of the terms of the Treaty of Le Goulet (see pages 42–4).[33] The Angevins seem to have accepted readily Capetian assertions of feudal suzerainty – or overlordship – over those territories (except Gascony) which comprised the Angevin 'empire' for two main reasons. First, as long as the French monarchy remained weak the Angevins probably gained more by the paying of homage than the Capetians, 'not least because the acceptance of homage conferred legitimacy [on the Angevins' status as continental lords] without imposing specific obligations'.[34] Second, frequently at odds among themselves, Henry II and his sons perceived the rendering of homage as a means by which they could strengthen their position in relation to claims made by other members of the family. For example, in the early years of his reign, having become a vassal of Louis VII, Henry II thereby ensured that the French king did not support claims to Anjou made by his younger brother, Geoffrey. Similarly, when Henry II refused to recognize Richard as his heir, the latter 'unbuckled his sword and stretching out his hands did homage to the king of France', hoping to bolster the legitimacy of his claim by doing so.[35] However, preoccupied with internecine family strife, it seems that the Henry and his sons were slow to appreciate the potential dangers of undertaking fealty to the French monarch: as vassals in the feudal hierarchy of France, the Angevins provided their overlord with the potential legal means of interfering in the Angevin dominions. This meant that existing hair-line cracks in the 'empire' would almost certainly become open fissures with more capable leadership than that demonstrated hitherto by Louis VII. It was John's ill-fortune that his reign coincided with that of Philip Augustus (r. 1180–1223) and that he consequently had to face more accomplished French leadership than any of his predecessors.

At the beginning of his reign Philip ruled little more than the Île-de-France (see Figure 3, page 24). By 1223, through a combined policy of judicious marriage and effective warfare, the royal demesne had been significantly expanded so that it was perhaps four times larger than it had been in 1180. Already, by the end of the first decade of the reign, it is estimated that Philip had increased royal revenues by 22 per cent. (By 1223, upon the acquisition of much of the Angevin 'empire', French revenues had increased by 72 per cent when compared to 1180.)[36] For this reason, Turner and Heiser believe that 'the period when England and the Angevins' continental possessions first began to split apart, abetted by a newly strengthened Capetian monarchy, can be viewed as starting with Philip Augustus' accession in 1180'.[37] As his revenues grew so did Philip's ability to demonstrate his superiority over all the lay lords in his kingdom by insisting that he arbitrate between them and by demanding their attendance at his courts – just one of the reasons why Philip's latest biographer concluded that 'there can surely be no doubt that Philip II had been a great king'.[38]

Simultaneous with the ongoing augmentation of the Capetian royal demesne, it seems the actions of Abbot Suger and the monastery of St Denis enhanced Philip's authority by means of a concerted propaganda campaign. Suger, in the years before the middle of the eleventh century, had sought to enhance the status of his monastery. Amongst other things, he rebuilt it in what is widely recognized as being the first example of Gothic architecture and asserted that the monastery had direct links with Charlemagne, the Frankish ruler (768–814) whose empire had united most of Western Europe for the first time since the Romans.[39] Since many of the early Frankish kings were buried in St Denis, Suger thus initiated a slow burning refurbishment of the image of monarchy from which most historians agree that Philip significantly benefitted.[40] Philip's reputation was also enhanced by the writing of Rigord (1150c.–1209c.), a chronicler resident at St Denis who wrote a largely very favourable chronicle of the life of the French king. It is significant that John had no such 'spin doctor' of his own.

Thus, even before the accession of John in 1199, Philip had grown sufficiently strong to exploit his position as overlord, to use it as 'a powerful weapon for subverting [his] English rivals' authority, affording a pretext for intervention in the Angevin provinces of western France'.[41] This is the crucial point: having readily become vassals of the Capetians, any violation of feudal custom by the Angevins meant that Philip, as overlord, could act with legal authority against an Angevin ruler. Increasingly, the royal court at Paris became an alternative power to which subjects of the Angevins felt they could appeal, which is exactly what the Lusignans did in 1202, with devastating consequences (see pages 44–5). This is the context in which Hollister, though perhaps allowing himself to be overly influenced by the advantage of hindsight, thought Henry II's act of homage in 1156 to have been 'precedent shattering' and considered that it 'marks the death of the Anglo-Norman regnum… From the beginning the Angevin kings had, for their own purposes, recognized the Capetian suzerainty; in the end it was the instrument of their undoing.'[42] Most historians have agreed with Hollister. 'Capetian suzerainty was an insurmountable barrier' concludes R. V. Turner and R. Heiser, 'preventing the Angevins from moulding their possessions into a coherent whole; and coupled with the Plantagenet propensity for family rivalries, it spelled disaster for their 'empire'.[43] Similarly, D. Carpenter believes 'the result [of French suzerainty] was that Henry II was now restricted by the oath of loyalty he had sworn, and punishable by forfeiture of his fiefs for its breach. Under his son John, that is exactly what happened'.[44] J. C. Holt concluded that 'the main weakness of the Plantagenets and the main strength of the Capetians lay in the feudal suzerainty of the King of France'.[45] Also in agreement is M. Aurrell, who believes that 'too much can never be made of their [i.e. the Angevin kings] subordinate status [to the Capetians], which deeply compromised the future of the so-called Plantagenet Empire'.[46]

J. Gillingham, however, cautions against accepting this interpretation of the significance of homage in the fall of the Angevin 'empire'. By revisiting the evidence he argues that 'the whole notion of a line of development [of homage and the consequently steadily increasing definition of the French king's rights] is a figment of the imagination of historians'.[47] He argues instead that 'whether or not their dukes or counts knelt in homage to the king of France, it would always be possible for the king [of France] – if he wished – to find legitimate reasons to intervene within those duchies and counties, and whether or not he could depended upon matters such as material resources and personal qualities'.[48] By thus removing French suzerainty as a structural reason for John's loss of the continental possessions, Gillingham is more easily able to make his favoured argument that that event came about because 'one of the ablest and most ruthless kings ever to rule France happened to be opposed by one of the worst kings ever to rule England'.[49]

However, Gillingham perhaps rather over argues his case. There is no doubt that the French king's position as overlord did in fact provide a legal justification for the invasion of Normandy and other Angevin territories, but Gillingham's argument that 'it would always be possible for the [French] king to find legitimate reasons to intervene' is too dependent upon speculation to be convincing. Moreover, it is the theme of this book that in a number of areas John's actions and achievements free him from the label of 'worst king'. And, if this label does not stick, then there must be reasons other than the qualities of John for the loss of the continental territories.

Chapter 4

WAR OF SUCCESSION AND THE LOSS OF CONTINENTAL TERRITORIES, 1199–1204

Timeline

1199

April–June	First phase of the war of succession
6 April	Death of Richard
14 April	John secures treasury at Chinon
20 April	Arthur pays homage to Philip
25 April	John invested as Duke of Normandy
27 May	John crowned king of England
24 June–16 August	Truce with Philip
July	Eleanor of Aquitaine pays homage to Philip
September–January 1200	Second phase of the war of succession
September	Eleanor makes over her inheritance to John as her rightful heir
22 September	William des Roches defects from Philip; John gains possession of Arthur and Constance
23 September	Arthur and Constance escape from John

1200

January–June	At some point during this time Hugh de Lusignan was betrothed to Isabella of Angoulême
January	New truce agreed with Philip
January–May	John on progress in England
22 May	Treaty of Le Goulet
June–August	John on royal progress in France accompanied with an army

24 August	Marriage of John and Isabella of Angoulême
8 October	John and Isabella crowned at Westminster
Autumn–Easter 1201	John tours England

1201

Easter	John orders his English vassals to muster as an army and meet him at Portsmouth
August	Death of Constance
Summer	Counts of Boulogne and Flanders leave on crusade

1202

28 April	John refused to present himself at the French court in order to answer the charge that he was a contumacious vassal. Philip therefore pronounced the confiscation of all the fiefs of John
Spring	Philip launches a series of campaigns against castles in eastern Normandy; Arthur, allied with dissident Angevins and Poitevins, attack south of the Loire
July	Philip knighted Arthur and received his homage for Brittany, Poitou, Maine and Touraine
30 July	John learned that Eleanor of Aquitaine was under siege at Mirebeau
1 August	John relieves Mirebeau and captures many important prisoners, including Arthur and the Lusignans. Defection of William des Roches to Philip

1203

Easter	Arthur disappears from his prison at Rouen, rumoured to be murdered
August	Philip begins the siege of Chateau-Gaillard
5 December	John leaves Normandy, not to return to the Continent until the campaign of 1206

1204

6 March	Surrender of Chateau-Gaillard
1 April	Death of Eleanor of Aquitaine
24 June	Surrender of Rouen
August	Philip establishes his authority over much of Anjou

A) Narrative: Succession and War, 1199–1204

i) Succession Resolved, 1199–1200

Richard died on 6 April 1199 aged forty-one, the crossbow wound he had received whilst besieging the castle of Chalus inducing a fatal case of gangrene. Since Richard had not produced an heir, John was now in a position to lay claim to the 'empire', though he had a rival to this inheritance in the form of his nephew, Arthur of Brittany, the son of Constance and John's brother Geoffrey. Uncertainty as to whom had the stronger claim in these circumstances – either the younger brother of the dead king (known as the cadet) or the child of a dead elder brother (known as the representative) – bedevilled the succession until the mid-thirteenth century (an issue which became known as *causus regis*). For this reason William the Breton, a contemporary chronicler usually sympathetic to Philip, believed that John succeeded 'under the most inauspicious circumstances'.[1] Later historians have generally supported this interpretation. For instance, H. G. Richardson and G. O. Sayles argue that John was indeed faced with a 'tangled and formidable situation'.[2]

With no clear legal resolution, a variety of factors and customs came into play to determine the succession in 1199. These included: the wishes of the late king, the sentiments of the leading barons and the practical issue of the ages of those contesting the inheritance. Only in this last respect did John have a clear and immediate advantage, being twenty-one years older than his twelve-year-old rival. Although John's claim to the 'imperial' inheritance had been strengthened by Richard who, on his deathbed, seemingly bequeathed his inheritance to John, the impact of this bequest was diminished by Richard's earlier agreement in the Treaty of Messina (1191) formally to recognize Arthur as his heir. For the baronage, the answer to the question of who had the better right to succeed varied from place to place in the 'empire'. Thus, it is usually asserted that Arthur's claim to Brittany was unimpeachable whilst in each of Maine, Anjou and Touraine he could claim to have custom on his side. Meanwhile, John could feel reasonably assured that feudal custom provided him with the stronger claim to England and Normandy. The debate, however, was ongoing and fluid, so much so that, as Painter has observed, 'any prelate or baron of the Plantagenet lands could convince himself without much difficulty that either John or Arthur was Richard's rightful heir'.[3]

In a dramatic, though almost certainly imagined scene, the biographer of William Marshal, Earl of Pembroke, allows us to eavesdrop on the crisis of

1199. Upon learning of the death of Richard, Marshal visited Hubert Walter, the archbishop of Canterbury, late at night on 10 April and told him, 'we must lose no time in choosing someone to be king'. 'I think', said Walter, 'that Arthur should rightfully be king'; to which Marshal replied, 'To my mind that would be bad; Arthur is counselled by traitors; he is haughty and proud; and if we put him over us, he will only do us harm for he does not love the people of this land. He shall not come here by my advice. Consider, rather, Count John: he seems to be the nearest heir to the land which belonged to his father and brother… Undoubtedly a son has a better claim to his father's land than a grandson; it is right that he should have it.' Walter responded to this by saying 'So be it then – but mark my words, Marshal, you will never regret anything in your life as much as this.'[4] Although this last line encourages us to be cautious about trusting this source, sufficient other evidence exists to allow us to imagine that this was a typical scene played out amongst the political elite. Discussions elsewhere ran to a different conclusion and thus on 18 April 1199, the barons of Anjou, Maine, Touraine and Brittany decided to support Arthur. Finally, on 20 April 1199, Arthur, Duke of Brittany, did homage to Philip.

There is, however, a further factor which determined the outcome of a contested succession – the speed and resolution with which those with a claim acted. In the difficult circumstances of April 1199, John did not sit on his hands. Upon learning of the death of his brother, John (who was at the time visiting Arthur in Brittany) immediately sent Marshal and Walter to England in order to preserve the peace whilst he himself rode for Chinon and seized the Angevin treasury. This 'was a prudent move for anyone who wished to control the springs of government', observes W. L. Warren.[5] John also secured the castles at Loches and Chinon, which were of strategic importance in terms of control over the Loire valley. Even so, just a week after Richard's death, John was driven back to Normandy by forces loyal to Arthur. He and his mother descended upon Angers at the head of a force of Bretons whilst Philip – acting on the pretext that as feudal overlord he had a right to intervene in the succession dispute – launched an attack on the Évreux region and simultaneously lent support to assaults on Le Mans and Tours. There was suddenly a real threat that the Angevin 'empire' would be snapped in two, fracturing along the line of the Loire valley (see Figure 4, page 41).

Recognizing that he would need a stronger authority to fight off these threats, John had himself invested as Duke of Normandy in a ceremony at Rouen on 25 April 1199. Then, after razing the castle and city walls at Le Mans in revenge for that city transferring its allegiance to Arthur, John crossed to England to be crowned on 27 May. Leaving Aimeri de Thouars

Figure 4. Preliminary moves in the war of succession, April to September 1199 (courtesy of Yale University Press)

(whom John had appointed Seneschal of Anjou in opposition to Arthur's and Philip's nominee, William des Roches) to attack Tours in an attempt to capture Arthur, John was back on the Continent within three weeks where he fought vigorously to hold off Philip in the Évreux region.

In this period of confused scrambling John also benefitted from the actions of his mother Eleanor of Aquitaine, who, upon learning of the death of Richard, sent a force into Anjou headed by the famous mercenary, Mercadier. Later, in July, she renewed her homage to Philip, an act described by one historian as 'a diplomatic masterstroke' because it removed justification for Philip's intervention in Aquitaine.[6] Cleverly, she then ceded Poitou to John and later received it back from him for life. For as long as she lived, Aquitaine was likely to remain loyal to John's cause. These actions collectively were sufficient to bring Philip to the negotiating table and on 24 June a truce was arranged, to last until 16 August, thereby providing John with 'nearly two months in which to mature his plans and increase his forces'.[7]

When fighting was renewed the advantage lay with John, not least because the unreasonably harsh demands Philip had made of John during the negotiations encouraged 'such of the counts and barons of the realm of France as had been in alliance with King Richard' to transfer their allegiance to John.[8] (It seems that bribes helped also.) Thus, in September, with the bulk of the Franco-Norman frontier protected by the counts Baldwin of Flanders and Renaud of Boulogne, John headed south with 'the initiative clearly in his hands'.[9] Philip followed and razed the castle of Ballon, at that time held by one of John's adherents. This action triggered an event which significantly strengthened John's position: William des Roches came over to John.

As the most powerful baron in Anjou and in effect the commander-in-chief of the Arthurian forces, des Roches claimed the castle of Ballon as his own. He thus asserted that Philip, by destroying it, had acted unreasonably. This, though, was perhaps not the real reason for des Roches changing sides. It seems more likely that des Roches, always pragmatic, understood the extent of John's recent successes and believed that his own authority was more likely to be enhanced by his association with the Angevin sovereign than the Capetian. Therefore, in return for being granted the Seneschalship of Anjou and the town of Le Mans, des Roches offered to arrange a settlement between the Bretons and John, including the presentation of Arthur and Constance as prisoners. The deal was struck on 22 September. A great triumph had been achieved.

It was short lived. The elevation of des Roches had occurred at the expense of Aimeri de Thouars. John felt sufficiently strong not to have compensated Aimeri – in fact, it would have made him appear weak if he had done so. However, the one time seneschal – smarting at the elevation of des Roches – struck back by slipping away to Philip, taking with him Constance and Arthur. Nonetheless, John's energetic campaigning had put him in a very strong position. Moreover, having witnessed the inconstancy of leading elements of the Arthurian party, and from January 1200 labouring under an interdict, the French king was disinclined to continue the war and a truce was thus reached in January 1200. This truce culminated in the Treaty of Le Goulet of 22 May.

John won highly significant concessions from Philip in the Treaty of Le Goulet. Notably, Philip accepted John's succession to all the Continental Angevin territories – Normandy, Anjou and Aquitaine – and Arthur was to have only Brittany and to hold it as John's vassal. By these terms John won the war of succession and set off to advertise his authority in person by undertaking a grand tour (see Figure 5, page 43). Yet Philip could also claim to be the winner from the Treaty of Le Goulet. Not only did John acknowledge Philip as his overlord and accept that he held his Continental territories directly from him, but also he agreed to pay the substantial succession relief of 20,000 marks sterling and recognized the French court as having supreme jurisdiction to resolve disputes between vassals. Moreover, by agreeing to recognize the counts of Flanders and Boulogne as vassals of Philip,

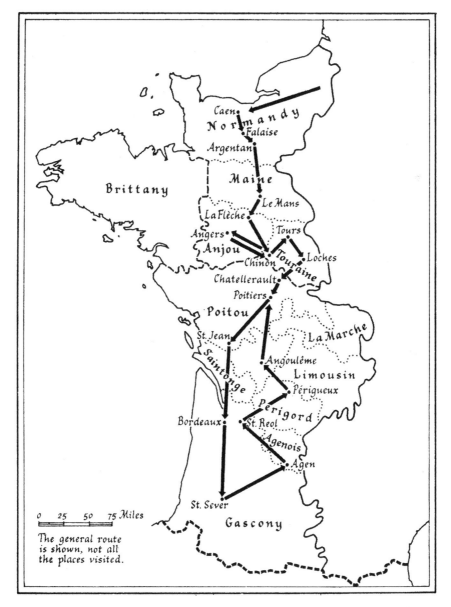

Figure 5. John's itinerary through his French dominions in the summer of 1200 (courtesy of Yale University Press)

John could not henceforth mobilize them on his behalf, depriving himself of the Ricardian anti-French alliance system that had done so much to restrain French ambitions in the second half of the 1190s. John also accepted significant territorial changes that were not in his favour. In particular, Philip successfully claimed the Norman border region of the Evrécin and the Vexin, except for Les Andelys, where Chateau-Gaillard was sited.

ii) Succession Disputed, 1200–1202

In 1200 John had been married to Isabella of Gloucester for eleven years. However, since she was in fact a cousin and the required dispensation for the marriage from the pope had never been received, John was quickly able to obtain an annulment. On 24 August 1200 he married Isabella of Angoulême.

Isabella was the sole heiress to Angoulême, a substantial province (immediately south of Poitou sitting astride the River Charente) from which the counts had grown wealthy on account of the profits from trade routes crossing their land. The counts of Angoulême thus retained a considerable degree of autonomy from Plantagenet control, despite regular military campaigns by both Henry II and Richard.[10] At some point in the first six months of 1200, Isabella was betrothed to Hugh de Lusignan, a neighbouring lord who had recently added the Lordship of La Marche to his holdings. Clearly, as a study of the map reveals, the potential unification of the three lordships of Angoulême, Lusignan and La Marche represented a threat of the greatest order to King John (see Figure 2, page 3). It would mean that Hugh would become master of most of Poitou – a territory of key importance to the integrity of the Plantagenet dominions in France – and would thereby acquire authority akin to the hereditary Plantagenet dukes of Aquitaine. In short, for Isabella to have married Hugh would have brought disaster for John. For these reasons John thwarted Hugh's prospects by marrying Isabella himself, a development that R. V. Turner believes was 'an astute diplomatic move'.[11] Yet, other historians have criticized John for this very act, following Roger of Wendover's line that 'this marriage was afterwards very injurious to the king as well as the kingdom of England'.[12]

'It was a fateful marriage' asserts Warren, who goes on to claim that 'the loss of the continental dominions stemmed from it, or so at least most contemporaries firmly believed'.[13] Cheated of Isabella and her inheritance, Hugh had an obvious grievance and therefore, as a Poitevin vassal of John, brought an appeal to the Angevin's court in 1201.[14] John, however, met this challenge by denying redress in court and instead invited the Lusignans to a judicial duel with royal champions (i.e. trial by battle). He simultaneously instructed his officials to do all the harm they could to Ralph, the brother of Hugh, who possessed the lordship of Eu in Normandy. Faced with this response from John – Warren believes that it amounts to 'stupid provocation' – the Lusignans appealed to their supreme overlord, Philip Augustus.[15] John, as a vassal of Philip, a status recently renewed in the treaty of Le Goulet, now found himself summoned to the French court shortly after Easter 1202. However, John refused to appear, alleging that as Duke of Normandy he was not obliged to fulfil the demands of his overlord anywhere other than on the Franco-Norman border. Philip countered this objection by stating that John was being summoned as Lord of Aquitaine and Anjou, a response which most historians claim John should have anticipated since it was an 'obvious reply'.[16] Duly adjudged to be a contumacious vassal, John was declared to have forfeited his fiefs of Aquitaine, Poitou and Anjou. In this way Philip was given a legal pretext for invading the Angevin territories (see Appendix, Document 5).

Philip thus squared his differences with the church and, fortuitously if not by design, the counts of Flanders and Boulogne – each of whom had previously acted so vigorously on behalf of King Richard – heeded Pope Innocent III's call for a new crusade and left the North European stage. Meanwhile, John's nephew Otto IV of Brunswick became more focused on his rivalry with Philip of Swabia just at the moment John needed him free to act on his behalf. An even greater concern to John was the person of Philip Augustus: as Warren points out, 'it was no mere neighbouring prince of comparable age and experience with whom John trifled in 1201–2, but a man who felt himself to be the heir of Charlemagne'.[17] Perhaps above all, this heir of Charlemagne was finding new ways of mobilizing French resources so that, according to some historians, the Angevin resources available to John were now much less than those of the Capetians (see 'Interpretation' pages 57–62). In the struggle that was about to commence, John was in these ways severely handicapped. He nonetheless got off to a spectacular start.

iii) War with France Stage One, Spring to Autumn 1202

By 1202 John had already demonstrated that he was not without ability in military affairs. His mustering of forces in 1199 and his subsequent progress through Aquitaine was impressive. Then shortly after Easter 1201, as tension developed as a consequence of his marriage, he summoned his English vassals to Portsmouth to provide him with a feudal host. However, recognizing that a feudal army was by no means the best element with which to wage war, John demanded money instead and sent his vassals home – an arguably forward-thinking policy.

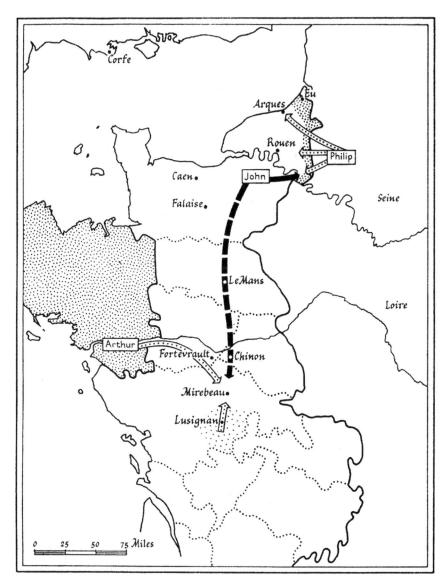

Figure 6. War with France phase 1, spring to autumn 1202 (courtesy of Yale University Press)

During the first six months of 1202 John was resident in Normandy with his army of mercenaries. For over a decade Philip Augustus had been launching raids into Normandy with relatively little success. Now, however, in less than three months, aided by the rebel count of Eu he had subdued the duchy's entire northeastern march. By the end of July he was besieging the important castle of Arques near Dieppe (see Figure 6). John, though, was proving resilient. Having given orders that French ships off Arques should be harassed, he was also intent upon cutting Philip's supply lines on land. Meanwhile Arthur, aided by rebels in Poitou and Maine, had invaded the Loire valley region and by the end of July had trapped Eleanor of Aquitaine in the castle at Mirebeau. John was at Le Mans when William des Roches brought him this news. Within forty-eight hours the John had covered the eighty miles to Mirebeau and by doing so had earned himself the advantage of surprise: Arthur and his adherents were apprehended whilst having breakfast. In exultant mood, John informed the English barons that 'there we captured our nephew Arthur…and Geoffrey de Lusignan [uncle of Hugh and Ralph], Hugh de Lusignan, Andrew de Chauvigni, the viscount of Chateleraut, Raymond Thouars, Savary de Mauléon, Hugh Bauge, and all our other Poitevan enemies who were there' – perhaps 200 knights in all.[18] It was an astonishing haul: 'a first-rate achievement; well nigh miraculous some thought'.[19] In this single episode the leadership of the Poitevan and Breton rebels had been disorientated. Arthur and the Lusignans were imprisoned in Falaise; the non-ransomable prisoners were sent to Corfe castle in England. Meanwhile, in Normandy, a shaken Philip called off the siege of Arques and withdrew.

So great was John's success that, as Powicke pointed out, 'it might have been expected that [this victory] would have secured his rule throughout Normandy and Aquitaine for the next few years'.[20] That this did not transpire was in large part because of the transfer of allegiance of William des Roches back to Philip, combined with the fact that John allowed himself to be implicated in the probable murder of Arthur.

iv) War with France Stage Two, Autumn 1202 to December 1203

In 1202 John should perhaps have been more alert to the fact that William des Roches had by that time already changed sides, dropping his allegiance to Philip in favour of John. Since doing so he had fought vigorously for John and there is no doubt that the success at Mirebeau, where he knew the topography, was substantially because of his contribution. Indeed, the explanation for des Roches' vigour is that John had promised him he would control the fate of Arthur, a control which carried with it diplomatic clout and the prospect of substantial monies obtained from ransom demands. Thus, when John removed Arthur to Falaise, des Roches withdrew his support. Historians have offered a variety of explanations for John's action, many asserting that the aftermath of Mirebeau revealed in John self-destructive tendencies so severe that they prove him unfit to govern. Warren's diagnosis is apparently compelling: he talks of John suffering from 'over-confidence born of success, and his inveterate distrust of powerful subjects'.[21] Yet we can perhaps forgive John for being distrustful because des Roches had already demonstrated he was something of a weathercock of fortune. Moreover, des Roches was increasingly a threat to John. During the summer of 1201 he married Marguerite de Sable and by this means acquired a vast landholding which meant that overnight des Roches became one of the greatest barons of Anjou and Maine and relative-in-law to the most exclusive house of the region. To have granted this man control over the person of Arthur who, as we have seen, had a powerful claim upon the inheritance that John insisted was his alone, was unthinkable – it would have provided des Roches with the means to destroy the Angevin dominions. Moreover, for as long as the king possessed the person of Arthur he had a powerful means by which to coerce the loyalty of the Bretons.

It is then clear that the ambitions of des Roches needed constraining. Whilst it is perhaps equally clear that the means by which John sought to clip these ambitions lacked delicacy, it is a false judgement – arrived at only with the benefit of hindsight – to assert that John's treatment of des Roches was 'fatuous folly'.[22] Arguably, with Philip outmanoeuvred and the rebels leaderless, this was in fact the best moment to strike at des Roches. It is in this context that we should also understand John's decision to release the Lusignans in early 1203. Most authorities have chosen to follow the judgement of the biographer of William Marshal in his expression of horror that John should in this way 'put a head back on the trunk of Poitevin disaffection'.[23] However, we should be alert to the fact that we first learn of this remark in an account published only after Normandy has been lost. At the time John was careful to obtain from the Lusignans oaths of loyalty, secured by the granting of castles and hostages. Though many broke their word, not all did so – Savary de Mauléon, for instance, remained faithful to John throughout all his later troubles. Defections and disloyalty in all parts of John's dominions in northern France now became endemic, inspired in part by intrigue sponsored by Philip but also by rumours of John's mistreatment of prisoners, particularly Arthur.[24]

Just before Easter 1203 Arthur of Brittany disappeared (see Appendix, Document 6). Possessed of motive and opportunity, John (like Richard III) has been condemned as the killer of his nephew; and the reputation of John (like the reputation of Richard) has been indelibly stained by this accusation. The Margam annals gives us the best description of the supposed murder of Arthur: 'After King John had captured Arthur and kept him alive in prison for some time, at length, in the castle of Rouen, after dinner on the Thursday before Easter [3 April 1203], when he was drunk and possessed by the devil, he slew him with his own hand, and tying a heavy stone to the body, cast it into the Seine.'[25] In contrast, as J. T. Appleby suggests, 'when all is considered, the possibility that Arthur died in sickness, or in an accident whilst attempting to escape, as John's friends asserted, seems at least as likely as any of the ingenious explanations contributed by those with cause to malign him'.[26] On the other hand, the fate of the wife and children of William de Briouze lend ominous support to the validity of the accusation that John killed Arthur. William de Briouze had actually captured Arthur at Mirebeau and was frequently at John's side until 1207, when for some reason he fell from power. When John demanded that William surrender his sons as hostages to demonstrate his loyalty, William's wife Matilda refused. We can speculate that her action was inspired by the fact that she knew, via her husband, of the fate of Arthur and thus feared for the well-being of her sons. Indeed, Matilda and her eldest son were latterly imprisoned and starved to death; William eventually fled to the French court and died abroad (see pages 86–91).

There were, nonetheless, powerful – legitimate – reasons for John to have killed Arthur or, more likely, to have issued orders for him to be killed. After all, despite the fact that Arthur paid homage to John, the nephew had rebelled against the uncle, and had done so in collusion with Philip. Indeed, Arthur had been captured whilst fighting against John and could have been legally condemned to death. It was thus clear that for as long as Arthur lived John's claim upon the Angevin dominions would be insecure. There is even chronicle support for this interpretation. The Barnwell chronicler 'chose to reflect that the anonymity of Arthur's grave was just reward for his pride'.[27] 'Arthur was no innocent victim', concluded Roger of Wendover. 'He was captured at Mirebeau, a traitor to his lord and uncle to whom he had sworn homage an allegiance and he could rightly be condemned without judgement to die even the most shameful of deaths.'[28] Arguably, John's mistake was not the removal of Arthur but the fact that he allowed himself to be implicated in his nephew's disappearance.

Encouraged by renewed and widespread disaffection in John's territories, especially in Poitou and Anjou, Philip took again to his favourite campaigning territory in the Spring of 1203: Normandy. For Normandy to fall it was necessary to take Rouen, the duchy's capital. Standing in the way, however, perched high – as if 'rising to the stars', said William the Breton – on a dramatic outcrop of land above the Seine roughly half way between Rouen and Paris, was Chateau-Gaillard (see Figure 7, page 50).[29] Built by Richard with no expense spared, it was a significant defensive obstacle. Moreover, it had a system of supporting castles which would have to be overcome. But one by one these quickly surrendered: Beaumont-le-Roger; Montfort-sur-Risle and above all Le Vaudreuil, recently strengthened by Richard. 'In the last analysis', observes Warren 'Normandy was lost behind the castles in the hearts of the Normans themselves before

Figure 7. War with France phase 2, autumn 1202 to December 1203 (courtesy of Yale University Press)

Philip launched his attack.'[30] Desertions amongst the Breton and Angevin baronage, apparently particularly motivated by mounting anxiety over the fate of Arthur, seem to have spread to the Norman baronage. Indeed, the biographer of William Marshal says that treachery ran through Normandy like an epidemic. Gervase of Canterbury and the Barnwell chronicler assert that treachery among the Normans was so prevalent that resistance to the French invasion was impossible. The impact of these defections upon John unsurprisingly sapped his resolution and encouraged him to be suspicious of all around him.

Ralph of Coggeshall averred that the king 'could bring no help to the besieged because he went all the time in fear of his subjects' treason'.[31] This was not completely true. When Philip began his siege of Chateau-Gaillard in late August 1203, John devised a plan of relief that was at once bold and daring. The plan only failed because the current of the Seine meant that the amphibious part of the relief force could not keep pace with its counterpart on land led by William Marshal, allowing Philip to pick off each independently of the other.

v) War with France Stage Three, Summer 1204

It is too easy to accuse John of flight when he returned to England in December 1203. He was right to be confident that Chateau-Gaillard could yet hold out, not least because it was commanded by a loyal Englishman rather than a Norman; even if it did fall John had ensured that Rouen's defences had been stiffened so that the city was practically impregnable. Moreover, his last act before leaving for England had been to fortify the River Touques,

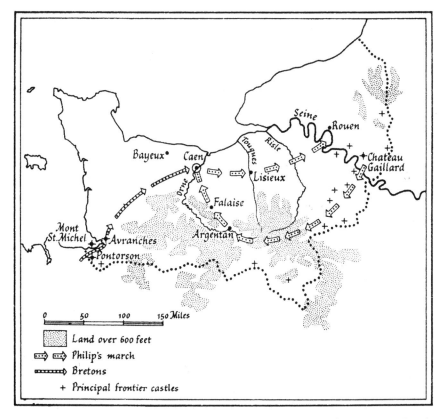

Figure 8. War with France phase 3, summer 1204 (courtesy of Yale University Press)

suggesting that John intended to use western Normandy as a springboard for a renewed attack against Philip in the new year. Normandy could look after itself, particularly since this was not now the campaigning season, whilst John raised new resources in England. In a meeting in January 1204 with the English barons, John persuaded them to make a substantial payment of scutage (see page 121) and royal officials successfully collected heavy levies ('tallages') from towns, amongst a variety of other emergency taxes.

With everything arranged, John was ready to return to Normandy in March 1204, when he learned the devastating news that Chateau-Gaillard had succumbed to Philip's siege engines. Even more damaging, however, was Philip's next move: instead of moving on to Rouen as expected – where he would in all likelihood have endured a lengthy siege and thus allowed John time to return to Normandy with new forces – Philip headed west (see Figure 8, page 51). The French king picked a route which rendered the newly fortified River Torques irrelevant and, eliciting the support of the Bretons, duly deprived John of his intended springboard. It was a dynamic strategic manoeuvre that Warren describes as 'a brilliant left-hook'.[32] Isolated, Rouen surrendered on 24 June 1204. Normandy was lost.

B) Interpretations: Why did John Lose Normandy?

i) 'Softsword'?

Older interpretations assert that the main explanation for the loss of Normandy was John's inadequacy as a ruler and a man. He was, it is alleged, neither a leader nor a soldier as evidenced by his decision to stop fighting in 1200, his marriage to Isabella and his seeming involvement in the murder of Arthur.

John's reputation has traditionally suffered from his decision to cease fighting in the spring of 1200 and to negotiate peace in the form of the Treaty of Le Goulet. Roger of Wendover talks of John's 'incorrigible idleness' and states that the king so preferred the company of his queen than the rigours of war that he must have been 'infatuated with sorcery or witchcraft'[33] (see Appendix, Documents 7 and 8). Gervase of Canterbury asserted that general gossip at the time was that John was 'Softsword' because of his decision to enter negotiations with Philip. A political song of the day chanted that 'No man may ever trust him / For his heart is soft and cowardly'.[34] In short, John is charged with laziness and cowardice. Yet this opinion has been formed, at least in part, by a dangerous over-reliance upon near contemporary chroniclers. In fact, if anything, the king suffered from energy, as the record evidence reveals (see Chapter 8). Coggeshall – normally critical of

John – concurs, stating that John 'ruled indefatigably'.[35] When John was back in England from December 1203 he was not, as Warren states, 'biting his nails' but systematically preparing a new assault upon Normandy.[36] Indeed, suggestions that King John was lazy, cowardly and irresolute fit unhappily with the John's determination to regain his lost territories which he evinced consistently after 1204, a determination so great that it provided the barons with a set of grievances which they articulated in Magna Carta. Moreover, as R. V. Turner has argued, John does not deserve the reputation for military incapacity. Turner points out that the traditional understanding of John as a deficient soldier is a consequence of historians 'misunderstanding the nature of medieval warfare'.[37] An opinion that insists that John was a poor soldier – 'Softsword' – has either to ignore, or falsely diminish, the efficacy of the Mirebeau campaign, the strategic insight revealed by the plan to relieve Chateau-Gaillard (K. Norgate considered this 'a masterpiece of ingenuity') and the forward-thinking decision to establish fortifications along the line of the River Torques.[38] King John 'like any capable general' observes Turner, 'had a sense of geography and an ability to plan a strategy to gain ground'.[39] This is not to deny that John was guilty of some military error – after all, war rarely goes according to plan – but it does encourage the exploration of other reasons for the loss of Normandy (see 'Interpretation' in Chapter 10 for a fuller discussion of the military ability of John).

One such alternative reason is obtained by an appreciation of the theatre in which the war was being fought. Whereas John had the disadvantage of a long frontier stretching from the River Seine to the River Garonne, Philip enjoyed the benefit of a compact centre in the form of the Île-de-France from which he could launch his attacks down either the Seine or Loire valleys. Moreover, whereas John had long unwieldy lines of communication and supply, ultimately stretching back across the Channel, Philip had significantly shorter, more manageable, lines of communication.

Rather than a consequence of any martial deficiency, it makes better sense to understand John's decision to negotiate in 1200 as an act of necessity dictated by 'an economy at full stretch and a Normandy suddenly weary of war'.[40] In these circumstances, says Warren, 'if John had tried a firm sword it would have shattered in his hand'.[41] In any case, although crowned, John had not yet imposed his authority on England. Therefore, in the months immediately following the truce, he spent time in England. In this respect Le Goulet looks like a strategic victory. Indeed, 'Softsword' appears critical only because we know that thereafter Normandy is lost and not regained – there is much to be said for the idea that in 1200 John was being prudent in preferring peace to war.

The details of the Treaty of Le Goulet have meant that historians have not been able to agree upon an interpretation of its impact. On the one hand scholars like E. M. Hallam and J. Everard believe that 'John made enormous allowances to Philip...which neither Richard nor Henry II would ever have considered. He rendered homage to the French king, he paid him an enormous relief, thus acknowledging Philip's right to decide the succession.' J. W. Baldwin supports this interpretation, arguing that 'By giving up Arthur, at least for a time, Philip had exacted from John the major military objectives he had been unable to win from Richard.'[42] On the other hand, R. Bartlett concludes his study by asserting that 'It appeared as if John had achieved a transmission of power virtually as complete as that of 1189' and D. Carpenter believes that it was Philip who had made the 'major concession'.[43] K. Norgate, usually critical of John, describes Philip's recognition of John as lawful heir to the Angevin territories as a 'personal triumph'.[44] Against this background, and supportive of the idea that Philip was a cunning opponent, a perhaps more helpful approach than seeking to identify a definitive winner and loser from Le Goulet, is the judgement provided by J. C. Holt: 'for John', he says, 'the treaty was a settlement; for Philip it was a springboard'.[45]

ii) The Lusignans

The established interpretation is that this 'springboard' proferred to Philip by the Treaty of Le Goulet was given greater effect because of the consequences of John's marriage to Isabella and his alleged involvement in the murder of Arthur. These are now examined in turn.

Chronicle opinion would have us believe a lurid picture of mad infatuation, of John as a twelfth-century Humbert Humbert.[46] Historians have not been able to prove Isabella's age definitively in 1200 but she was unlikely to have been more than fifteen and quite possibly as young as nine.[47] 'How happy it must make all latter day critics of King John', observes N. Vincent, 'to know that the king may have been guilty not only of cruelty and murder but even, possibly, of child molesting'.[48] Indeed, the chroniclers aver that John was beguiled by Isabella's beauty in 1200 and that a reason for the loss of Normandy was because he chose to lay in bed with her rather than prosecute the war against Philip. For reasons already outlined, we need to treat chronicle opinion with a great deal of caution and we should be mindful of the fact that marriages in this period were undertaken first and foremost for reasons of diplomacy. We should be alert, also, to judging early thirteenth-century actions against morals of our own day. In John's day, canon law stipulated an age of consent of twelve for girls and fourteen for boys. Marriage at an early age was commonplace: John's sister, Eleanor, was married to the king of Castile when she was eight and her husband was twenty-two; John's son, Henry III, married Eleanor of Provence when she was twelve and he was twenty-nine; John's daughter, Joan, was married to Alexander II, King of Scots when she was twelve and her husband was twenty-four; and John's youngest daughter, Eleanor, was married at the age of nine to the son of William Marshal, a man about fifteen years her senior. Moreover, Isabella did not give birth to her first child until 1207, suggesting that John abstained from sexual relations until that time.[49] All in all, it is possible to conclude that John's second marriage 'in no way offended against contemporary law or contemporary morals' even though it may do considerable violence to our own.[50]

John's apparent mistreatment of the Lusignans in light of his marriage – frequently asserted as the trigger cause for the loss of Normandy – is traditionally a key theme in the Bad King John school of history. Yet there are explanations for what appears at first sight to be a series of inexplicable actions undertaken by John. First, the Lusignans, kings of Jerusalem and Cyprus as well as lords of Lusignan, had long been rebellious vassals. For instance, in 1168 they slew Patrick Earl of Salisbury whom Henry II had appointed to govern Poitou and in 1188 Geoffrey de Lusignan had murdered the then Count of Poitou. (Since Salisbury was the uncle of William Marshal, John could expect to rely especially on the latter's support in his actions against the Lusignans.) John also had reason to believe that the Lusignans had kidnapped his mother in 1168, or at least sought to do so. John thus charged the Lusignans with long-standing treachery. In these circumstances, it was usual to prove the truth of such a claim by a duel to the death with royal champions. Trial by battle was thus certainly not intrinsically humiliating, though it seems that the Lusignans may have had a legitimate grievance because the champions John proposed for the duel were considered of insufficient status.

Second, it has been suggested 'with some reason that [the judgement of Philip's court in pronouncing John to be a contumacious vassal] was "quite revolutionary", as the principle [it espoused] had not previously been applied to magnate principalities. It is a measure of the extending power of the monarchy under Philip Augustus.'[51] In other words, there are grounds for arguing that the judgement of the court was unexpected. Certainly, John briefed the archbishop of Canterbury and the bishop of Ely to lay before his English subjects an account of the 'humility and moderation we bore ourselves before [Philip], and what insolence [he] always found in him, and how he openly acted against the terms of the peace which had been made and confirmed between us'.[52] Similarly, in a letter from 7 July 1202, in which John requested a loan from the Cistercian abbots of England, he lamented 'how the king of France contrary to the peace which was made between us... unjustly attacks us'.[53] Of course, we must be alert to the propagandist nature of these letters but they nevertheless carry some truth.

Third, we should not be blind to the notion that in 1202, unlike 1200, John deliberately sought war and that he may have been intent upon a showdown with Philip in order to gain revenge for all those occasions when the French king had manipulated Angevin rivalries to Capetian advantage. K. Norgate has speculated whether John had set upon a 'deliberate purpose of goading [the Lusignans] into some outrageous course of action which might enable him to recover La Marche and ruin them completely, or even drive them altogether out of the land'.[54] After all, in 1202 John had every reason to feel confident that he would be successful: his military campaign of 1199–1200 had gone well; Aquitaine appeared to be secure (at least as long as his mother lived) and Philip was mired in a struggle with the church over his bigamous marriage to Agnes of Meran. Moreover, Arthur's status as an alternative successor to Richard had been diminished by the Treaty of Le Goulet and Arthur's mother Constance, once consistently guilty of encouraging ambition in her son, had died in 1201. Lastly, until his death in 1202, Count Adhemar of Angoulême supported John against the Lusignans and seems to have taken command of the county of La Marche. In Powicke's judgement, John had 'secured a turbulent independent vassal as a strong ally'.[55] There were, then, plenty of reasons for John to feel emboldened to move against the Lusignans, perhaps with the intention of destroying them once and for all, and also to resist the strictures of his overlord, Philip. Moreover, the attack upon Eu made considerable strategic sense, sitting as it did at the mouth of the river Bresle (which in turn separated the French county of Ponthieu from the Duchy of Normandy).

iii) Fickleness and Faithlessness

As noted by the Barnwell chronicler (see page 6), John suffered from ill-fortune in the early years of his reign. Simple bad luck contributes to an explanation of the loss of Normandy. We have already observed the decision of the counts of Flanders and Boulogne to respond positively to the papal call for a Fourth Crusade, meaning that John was denied the possibility of opening a second front by forming with them an anti-Capetian alliance. Then, upon the death of Eleanor in April 1204, a significant legal obstacle to Philip's further progress into the southern territories of the Angevin 'empire' was removed, encouraging an even greater rate of defection from John amongst the Angevin and Poitevin political class – a process that was already afflicting the Anglo-Norman political nation. Indeed, it has been argued by S. Painter that the basic cause for the loss of Normandy was 'the unenthusiastic if not actually treasonable behavior of the Anglo-Norman baronage'.[56] The most spectacular instance of such behavior is offered by the action of the Count of

Alençon: in January 1203 John dined with the count only to learn two days later that he had transferred his allegiance to Philip.

From the spring of 1203 there was thus a steady hemorrhaging of support for John. Some historical opinion has suggested that the behaviour evinced by the Count of Alençon was the accepted and time-honoured form of conduct amongst members of the French political elite. Particularly in the southern parts of his dominions, as Turner puts it, John, 'had to contend with the legendary faithlessness and fickleness of the Poitevin nobles'.[57] No doubt, as William Marshal's biographer asserted, John, by his actions, 'had not been careful to avoid irritating people'.[58] Yet that is the nature of politics. Perhaps more palpable, helped by a propaganda machine first started by Louis VII, was the great and growing sense that the Capetian monarchy epitomized a social, intellectual and cultural renaissance with which the Angevins were not associated. Certainly, Philip's benevolent attitude towards the church, for example, was in marked contrast to John's and meant that many of the Norman clergy welcomed Philip's takeover of the duchy. Similarly, Philip's attitude towards baronial fortresses was less despotic than that of John, for whereas the Angevin sought to confiscate or raze such castles the Capetian accepted 'legal recognition of his overlordship without pressing for the same personal domination that his enemies preferred'.[59]

A consequence of the great and growing sense of treachery was that John increasingly hired mercenaries, foreign lowborn men, such as Martin Algais, Gerard d'Athée, Brandin and Lupescar (the 'Wolf'); and, since John realized that he could rely upon such men, he appointed them to positions which the established political elite would ordinarily have expected to occupy. This, coupled with the fact that mercenary captains pillaged and mistreated non-combatants and necessitated the levying of taxes, caused yet further disaffection with the Angevin cause. (Gérard d'Athée and his kinsmen were mentioned by name in Article 50 of Magna Carta. See page 146.) 'Do you know', says the biographer of William Marshal, 'why King John was unable to keep the love of his people? It was because Lupescar maltreated them, and pillaged them as though they were in enemy territory.'[60] A vicious circle had been set in motion.

iv) Structural Tensions and Finance

As pointed out in Chapter 3, some historians have argued that for structural reasons the loss of Normandy – indeed, the loss of nearly all the Continental dominions of the Angevins – had become an inevitability even before 1199. This 'structuralist' argument has centred in particular upon the availability, or otherwise, of revenue. In this respect J. C. Holt has argued that John failed to retain the Continental possessions he inherited because by 1199 England – and more especially Normandy – had been drained of resources by his predecessors whilst the revenues of the Capetian monarchy were simultaneously rapidly expanding. However, J. Gillingham contests this position, arguing that Holt has misinterpreted the evidence. He insists instead that a far more compelling explanation of the loss of the Continental territories is the inadequacy of John's leadership. It is worth examining these positions in some detail.

Even before John acceded to the throne it seems that England was financially exhausted. This appears to be well attested by contemporary and near contemporary observation. 'By these vexations [i.e. revenue raising devices]', noted the chronicler Howden, describing conditions in England in 1198, 'whether justly or unjustly, the whole of England from sea to sea was reduced to poverty'.[61] Coggeshall echoed this sentiment when he noted that 'No age can remember, no history can record an preceding king, even those who reigned for a long time, who exacted and received so much money from his kingdom as that King [i.e. Richard] exacted and amassed in the five years after his return from captivity.'[62] Chronicle evidence must of course be treated with great care, but later historians in general find themselves in agreement. 'Raising Richard's ransom required the imposition of staggering levies on his subjects and on the churches in his domains', observe Turner and Heiser.[63]

England's financial exhaustion came about for a number of reasons. In part it was because of the particular financial demands made by Richard, namely the funding of his participation in the Third Crusade and the consequent raising of a ransom of perhaps 100,000 marks (£66,000) to free him from the Holy Roman Emperor, Henry VI, after his capture as he returned from the Holy Land. In part it was due to a combination of increased silver supply and rising population that produced in England a long cycle of inflation, of the order of 100–200 per cent by the last two decades of the twelfth century. Perhaps most especially, it was also because of the rising costs of defending long and exposed 'imperial' frontiers against the increasingly efficient French government. The building of Chateau-Gaillard cost £11,500 – the equivalent of perhaps one third of the revenue of John by the end of his reign.

Financial exhaustion in England may not have mattered too much if significant amounts of revenue could nonetheless have been mobilized from other parts of the 'empire', particularly in the place it was needed most – Normandy. In fact, as demonstrated by the research of J. C. Holt, England was being bled white because of the impoverished condition of Normandy.[64] The Norman Exchequer Rolls for 1195 and 1198 reveal a duchy already squeezed to the limit, a consequence of what V. D. Moss has called the

'Norman fiscal revolution'.[65] In 1202–3 John was rapidly losing territory in Normandy and consequently it seems that 'King John could only extract [from Normandy] about approximately half the revenue that was raised by King Richard in 1198.'[66] 'By 1203, if not earlier', observes R. V. Turner, 'the Norman treasury was empty, and money had to be found in England for its defence.'[67] Evidence has not survived to allow for any definitive assessment of the extent to which other constituent parts of the 'empire' might have provided financial resources for the defence of Normandy, but there is a general consensus that any such revenues were insubstantial.

John not only had to deal with financial exhaustion in key constituencies of his 'empire' but also a Capetian monarchy that was newly rich, notably from new lands incorporated into the French royal domain in 1191 and more efficient sinews of governance. Comparison of Angevin and Capetian revenue has necessarily proved difficult, but nonetheless a number of recent studies 'point to stunning increases in royal revenues under Philip, whose innovations apparently ended the Angevins' superiority in resources, tipping the balance in the Capetians' favour by the first years of the thirteenth century'.[68] J. C. Holt estimates that the Angevin total revenues in 1195 were no more than 45 per cent of those of Philip; and, although enhanced, the equivalent figure in 1198 was 74 per cent.[69] N. Barratt believes that by 1202–3 Angevin revenue was somewhere between 71 per cent and 74 per cent of the Capetian total.[70] The latest biographer of the French King believes that 'even from the fragmentary records it is clear that [French] royal income was increasing progressively through the reign and at a considerable rate, a rise of 72 per cent between the beginning of the reign and 1203. It is also clear that it was a successful operation and more was collected than spent.'[71] In all, we are provided with the distinct impression that Philip's finances were adequate to his political designs against the Angevin lands on the Continent. Tellingly, whereas his predecessors had been unable to afford the cost of hiring mercenaries, Philip was able to hire a permanent force 2,500 strong. Moss' study of Capetian and Angevin financial wherewithal led him to conclude 'that any Plantagenet ruler, however able, would have failed to defend the Angevin "empire" in the first decade of the thirteenth century because of the impossibility of matching the Capetians' growing revenues'.[72] Against this background, John lost Normandy less because of any deficiency of leadership and more because he was financially out-gunned.

In this context, revenue raising devices so loudly complained of in Magna Carta (see pages 139–50) were applied with renewed vigour and do seem to have raised extraordinary amounts of money, particularly after 1194 (which appears as something of a watershed in English finance: before that year annual revenue was of the order of £12,000 p.a, whereas during the years 1194–9 average annual revenue was £25,000).[73] But such sums could only be extracted at a political cost which further loosened the political ties between England and Normandy, which were already diminished because of the well established and ongoing process whereby leading families chose to arrange their affairs in ways which did not sustain cross-Channel inheritances (see pages 28–30). Equal and opposite forces were at work. On each side of the Channel, the political will to maintain the Anglo-Norman regnum (the central fulcrum of the 'empire') was haemorrhaging in proportion to the rising costs of maintaining the arrangement. As R. W. Southern observed, 'there is a direct connection between the over-great financial and military burden of [the] Continental policy [required to maintain the Anglo-Norman regnum] and the failure of the English kings to create any warmth of sentiment operating in their favour among the most powerful classes of society'.[74] Arguably, the creation of any such 'warmth of sentiment' was pretty much impossible by 1199. It was John's bad luck that he inherited this condition.

John Gillingham, however, has robustly contested what he calls 'the orthodoxy of 1991 – that is, that by 1199 the Angevin Empire was incapable of paying for its own defence, and not even Richard's warlike spirit could have sustained it longer.'[75] There are two main aspects to his argument.

First, he argues that John mobilized more resources than other historians have allowed. Thus, he disputes a figure of £24,000 as the total English revenue for 1202–3. He advises that 'an unknown sum has to be added…in order to take account of the levy of a seventh on moveables [in 1203]' and he points out, with this factored in that total English revenue at this time may have been as high as £134,000, 'lending no support whatsoever to the notion that England in 1200 was more impoverished than in 1194'.[76] Gillingham protests that any suggestion that England was in a financial crisis 1199–1204 cannot be reconciled with the financial history of the second half of John's reign 'when royal revenue in England was to climb at an astonishing rate' and consequently produced many of the grievances articulated in Magna Carta.[77] Pointing out that the war in Normandy was episodic and localized, Gillingham also argues that this territory was probably not impoverished. Indeed, he believes that military spending on projects such as Chateau-Gaillard probably 'stimulated the Norman economy'.[78] Above all, Gillingham claims that other parts of the 'empire' – particularly Ireland, Anjou and Aquitaine – are likely to have made a much more substantial contribution to the Angevin coffers than other historians have assumed. 'A glance at the map', says Gillingham, 'would appear to suggest that revenues [from Anjou and Aquitaine] were considerable. The area contains some very fertile regions, notably the valleys of the Loire, the Charente and the Garonne. In the Loire valley were the vineyards of Anjou and Touraine and the great town of Tours, famous for its metalwork.'[79] The assumption is that tolls and duties will have raised significant revenue. Thus, it is unsurprising that 'on the Third Crusade [Philip] had cut a sorry figure, a lord outshone and outbid by his own vassal [i.e. Richard]'.[80] From all of this Gillingham is then able to draw the conclusion that 'if John was no match for Philip Augustus it was not because he had inherited inadequate financial resources; it was because he did not know how to rule'.[81] Or, as a monk from Clairmarais near St Omer put it, when John left Normandy: 'he was struck down by cowardice rather than lack of money'.[82]

Second, Gillingham refuses to accept comparative analysis which apparently shows Capetian revenue to have been greater than that of the Angevins. This, he asserts, is a claim that 'does not stand up'.[83] He concludes instead that 'there can be no doubt that c.1200 the overall resources of the Angevin Empire were a good deal greater than those at the disposal of Philip Augustus'.[84] He believes that Capetian revenues have been overestimated. He claims that that the alleged Capetian total revenue of 1202–3 (about £73,000) includes a substantial sum which 'might have been drawn from a reserve built up in the years of peace after 1198 or possibly money which Philip had borrowed, but it certainly should not be included in the revenue for 1202–1203'.[85] He also states that 'whilst it is true that Philip's territorial acquisitions in the northeast, notable around Amiens and Arras, meant that by the early 1190s he was wealthier than his father had been after 1152, this is far from proving that he was already as well off as the Angevins', not least because by 1200 'he had relinquished Aire and St Omer to the count of Flanders'.[86] This analysis allows Gillingham to argue that the 'collapse [of the 'empire'] is much more plausibly attributed to the question marks against John's personality than to any structural reasons'.[87]

Which of these two interpretations is the more valid, that put forward by Gillingham or that sponsored by Holt et al.? As all historians acknowledge, there are complex and significant difficulties involved in using the existing financial accounts to estimate revenues.[88] (Gillingham describes any such undertaking as 'an extraordinarily hazardous exercise'; J. C. Holt believes it to be 'a structure of guesswork of Byzantine complexity'.[89]) For instance, although accounts for the three main territories – France, Normandy and England – have survived for the same financial year (1202–3), the French account survives in isolation and therefore cannot easily be used to demonstrate Philip's revenue before 1203. Nonetheless, despite issues of technical difficulty such as this, recent scholarship by Turner and Heiser has concluded that 'nothing suggests that surpluses generated [in Greater Anjou] were sufficient for exporting sums to Normandy for expenditure on mercenary forces'.[90] In any case, it is particularly difficult to accept Gillingham's proposition that significant funds flowed north to Normandy from Greater Anjou and Aquitaine because the Angevins simply did not have the administrative machinery in these regions necessary to mobilize significant revenues. Finally, financial stability is not just a function of revenues but also of expenditure – and Gillingham overlooks this. The expense of the vast Angevin 'empire', and the specific problem of price inflation in England (see pages 131–2), added greatly to John's problems.

Chapter 5

EFFORTS TO REGAIN THE FRENCH TERRITORIES, 1205–1214

Timeline

1205	
Summer	Proposed expedition to France is called off
1206	John undertakes a campaign in the southwestern territories of France
1 August	Surrender of Montauban
26 October	Two year truce with Philip
1209	Otto crowned Holy Roman Emperor
1212	Welsh rebellion and conspiracy in England prevent continental expedition from sailing
1213	Further baronial recalcitrance prevents continental expedition from setting out
May	Battle of Damme
1214	
15 February	John lands at La Rochelle
17 June	John enters Angers but thereafter was unable to take Roche-au-Moine; anti-Capetian alliance mobilizes in the north
27 July	Battle of Bouvines
October	John returns to England

A) Narrative: The Course of the War, 1205–1214

John's overriding ambition after 1204 was to regain his French territories. The ultimate campaign to this end was fought in 1214, and culminated in the Battle of Bouvines, arguably one of the most important battles in European history.

The Christmas festivities of 1204, played out against what was turning out to be a ferociously cold winter, can have done little to raise John's spirits. It is customary for textbooks to talk of the 'loss of Normandy', but by the end of 1204 it was far worse than that. After the fall of Rouen in June 1204, Philip Augustus had pressed south so that in great swathes of the Angevin 'empire' men were recognizing the French king as their overlord. Not only had the whole of Normandy been overrun by the forces of Philip Augustus but also in the counties of Anjou, Maine and Touraine – the very heart of the Angevin 'empire' – only the fortresses of Chinon and Loches held out. Meanwhile, in Poitou, John continued to hold firmly only the port of La Rochelle (and the adjacent island, Île d'Oléron), the fortress at Niort and the county of Angoulême, the last of which could not be attacked with feudal propriety because it was held by John in right of his wife – unlike the rest of Aquitaine which had lost its protection from attack upon the death of John's mother, Eleanor, in April 1204. In Gascony, only a handful of towns retained their allegiance to John, most lords now recognizing Alfonso VIII of Castile, the husband of John's sister, Eleanor, as their new overlord. The only development from which John could gain any succour was a stiffening of resistance to Philip amongst the lords of Aquitaine, those lords recognizing that their interests were best served by the (mostly) absentee overlordship of John. For this reason, by the end of 1204/early 1205, the assault of Philip had run its course.

i) Issues of Allegiance

John had no intention of letting Philip Augustus keep what he had taken. Recognizing that Normandy could not be regained by means of an amphibious campaign, John sought to establish a secure land base in the Loire region from which he could launch an invasion of Normandy and in which he could most easily recruit mercenaries. It would also place him in the centre of the 'empire' and John might have expected that his presence there would stem the haemorrhaging of support recently witnessed.

In purely military terms there was much to recommend such a scheme; John's difficulty was how to win political support from the barons for his plan, few of whom had any interest in territories south of Normandy. As W. L. Warren says, 'Aquitaine was nothing to them. It was virtually a private concern of the king, a problem assumed by Henry II when he married Eleanor.'[1] John, though, must have hoped that his main ambition of winning back Normandy would earn political support because the Anglo-Norman regnum had been in existence since 1066. However, in this respect he was swimming against the tide of a process underway for at least the last fifty years, for the habit of Anglo-Norman families dividing their inheritances at the Channel was well worn (see pages 28–30). Others, apparently sensing which way the wind was blowing, had made private agreements that were inimical to John's ambition. Thus, during the siege of Arques in 1203, Ellis of Wimberville and Alan Martell, realizing that they both held similar amounts of land on each side of the Channel, agreed to an exchange so that henceforth Ellis held only English lands and Martell held only Norman ones. Consequently, after the loss of Normandy, neither had a reason to fight. By the early thirteenth century, only three Anglo-Norman barons still had substantial lands in Normandy – Ranulf de Blundeville, Earl of Chester (d. 1232), Robert de Breteuil, Earl of Leicester (d. 1204) and William Marshal, Earl of Pembroke (d. 1219). In April 1204, these last two, having been sent by John to discuss a settlement between the respective kings, seem to have used the occasion to make arrangements to their own advantage: they made a payment to Philip by which they escaped – though only for twelve months – the French king's demand that they pay him homage for their lands in Normandy. It was ominous for John that his leading barons were desirous of peace whilst he sought war.

ii) Prospect of a French Invasion

In the early months of 1205 John undertook a number of actions in response to reports that Philip Augustus was on the point of undertaking an invasion of England. Firstly, he insisted that all males over the age of twelve take an oath 'for the general defence of the realm…against foreigners and against any other disturbers of the peace'.[2] Secondly, each shire was to have a chief constable who in turn was to appoint constables for the hundreds, charged with mustering and supervising the local levies.[3] Thirdly, realizing that he would be best served by a small permanent band of knights (rather than the old feudal host who would traditionally only serve for forty days), John demanded that each shire now only send him one in every ten knights expected from the old feudal quota and that the other nine should pay 2s per day towards the 'running costs' of that knight. Historians have been generally critical of John at this time, R. V. Turner asserting that John's actions betray the king as having been 'anxious' and 'close to panic'.[4] In fact, this royal activity can better be understood as a coherent programme of highly pertinent measures, collectively another substantiation of what the record evidence generally demonstrates – in short, 'that it is probable that there had never been a king who devoted himself so keenly to the job of ruling'.[5] Indeed, all of this provides a counterweight to what Wendover would have us believe of John's actions at this time – that he was at leisure, 'enjoying all the pleasures of life with his queen'.[6]

iii) The Expedition that Never Sailed, 1205

By the early spring of 1205 John's instructions were no longer defensive in nature, in fact the very opposite: it was clear that he was now set on invading France and therefore quickly recognized the importance of developing the navy. Indeed, as early as 1204 he had some fifty galleys and had ordered the building of more, encouraging speculation among historians that 'it might almost be said that the history of the British navy begins with John'.[7] The record evidence testifies to a buzz of activity as provisions were marshalled, forces mustered and scutage collected. F. McLynn, usually a critic of John, concedes that all this produced 'the greatest force yet seen in English history'.[8] W. L. Warren concurs when he states that 'nothing hitherto had been seen like these preparations: they eclipsed even those for Richard's crusade in 1190.'[9] John had also moved to win baronial support for his invasion. The fact that he prepared fleets in both Portsmouth and Dartmouth has led to speculation that two separate expeditions were intended, the fleet at Portsmouth (under John's direction) to assault Normandy, and that in Dartmouth (carrying a mercenary force under the command of John's illegitimate son Geoffrey) to sail to La Rochelle. Although not tactically secure, a direct attack upon Normandy was clearly the best means of energizing the barons. By midsummer everything was ready.

The expedition never sailed (see Appendix, Document 9). The best explanation for this is that it was torpedoed by baronial recalcitrance, inspired perhaps by a lack of confidence in John's strategy, some cautionary words from Hubert Walter or the immense costs of the enterprise – as much as one quarter of the year's revenue was spent on this cause – but above all, by the example set by William Marshal.

In 1205 William Marshal, Earl of Pembroke was probably the greatest baron in England. Early in that year, with the deal he had cut with Philip twelve months earlier about to expire, Marshal had travelled to the French court (apparently with John's blessing). There, it seems he devised a bespoke form of liege homage paid to the French king for his Norman lands. S. Painter explains that this meant that 'if the French invaded England [Marshal] could fight against them, but he could not participate in John's attempts to recover his continental possessions [for that would provide Philip with a legitimate reason to seize his Norman lands]. The earl had definitely divided his allegiance.'[10] He had also secured a powerful reason not to accompany John. When John tried to insist that Marshal sail with him, the earl said to an assembly of barons 'Let this be a warning to you: what the king is planning to do to me he will do to every one of you when he gets the upper hand.'[11]

The fact that the king's most able and most powerful baron had done homage to John's enemy and refused to follow John into war inspires a good deal of sympathy for the king. The event marked the beginning of an estrangement between the king and Marshal which lasted until 1213; and it further confirmed John's growing belief that he would be better served by mercenary elements than by his barons. Meanwhile the castles at Chinon and Loches, unable to hold out any longer, surrendered.

iv) The Expedition of 1206

Against this background it is remarkable that John successfully undertook an invasion of France in 1206. Despite the disappointment of 1205, John's determination and nerve held steady. Over the winter of 1205–6 preparations were impressive and reveal a close attention to detail: defences of the Channel Islands were strengthened; eight substantial transport ships were made suitable for the king's use and in February John toured the north of England. Four days at York were followed by two at Knaresborough, two at Richmond, two at Bowes, then over the Pennines to Carlisle, Lancaster and Chester. This breathless itinerary was no doubt one of the reasons why now, unlike in 1205, the barons followed John: Angevin aspiration, spat out in one-to-one meetings, was a force of nature that few could resist.

Eschewing any thoughts of sending some of the force to Normandy, John arrived in the port of La Rochelle accompanied by several hundred vessels at the end of the first week of June (see Figure 9, page 68). The expedition seems to have had three main aims: to bolster the Angevin cause in Poitou; to thwart the progress of the king's brother-in-law, Alfonso of Castile (who was steadily imposing his authority on Gascony); and to gather information to facilitate a much bigger invasion at some later time.

The first of these aims was quickly achieved by a march that took John half way to Poitiers, travelling via the castle at Niort to deepen its defenders' loyalty for his cause. The second aim enjoyed spectacular success. Upon learning that the fortified town of Montauban in eastern Gascony was harbouring many of his enemies, John besieged it. On 1 August it surrendered to John after fifteen days, drawing begrudging respect from even Wendover who recorded that 'even Charlemagne could not subdue Montauban after a seven year's siege'.[12] This was enough to drive the Castilians from Gascony. Thereafter, John headed back north across Poitou and penetrated into Berry, a deed sufficiently impressive to persuade Aimeri de Thouars to once again support John. Then John drove on into Anjou, and in the second week in September held court at Angers, the old heart of the Angevin 'empire'. From there, a foray to the border with Maine was sufficient to bring Philip Augustus

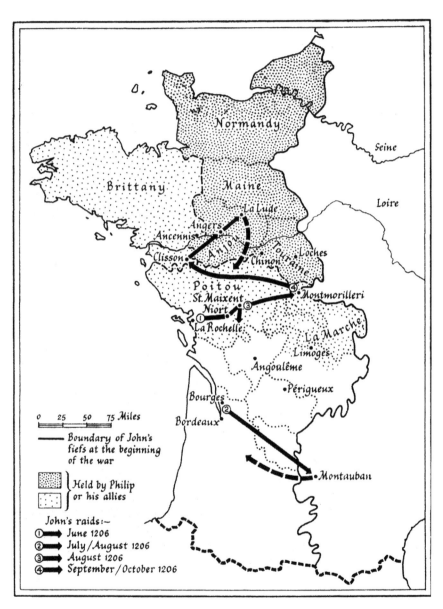

Figure 9. The expedition of 1206 (courtesy of Yale University Press)

to the negotiating table. On 26 October, a truce was arranged to last for two years. This, John estimated, would provide sufficient time to mobilize the greater resources that he now knew would be required for a more complete conquest, the third of his aims.

v) The Background to Bouvines

From 1206 John appears to have been clear in his mind as to the strategy required to bring down Philip Augustus. He thus determined to launch simultaneous attacks, one upon the northern French territories (with a probable ultimate intention of pressing on to Paris) and the other in the Poitou region, thereby forcing Philip to fight a war on two fronts and, by attacking in the north, appeasing those barons who had sat on their hands in 1205. John set about fashioning an anti-Capetian coalition to perpetrate the northern assault, while he himself prepared to lead a force in the south, determined to extend the success already achieved from the 1206 expedition. R. V. Turner judges that the whole scheme as it manifested itself in 1214 amounted to 'the largest military operation ever devised by an English or French monarch' and that preparations for the campaign 'show a capacity for planning on a grand scale'.[13]

A key part of these preparations was the raising of huge sums of money – perhaps 200,000 marks by 1214 – needed for assisting in the construction of an anti-Capetian coalition, building and equipping ships and hiring mercenaries. John was significantly assisted in the creation of this coalition by the actions of Philip. In the years 1211–13, perhaps over-confident after gaining Normandy, Philip seized territory belonging to Counts Renaud of Boulogne and Ferrand of Flanders. A consequence of these acts of 'brutal opportunism' was that these important princes of the Low Countries were pushed into John's camp.[14] John was also benefitting from changing events in the Holy Roman Empire. His nephew Otto – upon the murder of his rival Philip, Duke of Swabia – had finally been crowned emperor by Pope Innocent III in 1209. To cement an alliance, John sent Otto huge sums of money – on one occasion alone, 10,000 marks.[15] Though Otto's position was less strong as early as 1211 because he was by then excommunicate, and Philip Augustus was able to sponsor a rival to his authority, it seemed that John's coalition was nevertheless sufficiently robust to achieve its goal – to crush the king of France 'on the anvil of Poitou by a hammer from the Low Countries'.[16]

By 1212 John was ready: the coalition was in place, ships had been built and it seemed that Scotland, Ireland and Wales were quiescent (see Chapter 6). However, a sudden rebellion in Wales in 1212 followed by a serious conspiracy in England meant that John's plans for an invasion were put on hold.

A further impediment to the king's ambitions emerged in 1213 when elements of the barons argued – extraordinarily – that the terms of their feudal tenure meant that they did not have to undertake service in Poitou. Added to these developments within England, there was a sudden and real fear that Philip was about to invade (see Appendix Document 19). With papal backing, Philip was able to claim that he was launching a crusade against an excommunicate king. John, however, took the wind out his enemy's sails by submitting to the papacy in May 1213. Then, acting on the principle that attack is the best form of defence, John ordered out his fleet of 500 ships under the command of his half-brother, William Longespée, Earl of Salisbury. It achieved extraordinary success by destroying on 30 May the French fleet as it moored off Damme, a short distance off Bruges. Of the perhaps 1,700 heavily laden French ships, three hundred were cut adrift and a further one hundred were looted and set on fire. Philip, unable to get his remaining ships to safety, took the decision to burn them rather then risk them falling into enemy hands. The spoils were considerable: 'never had so much treasure come into England since the days of King Arthur', said the biographer of William Marshal. Count Ferrand took comfort from the event that confirmed he had made the right choice of ally – the day after events at Damme he came to ratify his alliance with John. 'It is surprising', says Warren, 'that a nation so proud of its naval history has not honoured John more.'[17]

vi) The Campaign of 1214

At last, in early 1214, the main body of the expedition under John set sail. According to Coggeshall it was composed of 'few earls, but an infinite multitude of low class soldiers of fortune' and 'an incalculable treasury of gold, silver and precious stones'.[18] The king arrived in La Rochelle on 15 February and thereafter – making his presence known by travelling extensively and rapidly, and by taking the castle of Milécu after a siege of only three days – he was able to stiffen Angevin authority (see Figure 10). He also took the Lusignan fortresses at Mervant and Vouvant and then secured the allegiance of these one-time enemies by arranging for his daughter, Joan, to marry the son of Hugh de Lusignan, also called Hugh.

With the southwestern territories of his dominions thus secured, John moved north, intent upon drawing into battle the French army that had been reported hovering in the territories just north of Poitou. Having won an important encounter at Nantes – at which John obtained some prisoners of significance – the town of Angers surrendered and the seneschal of Anjou, William des Roches, retreated to his new fortress at Roche-au-Moine. John duly laid siege, and when it seemed that it was about to fall, Louis, the son of

Figure 10. The Bouvines campaign, 1214 (courtesy of Yale University Press)

Philip (the French king having retreated north – see below), began to march to its relief.

John's success to this point had been extraordinary and thus provided him with a platform from which he could engage French forces with confidence. But as Louis drew ever closer the Poitevin barons, under that 'inveterate turncoat', Ameri de Thouars, melted away.[19] There is no evidence here of cowardice or lassitude on the part of John. Indeed, the Poitevins seem to have been disturbed by John's preparedness to do battle – Wendover asserts that the 'barons of Poitou refused to follow the king, saying that they were not prepared for a pitched battle'. Not for the first time they turned with the wind, perhaps sensing that if defeated in battle then their French overlord would seek harsh revenge whereas hitherto his authority had been notional rather than real. 'King John', continues Wendover in unusually sympathetic tone, 'knowing too well the accustomed treachery of the nobles of Poitou, although the capture of the castle [i.e Roche-au-Moine] was almost certain, retired in great annoyance from the siege'.[20] In the first week of July the English king was back at La Rochelle, perhaps beginning to realize that he faced an apparently insuperable structural issue.

In the meantime, at some point in late April, Philip had retreated to the north to deal with the invasion of the Earl of Salisbury, the Counts of Boulogne and Flanders and, John's nephew Otto, the Holy Roman Emperor. However, with disastrous results for the Angevin cause, Otto did not gather his forces before the third week in July, thus providing Philip with time to organize his host.

The armies met on 27 July at Bouvines (see Figure 11). J. Bradbury calls the ensuing battle 'one of the most decisive and significant battles in European history. At stake were the futures of France and the Holy Roman Empire, and indirectly of England and the Angevin Empire, as well as the counties of Flanders and Boulogne.'[21]

The French and their opponents each formed three main divisions at Bouvines, the former arrayed on the west of the battlefield and the latter on the east. Philip was in the centre of the French forces with, amongst others, William des Roches. On the French king's left were his Dreux relatives, whilst on his right were forces headed by the Duke of Burgundy and Guérin de Glapion, the bishop-elect of Senlis. Directly opposite Philip was Otto. On Otto's right were Renaud, Count of Boulogne and William Longespée; on his left was Ferrand, Count of Flanders. Estimates of the total size of the respective armies vary considerably, though J. W. Baldwin has recently concluded that 'the French fought with about 1,300 knights and 4,000–6,000 foot-sergeants [whilst the allies fought with] 1,300–1,500 knights and 7,500 foot-sergeants'.[22]

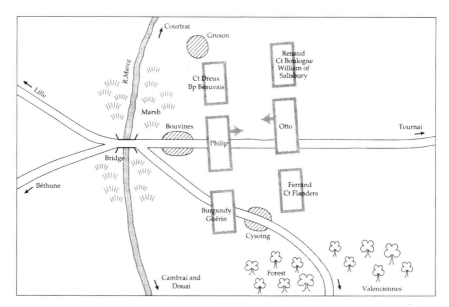

Figure 11. The arrangement of forces at the Battle of Bouvines, 1214

Although Philip himself was at one point unhorsed, the eventual outcome was an overwhelming victory for the French. A near contemporary account of Bouvines asserts that 'The providence of divine mercy ended this battle which had been fought...for the praise and the glory of Philip, and for the honor of the Holy Church. May its honor, its virtue, and its power remain through the infinity of centuries to come. Amen.'[23] Amongst the prisoners were the Counts of Boulogne and Flanders, as well as William Longespée, Earl of Salisbury. Otto, described by one historian as 'a worthless, inefficient, bungling, totally unreliable braggart', fled the battle.[24] In September, John had little choice but to agree a truce with Philip who, 'at a stroke had become the most successful royal commander in French history. Not one enemy, but virtually all his enemies, had been either destroyed or seriously weakened by his great victory.'[25] Arriving back in England in October, John knew that he would face baronial disaffection. Indeed, it was a short road from Bouvines to Runnymede.

Chapter 6

THE BRITISH PERSPECTIVE:
SCOTLAND, IRELAND AND WALES,
1199–1214

Timeline

1165	William the Lion's reign begins
1173–1174	William the Lion participates in the Great Rebellion against Henry II
1174	
December	Treaty of Falaise
1175	William the Lion swears fealty to Henry II at York
1189	Termination of Treaty of Falaise by Richard I
1199	Meiler Fitz Henry appointed justiciar in Ireland
1200	
21 November	William the Lion pays homage to John at Lincoln
1206	
9–12 February	John and William meet at York; inconclusive outcome
1207	
26–28 May	John and William meet at York; inconclusive outcome
1208	Beginning of the fall of William de Briouze
1208	Meiler Fitz Henry removed as justiciar in Ireland and replaced by John de Gray
1209	
7 August	Treaty of Norham
1210	
June–July	John campaigns in Ireland
1211	Guthred invades Scotland from Ireland and mobilizes support in Ross and Moray; John invades Wales on two occasions

1212

February	Marriage treaty between John's daughter Joan and Alexander, son of William the Lion
4 March	Alexander knighted by John
Summer	Guthred captured and beheaded; rebellion of Llywelyn the Great but a conspiracy against his person means that John calls off an intended invasion of Wales

1214

| 4 December | Death of William the Lion; accession of Alexander |
| 6 December | Alexander inaugurated as King Alexander II |

A) Narrative: The Celtic Fringe

By the end of the twelfth century a united Britain had yet to emerge. In Scotland there existed a royal dynasty discrete from the Angevins in England, though there were frequent marriage alliances between the two. Meanwhile, Ireland and Wales remained in a sort of half-conquered condition since the time of Henry II. Each was populated by a number of native princes, often at war amongst themselves but also trying to resist an ongoing process of colonisation by Anglo-Norman lords. When John came to the throne, a large area of south Wales and a substantial corridor of land between the Rivers Dee and Severn (a territory known as the Marches) had been conquered by Anglo-Normans. Many of these Anglo-Norman barons were also acquiring lands in Ireland (see Figure 12). A king of England needed to find a way of imposing his influence upon these different groups, in part because of an ever-present fear that they may lend support to his enemies and inpart because some of the Anglo-Norman barons – in the time of John, the Marshals, the Briouze and the Lacys, especially – were becoming so strong that they could ignore the authority of the Crown with impunity.

After John departed from Normandy in December 1203 his involvement in Britain was 'of an unparalleled intensity' when compared to his predecessors.[1] His principal aim in relation to Wales, Scotland and Ireland was to neutralize any potential threat to his authority, thereby ensuring that his intended invasion of the continent would not be undermined by rebellious elements at home. Simultaneously, John sought to increase his lands and revenues from Ireland and Wales. By 1212 his achievement was dramatic and comprehensive, and recognized as such by even chronicle opinion. 'In Ireland, Scotland and Wales there was no one who did not bow to the nod of the king of England', wrote the Barnwell chronicler, 'which, as is well known, was the case with none of his predecessors'.[2]

Figure 12. Anglo-Norman Ireland and its neighbours at the time of King John

i) Scotland

In 1199 England's relations with Scotland were fractious and had the potential to become very serious indeed. This was for two reasons. First, the king of Scotland, William the Lion (r. 1165–1214) continued to advance Scottish claims upon the northern counties of England – Cumberland, Westmorland, and especially Northumberland which William's father and brother had each possessed as an earldom at some time. Second, there remained the possibility that a resentful Scottish king would find common cause with an enemy, or enemies, of the English king. Indeed, this is exactly what had happened in 1173–4 when William had fought alongside the antagonists of Henry II in the Great Rebellion. On that occasion William had been captured at the Battle of Alnwick in 1174 and had been forced to agree to the Treaty of Falaise (1174) as the price of his freedom. According to its terms William was obliged to pay homage to Henry II, thereby recognizing the overlordship of the English Crown, and also to foot the costs of an English army of occupation. It was John's ill-fortune that Richard had terminated this treaty in return for 10,000 marks to fund his crusade, formally recognized in the Quitclaim of Canterbury on 5 December 1189. As W. L. Warren observes, 'King Richard, with typical cavalier disregard for long term interests, had thrown this advantage [of overlordship] away'.[3]

Despite the fact that William had been emboldened by the actions of Richard, John consistently outmanoeuvred his Scottish opponent. William had initially refused a summons to pay homage to John at York in March 1200, but by November – perhaps intimidated by the English king's achievement on the continent – William came to John at Lincoln. All demands for Northumberland were simply ignored. As D. Carpenter puts it, 'John brushed aside King William's renewed claims to the northern counties.'[4] John continued to play a brilliant game of procrastination, meeting with William in 1206 and 1207 ensuring that the northern king enjoyed neither 'quarrel or achievement'.[5]

Tensions, however, exploded in 1209. This was partly because it seems that William was harbouring fugitives and enemies of John (for instance, Stephen Langton's father had taken refuge in St Andrews in 1207). More especially, it was a result of the termination of John's two-year truce with Philip and the fact that William was prosecuting a scheme to marry one of his daughters to the French king.[6] Fearful of being simultaneously invaded by Scotland and France, John launched a pre-emptive strike. By August he was at Norham (on the Tweed) with a substantial army at his back, composed of English elements alongside Welsh princes and overseas mercenaries. It was sufficient to produce a Scottish capitulation so complete that the threat from William was effectively neutralized. According to the terms of the Treaty of Norham of 1209 John received both of William's daughters into his custody (along with thirteen other hostages) and extracted a payment of £10,000 over two years. Thus, as W. W. Scott notes, 'King William was now as effectively under King John's lordship as he had ever been under Henry II's'.[7] More generally, John's humiliation of William acted as an example to anyone who sought to advance his or her cause by rebellion.

In 1211–12 a threat to the succession of William's son, the thirteen-year-old Alexander, provided a vehicle for John to consolidate his position further. In January of 1211 Guthred MacWilliam, a descendant of the older line of Scottish kings, arrived in Scotland from Ireland and was able to mobilize considerable support in Ross and Moray. The most recent scholarship suggests that William now sought John's help, the price of which was an Anglo-Scottish marriage alliance. Thus, John's daughter, Joan, was betrothed to Alexander thereby drawing the Scottish kingdom yet closer to its Angevin neighbour (they were eventually married in 1221). As part of the marriage deal, in March 1212 Alexander appeared in London to be knighted by John. He was then sent back to Scotland with a force of mercenaries, having been accompanied by John as far as Hexham. In the event, Guthrum was betrayed and duly captured and hanged.

Alexander succeeded his father in 1214. The succession of his son was pretty much William's only achievement. At his death he had not recovered the northern counties of England; his daughters were not yet married and were still in England and John had knighted his son. Conversely, Angevin overlordship of Scotland was more dominant than ever and the prospect of a Franco-Scottish alliance had fully receded. John had done well.

ii) Ireland

In the immediate aftermath of John's expedition in 1185 (see pages 19–20), in the words of W. L. Warren, Ireland 'dissolved into a bloody free-for-all in which Irish princes [i.e. the native Irish] and [Anglo-Norman] adventurers from England teamed up indiscriminately against each other'.[8] Then, upon the death of Henry II in 1189, John used his authority as Lord of Ireland to reassert English lordship. K. Norgate observes that John 'granted a new and important charter to the city of Dublin in 1192', duly setting out the various privileges and immunities which its inhabitants would enjoy as well as granting them the right to establish guilds.[9] Other towns also developed by the granting of charters, or by the confirmation of existing charters: Waterford, Limerick, Cork, Dungarvan and Drogheda were all recipients of newly devised charters. John also authorized grants of estates to Anglo-Normans, the most substantial of which was that of 1194 when he gave away all of Connacht to William de Burgh. 'These land grants', observes S. Duffy, 'do appear to point to a more interventionist approach by John in Irish affairs following the death of Henry II'.[10] These grants resulted in a significant phase of castle building by the Anglo-Normans in Ireland, providing a means to 'bite and hold' new territories obtained.

On becoming king in 1199, John moved with determination and alacrity to impose his authority yet further upon Ireland, though his authorization of a newly vigorous programme of westward expansion led to a confused jostling for power amongst the leading Anglo-Norman barons – notably Meiler Fitz Henry, William de Briouze, William de Burgh, Philip of Worcester, Theobald Walter, Geoffrey de Marisco, John de Courcy and Walter and Hugh de Lacy. Perhaps, though, this was John's aim: ongoing differences between the Anglo-Norman settlers and the Native Irish on the one hand, and internecine disputes within each of these groups on the other hand, meant that John was able to play a game of divide and rule. As Carpenter puts it, the king 'cosseted or caned [either element] as seemed expedient' and was able to use the ensuing political divisions to his advantage to drive on with what Carpenter describes as 'forward policies'.[11]

John's representative in Ireland was Meiler Fitz Henry, justiciar there from 1199 until his removal in 1208. A provocative individual in many ways, he had been put in place to restrain the growing influence of the Anglo-Norman barons in Ireland. Though he made little progress in this respect, he nevertheless presided over the collection of significant amounts of revenue from Ireland, even levying the Thirteenth of 1207 which had also been instituted in England (see page 122). Other key developments also took place during this period. In 1203 John ordered that his justiciar take over the best ports and villages in Connacht and that the revenues extracted be used to build castles. From 1204 the king instructed the building of a castle in Dublin, erected to control the city, house the exchequer and store treasure. Another was built at Limerick, by its presence controlling the mouth of the important River Shannon. Initiatives in 1204 and 1207 provided for English laws and customs to be observed in Ireland, ensuring that 'lordship law was the king's law'.[12] The first Irish coinage was minted in 1207, each coin marked with the symbol of the harp. After Meiler Fitz Henry fell from power in 1208, he was replaced by the much more capable John de Gray (John's nominee for archbishop of Canterbury), who prosecuted yet further the programme of John. Wendover asserted that in Ireland John 'made and ordained English laws and customs, appointing sheriffs and other agents to govern the people of that kingdom according to English laws'.[13] It matters little that Wendover is not correct in his suggestion that John was the first to appoint sheriffs; more significant is that this comment, from a source usually critical of the king, shows begrudging respect.

In 1210, John made his second visit to Ireland. One explanation for the timing of John's appearance there was because William de Briouze, an English lord who had been declared a traitor, fled there in 1209 with his wife and children (see pages 86–91). In Ireland, William de Briouze received shelter from William Marshal and Walter and Hugh de Lacy the younger, respectively lords of Leinster and Meath (Marshal receiving Leinster after he had married Isabel de Clare, the daughter of 'Strongbow' in 1189). From John's point of view Ireland was now not only acting as a harbour for those who had fallen out of favour (Marshal had retreated there in 1207 after refusing to assist John on the Poitevan campaigns of 1205 and 1206) but also, and more worrying, was the fact that these individuals (all of whom had significant lands in Wales also) seemed to be coalescing in resistance to royal authority. At the end of 1206 John had instructed Meiler Fitz Henry to bring Marshal and Lacy into line, only for Meiler to suffer capture and witness the destruction of his estates. The new justiciar, John de Gray, was making progress in John's name but had reached the point where he needed an army at his back.

In addition to the above, Warren suggests that John had an ideological as well as political reason for his military undertaking of 1210. Taking into account that barons like Marshal, Lacy and Briouze had lost lands in Normandy after Philip overran northern France in 1204, Warren believes that 'Marshal's diligent concern with his Irish lordship suggests that he was trying to make his Irish estates render compensation for the loss of his estates in Normandy.'[14] To this end, he sought to undertake fresh conquests and implement further economic exploitation of the lordship. From John's point of view, each of these activities was antagonistic to royal policy which, recognizing that Ireland was not easily conquered, sought to win a measure of cooperation from the native Irish themselves. On the one hand therefore, after 1204 the Anglo-Norman barons in Ireland were increasingly determined upon conquest and exploitation of the native Irish, whereas on the other hand the royal ambition was assimilation of that element. Thus, it seems that John had a further reason for invading Ireland in 1210.

John landed at Waterford on 20 June and set about a nine-week campaign which was breathtaking in its scope and achievement. He had mobilized a feudal host and Flemish mercenaries numbering in total perhaps 1,000 foot soldiers and no fewer than eight hundred knights, carried over in a fleet of 700 ships.[15] D. Carpenter believes that it was 'probably the largest army ever seen in Ireland'.[16] The force was of sufficient size to confirm Marshal – ever the trimmer – that he was right in his decision now to drift back to support of the king. But when emissaries from Walter de Lacy offered complete submission John turned them down. He was determined on more than simply a show of strength: he dispossessed Walter and would not restore him until 1215. Hugh de Lacy, meanwhile, harbouring Matilda de Briouze and her sons in Ulster, put up resistance. John marched against him to great effect: Hugh de Lacy fled to Scotland. Impressive strategic vision, careful attention to detail and a policy of bringing many of the native Irish kings onto his side by treating them with favour, explain John's success. W. L. Warren concludes that 'the triumphant effectiveness of the expedition does not admit of any doubt'.[17] This is supported by R. V. Turner who believes that 'John made a strong impact in Ireland, perhaps stronger than any other medieval English monarch.'[18] Similarly, F. X. Martin believes that 'by any normal standards, John's success in Ireland was remarkable'[19] (see pages 164–7 for a fuller treatment of the military ability of John).

Having been brought into line in 1210, the Anglo-Norman barons in Ireland were among the most loyal in the crisis years in England from 1212. Indeed, in that year twenty-seven of them, fronted by William Marshal, declared in writing that they were 'prepared to live or die with the king and that till the last they would faithfully and inseparably adhere to him'.[20] Then, in 1213, facing a threat of invasion by Philip Augustus, John held a muster of forces to which John de Gray and Marshal provided 500 knights – practically the whole knights' service due from Ireland.

John's Irish policy in 1210 has traditionally been one of the few areas of royal policy which nearly all historians have tended to view favourably – even some chroniclers acknowledge John's achievement, albeit begrudgingly (see Appendix, Documents 16 and 17). Indeed, there has been remarkable unanimity that 'John, so often described as the worst of the kings of England, was, paradoxically, the best for Ireland.'[21] Fundamental to John's achievement in bringing the Anglo-Normans to heel is the belief that he established good relations with the majority of the native Irish kings as a key part of his strategy. In this respect, W. L. Warren concluded that John showed a 'marked favour' to the Irish kings and went on to develop 'close relations with their leaders'. In other words, John was implementing a forward thinking policy of assimilation. E. Curtis says that John came to Ireland, in part at least, 'to meet the claims of Gaelic kings versus Norman conquerors', and that 'while he displayed a gracious face to the Irish, John showed a stern one to his offending barons'. John's treatment of the native Irish, says Curtis, marked 'a great advance on his visit of 1185'. J. Lydon asserts that 'most of Gaelic Ireland seemed prepared to accept John'.[22] However, in an article published in 1996, S. Duffy argues that these conclusions are misleading because, as he explains, they rest upon an 'assumption which does not do full justice to the evidence of the Irish annals' and also that they ignore 'an important eye-witness account of the expedition preserved in a continental chronicle known as the *Histoire des ducs de Normandie et des rois d'Angleterre*'.[23] Duffy uses these sources to show that John's insistence on taking hostages as a demonstration of loyalty fomented disaffection in the native Irish Kings, Aed meith O'Neill and Cathal Crobderb O Conchobair. Duffy points out that this disaffection was so strong that 'within a year [of 1210] John's government had to sponsor invasions of both Connacht and Ulster in an attempt to bring the two kings to heel'.[24] This interpretation, however, provides only a slight corrective to the notion that 1210 was an out-and-out triumph. It remains the case that the majority of the native Irish kings do seem to have been won over by John. Moreover, Cathal, notwithstanding his later falling out with John, did offer the English king military support in 1210; and O'Neill seems to have helped John prosecute the war in Ulster in 1210. Perhaps above all, the size of force brought from Ireland to England by Marshal in 1213 – even Wendover acknowledges 500 knights and many mounted sargeants – suggests that Ireland was by that time free of troubles.[25]

iii) Wales

By the end of the twelfth century, Wales, like Ireland, was a patchwork quilt of principalities governed in part by native princes (who totalled at this time about twelve in number) and in part by Anglo-Norman barons known as Marcher lords.

In 1199 the most important of the various native Welsh princedoms were Deheubarth, Powys and Gwynedd. The first of these, however, had been fatally weakened by infighting following the death of its prince, Rhys ap Gruffydd, in 1197. The second was ruled by Gwenwynwyn (d. 1216). Llywelyn ap Iorweth (Llywelyn the Great, 1173c.–1240), the most powerful lord in North Wales whose military prowess and guile meant that he had the wherewithal to unite the Welsh into a single principality under his overlordship, ruled in Gwynedd. The native princes, frequently at war amongst themselves, also had to contend with Anglo-Norman penetration into Wales, ongoing since the time of the Conquest. This process of colonization meant that by the time John came to the throne a large area of south Wales and much of the border between England and Wales – the March – was controlled by a handful of Anglo-Normans. Prominent amongst these Marcher Lords were the Lacy, Briouze and Marshal families. Already possessing land in Normandy, from 1169 these Marcher lords had begun to expand into Ireland also – a development which acquired a new intensity after these lords lost their lands on the other side of the Channel in 1204.

For a number of reasons this situation posed a threat to King John. First, the native Welsh princes had only vague ties of personal dependence on the king and so could brook his authority with impunity. 'They recognized the dominance of the king', notes I. W. Rowlands, 'but did not conduct themselves as if subject to his domination.'[26] Second, the Marcher lords, if they were not already, clearly possessed the potential to become over-mighty. As great lords in their own right, they built castles and levied feudal hosts; it was the lord's law rather than the king's law that operated first and foremost in Marcher territories. Indeed, one Marcher lord declared in 1199 that 'neither the king nor the justiciar nor the sheriff ought to interfere in his liberty'.[27] In short, the Marcher lords had the means to blunt the will of the king. John thus moved to impose his authority upon his Welsh territories. 'John was confronted in Wales', observes I. W. Rowlands, 'by a duality of authority and lordship (Welsh and English) and by two foci of allegiance and obedience (native and settler).'[28]

John was keenly informed about Wales. He had obtained Glamorgan through his first marriage and, despite the annulment of the union with Isabella, he retained this lordship until 1214. Then, after the loss of Normandy in 1204, he visited Wales every year until 1211. Thus, duly aware of the in-fighting amongst the native princes, John made certain that these leaders submitted to him. He encouraged each to do so by apparently offering his support and favours: gifts, pensions, invitations to court and dynastic alliance. (In 1205 John's illegitimate daughter, Joan, was betrothed to Llywelyn the Great.) John ensured that the terms of submission were recorded in charters, which themselves were copied onto new Chancery Rolls (see page 115). By this means John made it clear that the native princes held their lands from him in return for homage and service and that a breach of this involved forfeiture. R. R. Davies regards these charters as 'menacing innovations' and concludes that they 'represented a palpable advance in the powers of overlordship'.[29] D. Carpenter judges that John by this means imposed his authority on the native Welsh with a 'new sharpness and precision'.[30] The status of the Welsh princes 'was being assimilated to that of English tenants-in-chief', observes I. W. Rowlands.[31] In effect, John was doing just what his rival, Philip Augustus, was also doing: bringing those vassals in peripheral territories under tighter control.

John's policy in respect to controlling the Marcher barons was to encourage rivalries between them and to counterbalance Marcher power with that of the native Welsh princes. Thus, he built up the power of William de Briouze and Marshal partly as a response to the growing authority of Ranulf of Chester in the north; and he maintained good relations with Llywelyn the Great – at least until 1210 – so that the Marcher lords had to contend with a powerful native prince.

The other means by which John imposed his authority was, of course, through military might. The fall of Briouze from 1208 (see pages 86–91), coupled with John's arrest of Gwenwynwyn, disturbed the equilibrium in a way that encouraged Llywelyn the Great to take advantage of the new circumstances thus obtained. He duly annexed southern Powys, marched into Ceredigion and rebuilt the castle at Aberystwyth. This was too much for John to bear and so, in 1211, full of confidence from his recent success in Ireland, he decided to move against his son-in-law. With Scotland cowed by the Treaty of Norham in 1209, John led two campaigns into Gwynedd in 1211, the second of which was devastating in its impact and thrust deeper into that part of Wales than any previous royal expedition. Llywelyn the Great was reduced to miserable surrender and had no means of protesting against crippling peace terms, which included the loss of huge territories in the northeast and west of Wales; the handing over of large numbers of cattle and the granting of hostages. 'This was royal overlordship with a vengeance', says A. D. Carr; 'John had gone further than any of his predecessors and had attained the strongest position yet held by the crown in Wales.'[32]

In fact, John's success was probably too great – or perhaps not great enough.[33] The harsh terms of 1211, coupled with Welsh resentment at the actions of the alien mercenary captains (Gerard d'Athée and Engelard de Cigogné, whom John had appointed as sheriffs of Hereford and Gloucester respectively) produced a backlash.[34] Llywelyn the Great led a rebellion in late June of 1212 when John travelled into the north of England. From John's point of view, Llywelyn's action must have been unexpected, for he had hosted Joan and his son-in-law in Cambridge as recently as Easter in that year. (Little wonder that the royal ability to trust was being incrementally diminished!) Nonetheless, the king's response was swift and brutal: he executed twenty-eight of the hostages he had taken the previous year – many of them, sons of Welsh princes – and he summoned the feudal host to Chester in August in readiness for another military campaign.[35] Moreover, a huge force of more than eight thousand labourers and craftsmen was assembled, ready to build the castles which would implant Angevin authority as firmly in Wales as the castles of Edward I were to establish that of the later Plantagenets.

The scheme of 1212 never took place, John's attention diverted by rumours of a conspiracy amongst the English barons which aimed directly at deposing him, perhaps even taking his life (see Appendix, Document

18). As the Barnwell annalist saw it, an element sought 'to drive [John] and his family from the kingdom and choose someone else as king in his place'.[36] Rumour abounded: Prince Richard (the king's second son) had been murdered; the queen had been raped; the king's treasury at Gloucester had been plundered. John ordered that no one be allowed access to his eldest son, Henry, who did not bear special letters authorizing a visit. At roughly the same time, a hermit called Peter of Wakefield predicted that John's reign would not last for more than fourteen years – and suffered with his life for doing so (see Appendix, Document 20). In this febrile atmosphere on 16 August John thus abandoned his proposed assault on the Welsh, stood down his army (elements of which he was suspicious) and turned his face to England. His call for hostages from those he most suspected produced the flight of Robert Fitz Walter and Eustace de Vesci, the former – protesting that he could not serve an excommunicate king – made his way to France and the latter to Scotland. (Both were to make their way back to England as part of the terms of raising the Interdict, agreed by John in 1213, and were to feature prominently in the rebellion of 1215.) John ordered that Fitz Walter's two castles be razed, Benington in Hertfordshire and Castle Baynard in London. This is also the moment at which Wendover alleges that Geoffrey of Norwich, perhaps having expressed doubts about serving an excommunicate king or in some way having allowed himself to be implicated in the actions of Robert Fitz Walter, met his fate – he was allegedly imprisoned at Norwich and slowly crushed to death by a cope of lead (see Appendix, Document 13). Though there is much to doubt about this story (see page 105).

Having extinguished the conspiracy, the Barnwell annalist says that John proceeded to make some concessions, such as limiting the severity of the actions of the Forest commissioners (see Appendix, Document 21). As for Wales after 1212, events developed in such a way in England that by 1213 the Welsh were able to recover all that they had previously lost; and in 1215, they secured a number of concessions in Magna Carta (see pages 139–50).

B) Interpretations: The Breaking of Briouze, A Case Study

The above has made mention of William de Briouze as one of the great Anglo-Norman barons who held lands in Normandy, Wales and Ireland. As a consequence, he was a powerful subject; by 1208, in the eyes of King John, he had become an overmighty subject and therefore John proceeded against him. William was forced into exile and his wife and eldest son were incarcerated and starved to death. S. Painter judges that 'the quarrel with William de Briouze and his family was the greatest mistake John made during his reign. It should have been avoided at any cost. For one thing it made his cruelty known to all his barons… Then there is a clear, though tenuous thread, linking the Briouze affair to the great baronial revolt [of 1215].'[37] (Clause 49 of the Magna Carta obliged John to promise that 'We will at once return all hostages and charters delivered up to us by Englishmen as security for peace or for loyal service.') The nature of Painter's judgement demands that any student of John examine more carefully the case of William de Briouze and the notion of hostage taking as a political act in the early medieval period.

Until about 1206 William de Briouze had acted as a loyal servant of John and his elder brother, Richard the Lionheart. He had fought on behalf of the latter against the native Welsh (campaigns in which he had proved successful in defending and extending England's frontier) and in Normandy in 1194 and 1199. Upon the death of King Richard, Briouze played an important part in winning support for John. Thereafter, in John's early years, he became an almost constant companion of the king, as evidenced by the fact that he was one of the most frequent witnesses to the king's charters. William was rewarded for his service to John by significant grants of land in the Welsh Marches and Ireland. For example, in 1203 the king granted Briouze the Gower with the castle of Swansea, and the castle and manor of Kington in Herefordshire. But Briouze also gained territories by offering fines (in effect, bribes). For instance, in 1206 he offered John a fine of 800 marks plus a number of horses and hunting dogs in return for the three Welsh castles at Grosmont, Skenfrith, and Whitecastle in Gwent, holding them by the service of two knights. Meanwhile, in 1201, John had granted the Irish honour of Limerick to Briouze in exchange for an offering of the huge sum of 5,000 marks, payable at 500 marks annually. Then, by judiciously marrying his daughter Margaret to Walter de Lacy, the Briouze influence grew greater still.

Like Briouze, Walter de Lacy held significant territory in the Welsh Marches and also in Ireland, where he held the Lordship of Meath and his brother Hugh was Lord of Ulster. There seems to have been a mutual arrangement between the two families that while his son-in-law Walter was driving forward his interests in Meath, Briouze looked after Lacy interests in Wales. Thus, for this reason, in July 1207 Briouze took custody of the Lacy castle at Ludlow, Shropshire.

All in all, according to the *Oxford Dictionary of National Biography* (DNB) entry on Briouze, by the beginning of his fall in 1208, Briouze had by these means 'continued to add to his family's holdings until he held as fiefs or custodies 325 knights' fees and sixteen castles in England, Wales, and Ireland, reaping a yearly income of over £800. He lacked only the title of earl to denote his ranking among the greatest magnates.'[38] It is clear that William de Briouze had grown so powerful that he represented a threat to royal authority. Already, in late 1206, John had ordered Meiler Fitz Henry to attack the Briouze lands in Limerick.

Thus, according to Wendover, in 1208 the king 'sent an armed force to all the men of rank in the kingdom, especially those of whom he was suspicious, and demanded hostages of them, by which he could…recall them to their due obedience'. When the king's force came to Briouze, Matilda, William's wife, refused to hand over hostages: 'I will not deliver up my sons to your lord, King John, because he basely murdered his nephew, Arthur', she declared. When John heard this he was 'seriously enraged' and sent a force to seize William and his family, but they had already fled into Ireland where they were received by William Marshal in the spring of 1209 and given asylum by Walter de Lacy.[39] After a hasty meeting between John and William de Briouze proved inconclusive, John proceeded into Ireland in 1210 and Walter, Hugh and Matilda and her sons fled before him (though not William, who had already returned to Wales). Matilda and her sons were eventually captured in Galloway, from whence she and her eldest son were taken and imprisoned in the dungeons of either Windsor castle or Corfe castle in late 1210 where they were probably starved to death.[40] In the meantime, Briouze had fled into France. He died at Corbeil outside Paris on 4 September 1211, and was buried in the abbey of St Victoire at Paris.

The weight of recent scholarship offers pretty much unanimous agreement with Painter's judgement about John's treatment of de Briouze. B. W. Holden, for instance, asserts that 'the destruction of the house of Briouze is one of the most important events of King John's reign'.[41] D. Carpenter says it was 'a shocking and unprecedented crime'.[42] 'One of the grimmest examples of the king's merciless love of cruelty', judges A. L. Poole.[43] F. McLynn employs the fate of Briouze to argue that John was an 'all-devouring Moloch of wards and hostages'.[44] 'It was most likely the callous treatment of de Briouze and his family that finally convinced the baronial rebels in 1215 that John must be deposed', says F. X. Martin.[45]

Nevertheless, there are ways in which John's reputation can be redeemed against this barrage of criticism. First, the issue of hostages is worthy of further consideration. If Wendover is to be believed, it was Matilda's refusal to offer her sons as hostages as a means of ensuring the loyal behaviour of their father that initiated the conflict. From a twenty-first century perspective, the use of hostages in this way is reprehensible and morally objectionable. In the opening year of the early thirteenth century, however, the taking of hostages by the king in order to compel loyalty from his subjects was nothing new. In fact, it was expected. 'He is no king that has not hostages in chains' was very much the sentiment of the Norman and Angevin periods.[46] For instance, Henry I had demanded hostages before he would release Waleran of Meulan and King Stephen demanded the same before he would free Ranulf (II) of Chester. In 1144, when Nigel, bishop of Ely, had made terms with Stephen, not only did he agree to pay the king £200 but also he was forced to surrender his son as a hostage – and this was for the second time. William Marshal had himself been employed as a hostage when he was aged about five years old.

Hostages faced very real dangers – that, after all, was the point of the hostage-taking process. Of the twenty-two hostages that Henry II had taken from the Welsh, he ordered in 1165 that the males amongst them – some of them sons of princes – be blinded and castrated and that the females should have their noses and ears cut off. William Marshal had been lucky to survive his experience. He had been surrendered by his father to King Stephen as part of a truce. When Marshal's father broke the truce, Stephen was seen as weak for refusing to hang the boy, even though William's father seemed unconcerned about the threat to his son's life, asserting that 'he still had the anvil and hammer to forge better ones'.[47] It is true that John made more systematic use of hostage taking than had his predecessors but the Briouze incident is too frequently dealt with by historians away from this broader context. Indeed, Holt concludes that John's practice of demanding hostages 'seems to have been a normal disciplinary method of government [at this time]'.[48] Hostage taking was par for the course; and, if a deal was broken, then all parties expected violence. It will not do to charge John with 'a love of cruelty' when hostage taking is evaluated in this way. If John is guilty of cruelty, then what of Richard in 1191 when, following a dispute about the terms upon which Acre had been surrendered, he ordered the killing of 2,700 Muslim prisoners? What of Henry V, who during the Battle of Agincourt in 1415 ordered the killing of several thousand French prisoners?

Second, we must remain alert to the bias in the chronicle accounts of the fate of Briouze and his family and the picture they paint of a family hunted down by a paranoid king, unable to brush aside Matilda's accusation of parricide. (If the granting of hostages was refused, then the king had little choice but to hunt them down and take them by force – he would appear critically weak if he did not do so.) Some chronicle opinion, seeking to disparage the reputation of John, insinuates that John was involved in the killing of Arthur. And yet all that can really be said against John is that he allowed himself to be implicated in that event, not that he was absolutely the perpetrator. Moreover, while the chronicle accounts use the Briouze incident to assert John's alleged insensitivity to the chivalric parameters of the age, they do not consider that perhaps Matilda herself did not quite fit the chivalric ideal. No mention is made of the fact that she had successfully defended Painscastle in 1198, earning for that fortification the name 'Matilda's Castle'. Wendover, in describing Matilda's reaction to the royal messengers when they demanded hostages, uses the word 'sauciness', which perhaps can equally be read as 'forthright'. He then goes on to say that 'her husband, upon hearing her speech, rebuked her'.[49] From John's point of view it seems that Matilda may have been of a greater concern than her husband – when Briouze came to John as the king was embarking for Ireland and offered to make peace for 40,000 marks, John replied that since the real power lay with Matilda he should cross and settle his differences with her in Ireland. We should appreciate that it seems as though 'Matilda wore the trousers'.

Third, John had the law on his side in his pursuit of Briouze, who, after all, was a debtor. J. A. P. Jones points out that 'John had to make an example of William or other barons would refuse his future financial demands; his treatment of William was more in line with Exchequer practice than the arbitrary proceedings of an oppressive monarch.'[50] After the fall of Briouze, John issued a document addressed 'to all who may read it'. This royal statement, witnessed by a dozen great men, presented the pursuit of Briouze and his family as 'according to the custom of England and the law of the exchequer'.[51] The document stated that Briouze had resisted paying in full his fine for Limerick, a total of £3,333 payable at £666 per year. At the beginning of 1207 only £468 had been paid. Of course, considering the purpose and provenance of this document we are right to be suspicious of its content, and it is telling that John felt it necessary to produce it at all. Indeed, B. W. Holden believes that it 'must be seen as an impressive example of early thirteenth century spin'.[52] Nevertheless, as K. Norgate points out, 'it is hardly conceivable that so many witnesses of such rank and character…should have set their hands to it if it contained any gross misrepresentations of matters which must have been well known to most of them'.[53] When John instructed Gerard d'Athée to distrain (confiscate) Briouze's possessions and take three of his castles, he was not acting in a uniquely tyrannical way; rather, this was normal procedure in such a case. Moreover, it seems that on several occasions Briouze went back on his word, failing to meet John as had been agreed and once even attacking castles which he had earlier agreed to hand over.

Finally, John's suspicions about the loyalty of Briouze had some justification. The king had only recently quarrelled with William Marshal who, having done homage to Philip Augustus in 1205, had refused to support John's Poitevin expeditions in 1205 and 1206. Consequently, Marshal had sought refuge in Ireland – and Marshal was the very person with whom Briouze had sought sanctuary. With both these men and the Lacys owning lands in Ireland and Wales, John needed to take determined and drastic action. As we have seen, after the loss of Normandy key Anglo-Norman barons looked west and successfully acquired huge estates in Wales and Ireland, allowing them potentially to operate independently of the king. Moreover, by the early spring of 1208 John was anticipating the issue of the papal interdict (see page 103) and was fearful that as a consequence of this the barons of England would consider themselves absolved from allegiance to him. For all these reasons it is possible to question the judgements of the historians referred to on page 88.

Chapter 7

SACERDOTIUM AND REGNUM, 1199–1214

Timeline

1164	Constitutions of Clarendon
1166	*Cartae Baronum*
1170	Murder of Becket
1198	Innocent becomes Pope; dies 1216
1205	
13 July	Death of Hubert Walter, archbishop of Canterbury
Mid-July	Monks at Canterbury elect their sub-prior, Reginald
11 December	John obliges monks to elect John de Gray
1206	
December	Innocent invalidates election of Reginald and John de Gray and appoints Stephen Langton
1207	
17 June	Innocent consecrates Langton at Viterbo
August	Innocent instructs bishops of Ely, London and Worcester to threaten John with the imposition of an interdict
1208	
18 March	John appoints commissioners to confiscate property of any churchman who fulfils the demands of an interdict
24 March	Innocent pronounces an interdict
1209	
8 November	Innocent pronounces John excommunicate
1212	
Midsummer	Rumours of domestic conspiracy

1213
    Spring   Fears of French invasion
    15 May   John submits to Innocent
    9 July   Langton enters England
1214
    2 July   Interdict lifted
1215
    4 March   John takes crusader's oath

A) Narrative: Key Features of the Church and John's Relations with the Papacy

In the Middle Ages the relationship between church and state, *sacerdotium* and *regnum*, was inherently combustible and, as such, it was not unusual for conflagrations to take hold. Indeed, as will become clear, so much was at stake for each of the parties that it is perhaps surprising that the early medieval politico/religious landscape was not illuminated by these flames more frequently than actually occurred. This is not to diminish the fact that each of John's predecessors at some point experienced tensions with the church, the most recent of which had been the rivalry played out between Henry II and Becket, culminating in the dramatic murder of the latter in 1170. The nature and intensity of these tensions was determined by the variable interaction of principles and personalities. From the point of view of the papacy, the typically Angevin characteristics of King John were likely to result in abrasive relations; but the personality of Pope Innocent III (1198–1216) was guaranteed to exaggerate elements of those characteristics. In the sermon he preached at his consecration, Innocent asserted that the pope was 'less than God, but greater than man, judge of all men and judged by none'.[1] A week later he underlined his position in a letter to the archbishop of Ravenna: 'the liberty of the Church is nowhere better served than where the Roman Church obtains full power both in temporal and in spiritual matters'.[2] Unsurprisingly, a recent biographer of John has concluded that the king 'had the bad luck to be a contemporary of Pope Innocent III, one of the most ambitious and aggressive of the lawyer-popes who occupied the papal throne in the high Middle Ages'.[3] As a feudal overlord in his own right, the pope could mobilize substantial resources and put armies into the field of battle. Moreover, possessed of the ability to instruct the clergy to cease performing divine service and the ability to expel rulers from the church (powers known as interdict and excommunication respectively), the papacy had the wherewithal to destabilize regimes, even to bring them down.

The next few pages lay out the context in which John's contest with the papacy was fought.

i) The Regular Clergy

The medieval church in England was composed of two sections, the monastic orders and the clergy – known respectively as the regular and secular clergy. The regular clergy had grown in number and nature since 1066. At the time of the Conquest, Benedictine foundations dominated monastic life in England, so-called because they structured their day according to regulations composed by St Benedict of Nursia (d. 547). Benedictine monasteries thus number among some of the oldest and most distinguished in England such as Glastonbury, Bury St Edmund's, Peterborough abbeys and the cathedral priories of Canterbury, Winchester, Worcester and Ely.

During the twelfth century, a revived spirituality across society led to the breaking of the Benedictine monopoly by new orders intent upon adhering to their different and particular interpretations of the Rule of St Benedict. Prominent amongst these were the Cluniacs and Cistercians, though there were also others, semi-monastic in nature, such as the Augustinians, who abided by the Augustinian Rule (named after St Augustine, d. 430) and called themselves canons rather than monks. Women as well as men were newly attracted to this life of religious seclusion. In the century prior to 1216 it has been estimated that the number of nuns swelled from 440 to 3,000 and that the number of men living in monastic communities grew from around 2,700 to 9,700.[4] Consequently, by the time of King John the English landscape (and to a lesser extent the Welsh, Scottish and Irish also) had become studded with new monastic houses.

By far the most dominant and successful of these new foundations were the Cistercians: in the twenty years from 1132 some forty Cistercian houses were founded, including in their number Rievaulx and Fountains in Yorkshire. Many of these houses depended upon the charitable endowment of land by a lay lord for their initial foundation.[5] In an age where nearly everyone believed that 'alms extinguish sin as water does fire', some monasteries attracted substantial donations and thus came to control huge areas of territory, thereby growing very rich. The heads of these larger religious communities – the abbots and abbesses – were not only responsible for setting the spiritual tone and maintaining the moral discipline within their houses in accordance with the strict rules of their order but, having sizeable landed estates to run, they were also important figures on the larger stage of the early medieval polity. Many of the major Benedictine foundations were required to perform military service to the Crown in return for their land, while the Cistercians faced additional taxation. Moreover, since it was not uncommon for these regular clergy to be governed by a mother house in Europe – the Cluniacs looked to Cluny; the Cistercians to Citeaux – there existed a centripetal force that was potentially antagonistic, and in conflict with, the English Crown. Indeed, by the early thirteenth century the Cistercian abbots met yearly at Citeaux, where, amongst other things, they promulgated legislation for their order; and there were also annual visitations from Citeaux to the daughter houses. 'Never before', notes N. Saul, 'had such elaborate machinery been established to unite the houses of an international order'.[6]

ii) The Secular Clergy

A description of how the secular clergy were organized is also important for an understanding of John's relationship with the church.

By 1199 England had for some time been divided into about 9,000 parishes, the basic administrative unit through which the church provided for the religious needs of ordinary people. Parishes were of varying territorial extents but had on average about four hundred members. The focal point of each was, of course, the parish church itself. This had frequently originated as the private chapel of the local landlord but had subsequently acquired a communal status. 'Everywhere', recorded William of Malmesbury writing about the early twelfth century, 'one could see churches rising up'.[7] During the twelfth century many of these parish churches were refashioned and extended, reflecting the piety of the parishioners, new styles in church architecture, and rising populations. The upkeep of these churches, and any rebuilding, was mainly the responsibility of the local lord and parishioners, who would make charitable bequests and donations for the purpose.

Each parish church had a priest. He was appointed in the first instance by the person who held the advowson (right of appointment) of the church – usually a local landlord – but the bishop made the formal investiture and appointment. Parishioners resorted to their church on a Sunday where they witnessed – and once a year, on Maundy Thursday, participated in – the sacrament of Mass presided over by the priest. The priest was at the core of life in the parish: he cared for the souls of all of the parishioners, living amongst them and providing moral guidance and direction; he visited the sick and distressed; he interpreted events of daily life, saying prayers for the living and for the souls of the dead; he led services on holy days, and administered baptisms, marriages, churchings, deaths, and burials. The church was very much the warp and weft of everyday life.

Nevertheless, few priests received any training and most were illiterate. There was little close supervision of those in the priesthood. Unsurprisingly, therefore, even though canon law stipulated that priests should remain unmarried, many had female 'companions of the hearth' and children. Gerald of Wales describes the 'houses and hovels of parish priests filled with bossy mistresses, creaking cradles, newborn babies and squawking brats'.[8]

In an effort to improve consistency and quality in the work of priests, and to maintain and enforce moral discipline, the English church was organized into a distinctive hierarchical structure. The bottom layer – the parishes – were grouped together to form deaneries, presided over by a dean, and several deaneries were grouped together to comprise an archdeaconry, in turn presided over by an archdeacon (appointments to these positions were made by a bishop). A number of archdeaconries combined to establish an administrative unit known as a diocese or see, governed by a bishop. At the time of John's accession there were seventeen dioceses, the average size of which was about 3,000 square miles and each thus presided over a large number of parochial units – for instance, the diocese of Lincoln comprised 1,600 parishes. The sees of Carlisle, Durham and York were governed by an archbishop based at York; the others were governed by an archbishop whose see was at Canterbury and which, in the eleventh century, under the leadership of Archbishop Lanfranc (1070–1089), had imposed its precedence over York. Overall, this structure was sufficiently robust to provide a rudimentary system of quality control – it allowed information about important issues to work its way up to the bishops and their leading officials, and it allowed messages and directives to filter down. Also, it was overlain by a hierarchy of church courts, dealing with moral and spiritual offences with an ultimate right of appeal to Rome.

The English church was not only well organized but it also grew wealthy thanks to endowments it received, given in the expectation that gifts to the church would extinguish the sins of the donor. Consequently, as early as 1086, as revealed by the Domesday survey, the church already owned one-fifth of the landed wealth of England. These permanent endowments of land provided a regular income for the monastic houses, and for the episcopal office holders. Parish priests, meanwhile, received payment from the tithe, a locally raised tax amounting to a tenth of the agricultural produce produced by parishioners and rendered to the church. They also received an income from the glebe land attached to the parish church and other petty fees and donations.

Bishops were therefore required to run their dioceses as befitting major religious leaders, yet their status as important landowners meant that they were also tenants-in-chief. As such, they owed feudal and military obligations to the king because the tenurial revolution following 1066 meant that all land was ultimately held of that office. As described by R. Bartlett, a newly appointed bishop 'would immediately become a major landlord, a local, perhaps regional, and possibly national potentate, and a master of knights, castles and money as well as religious director of his see'.[9] Bishops were thus liable to lead armies, serve in offices of state, provide counsel and go on diplomatic missions.[10] In common with the lay tenants-in-chief, bishops were obliged to supply quotas of knights (the *servitia debita*) as stipulated by the Crown. When Henry II investigated and recorded these obligations in 1166 in a document known as the *Cartae Baronum* it revealed just how extensive was the authority and status of the church. For instance, the *Cartae Baronum* showed that the bishoprics of Canterbury, Winchester, Lincoln and Worcester each owed 60 knights. Indeed, it reveals that all the bishoprics and abbeys that sent details to the king in 1166 rendered roughly 775 knights of the 5,000 or so owed to the Crown by all the tenants-in-chief at that time; around 15 per cent of the total.[11]

Having established an administrative web sufficiently robust that any touch at the centre would quickly be transmitted to its outer parts, and led by bishops, who, as ecclesiastical barons, had similar authority and status as their lay equivalents, the English church was necessarily central to the Crown's ability to deliver good governance. Moreover, empowered by their literacy, leading clergy were appointed to offices of state and thus played an important role in the administrative machinery of government. In John's reign, Hubert Walter was archbishop of Canterbury and chancellor; Peter des Roches was bishop of Winchester and justiciar; William Wrotham was archdeacon of Taunton and organizer of the navy; and William of Ely was archdeacon of Cleveland and treasurer. Leading clergy were therefore in a variety of ways central in assisting the monarch in governing the country. As such, it was of the greatest importance to the authority of the Crown that it should be able to appoint men of its choosing to high ecclesiastical office.

The leading clergy thus wore two hats, one as agents of the Crown and the other as agents of the papacy. It follows that their responsibilities and loyalties sometimes conflicted. For example, they were charged by the pope with implementing canon law. Ecclesiastical jurisdiction (dispensed through courts over which bishops presided) touched on many areas of life, such as murder, marriage, wills and defamation – issues which could also be the subject of royal justice. Religious courts generally dispensed more lenient judgements and sentences than the secular courts and so it began to seem to the Crown that anyone claiming to be a cleric could thus escape royal justice by seeking trial in a church court and ultimately even resorting to Rome in cases of appeal. Developments such as these besmirched the Crown's reputation as a provider of justice and good governance, and had to be resisted strongly; but, from the point of view of the papacy, the jurisdiction of the religious courts equally had to be purposefully maintained, even advanced.

In short, as spiritual leaders, bishops and abbots were primarily answerable to the papacy; as landholders and secular office holders, they were principally answerable to the Crown. There was thus the potential for conflict and ambiguity in their relationship with the Crown. This difficulty was especially evident in who exactly had the final say in appointing these major office holders, an ongoing struggle known as the Investiture Contest. A central feature of the quarrel was that the granting of such positions endowed the giver with potent patronage and thus a mechanism to compel allegiance – appointments to dioceses and leading abbeys were as much about building/ rewarding loyalty and appointing competent individuals, as about personal piety, spiritual holiness and flair as ecclesiastical administrators. Moreover, once appointments to these positions had been made they could not easily be unmade. Hence, it was of vital importance that the 'right' appointment occurred.[12] But what was the 'right' appointment from the point of view of the Crown was not necessarily the right appointment from the point of view of the church, and vice versa.

Unsurprisingly, therefore, by the time of John's accession there had been considerable chaffing between church (*sacerdotium*) and state (*regnum*) over which had the greater authority to appoint to high ecclesiastical office. As recently as 1164, in a powerful bid to win the initiative, Henry II had asserted what he considered to be the royal customs in the Constitutions of Clarendon. Becket's decision to reject these ultimately led to his murder in 1170. Clause 12 is of particular relevance because of the bearing it has on events in John's reign. It stated that:

When an archbishopric or bishopric is vacant, or any abbey or priory of the king's demesne, it ought to be in his own hand, and he shall receive from it all revenues and profits as part of his demesne. And when the time has come to provide for the church, the lord king ought to summon the more important of the beneficed clergy of the church, and the election ought to take place in the lord king's chapel with the assent of the lord king and on the advice of the clergy of the realm whom he has summoned for the purpose. And the clerk elected there shall do homage and fealty to the lord king as his liege lord for his life and limbs and his earthly honour, saving his order, before he is consecrated.[13]

These statements, however, only served to formalize the nature of the debate rather than to resolve it and tension remained significant and persistent. This can be sensed particularly in the writ issued by Henry II in 1172 by which he instructed his 'faithful monks' who were at that time considering who to appoint to the vacancy at Winchester, that 'We order you to hold a free election, but nevertheless forbid you to elect anyone except Richard my clerk, the archdeacon of Poitiers.'[14] A similar tone was adopted by Richard I in 1195 when he wrote to the bishop of London about a vacancy at Durham: 'Therefore we have decided to ask you to make careful provision to guard against any diminution of the right and dignity which our ancestors had in the choice of bishops in England and which is due to us… For we should not for any reason allow these monks [of Durham] to act to the detriment [of] our honour in the election of a bishop, and if by chance such action were taken it would have to be annulled at once.'[15] Thus, when John chose to use similar language against the monks at Canterbury in December 1205 after they failed to support the royal nominee, John de Gray, it was neither unexpected nor unusual. What was bracingly different on this occasion was the attitude adopted by the papacy. Whereas his predecessors had been pragmatic rather than pugnacious, Innocent chose to proceed by adhering rigidly to the letter of canon law. This action flew in the face of a century-and-a-half of custom and practice, and it is certain that it would have been robustly resisted by any medieval monarch.

iii) John's Relations with the Papacy, 1199–1205

All historians agree that the new pope, Innocent III (1198–1216), sought to reassert and extend the authority of the papacy, reviving a process initiated by Gregory VII in the late eleventh century. Nonetheless, this did not immediately result in difficult relations between the new pope and the new king of England. In fact, when John sought to annul his marriage to Isabella of Gloucester it was quickly and smoothly achieved by tribunals of bishops acting on behalf of the papacy in Normandy and Aquitaine. These clergy did not feel it necessary to refer the issue to the papacy and John did not suffer the difficulties that Philip Augustus encountered when he sought an annulment of his second marriage.[16] Moreover, at the start of John's reign, the succession question to the Holy Roman Empire produced a community of interest between the papacy and the English Crown. Innocent sought to secure the election of John's nephew Otto of Brunswick as Holy Roman Emperor as opposed to Philip of Hohenstaufen, the candidate supported by the out-of-favour Philip Augustus. Finally, even as the Canterbury election crisis was gathering momentum, the contested election of Peter des Roches (John's candidate) to the see of Winchester was confirmed by the papacy.[17] Yet there were also tensions. We can speculate that John's promise, according to the Treaty of Le Goulet (1200), not to support Otto must have had a negative impact upon relations with Innocent. During his time as Lord of Ireland,

John had angered Innocent by forcing the archbishop of Dublin into exile in 1198 and again in 1202. More damaging still was Innocent's response to the events in Normandy 1202–5: the pope refused to condemn Philip Augustus and stated that the French king's actions could be justified by *ratio peccati* ('reason of sin'). John's weakened position also explains events in the bishopric of Seez in Normandy. After the existing bishop's death in 1201 the monks in the chapter at Seez, without consulting John, proceeded to elect one of their own number, Sylvester. Unsurprisingly, upon learning of this, John insisted that his own nominee, the dean of Lisieux, should be elected. In the end he was forced to accept the election of Sylvester, despite this being 'contrary to the dignity and liberty of ourself and our land'.[18] (R. V. Turner believes that this outcome 'may have convinced the pope that he could pressure the king into accepting Stephen Langton at Canterbury'.[19]) Then, early in 1205, when the Norman bishops sought papal direction as to whether they should render fealty to Philip, the pope responded by telling them to do what law and custom demanded. According to Cheney, this amounted to 'an abnegation of authority, a ceremonial hand-washing'.[20] As such, Harper-Bill concludes that 'it may surely have been a contributory factor in John's rejection for the archbishopric of Canterbury of a papal nominee [i.e. Langton] who had been so long in Paris'[21] (see below page 102).

iv) John's Relations with the Papacy, 1205–1214

Hubert Walter, archbishop of Canterbury and chancellor, died on 13 July 1205. 'Now for the first time I am King of England', exclaimed John according to Matthew Paris.[22] On 15 July the king arrived in person at Canterbury and no doubt made it clear to the monks of the chapter that he expected them to elect his favoured candidate, the current bishop of Norwich and royal secretary, John de Gray, as Walter's successor. 'There was no man in England whom King John trusted so completely and so consistently as he did John de Gray', asserts Painter.[23]

Procedural issues, however, now intervened to complicate what John must have anticipated would be a straightforward 'election' of the sort enjoyed by his predecessors. On this occasion the bishops of the archdiocese argued that they had a right to participate in the election of a successor to Hubert. An appeal was thus made to Rome by the bishops and the monks of Canterbury Cathedral Priory in an attempt to sort things out. In the meantime, seeking to outflank John and the bishops, a faction of monks secretly elected their sub-prior, Reginald. Upon learning of this, John travelled to Canterbury and unleashed some typically Angevin authority: in his presence on 11 December 1205 – in a process in which the bishops took no part – the monks unanimously elected John de Gray. All that was now needed was papal confirmation of the done deed, increasingly a formality.

Innocent, the lawyer pope, concluded that neither election was valid because each had taken place whilst the whole procedure was under review. In December 1206 the pope met with a new delegation of monks from Canterbury in Rome and he asked them to vote again, there and then. When they divided evenly on Reginald and de Gray, Innocent insisted upon the election of his own candidate, Cardinal Stephen Langton, telling the monks not to be fearful of John because 'it is not the custom that the consent of princes is to be waited for concerning elections made at the apostolic see'.[24] It was a 'naively imperious' stance, to which John's reaction was predictable.[25]

Upon learning of this outcome, John was 'exceedingly outraged', a response which no doubt would have been espoused by any of his predecessors.[26] The king now commanded knights to travel to Canterbury to order 'the prior and monks to depart immediately from the kingdom as traitors to the king's majesty'.[27] As Painter observes, Innocent's action had 'raised an issue that constituted a vital threat to the political authority of the king of England'.[28] In other words, the pope had started a war.

War was inevitable not only because of the principle that was at stake but also because of the nature of the person of Langton, the choice of whom was wholly unacceptable to the English king. Langton – an Englishman and renowned teacher – had been resident in Paris for perhaps thirty years and had for some time enjoyed the patronage of Philip Augustus, receiving from him the benefice of Notre Dame. Thus, added to the sensation that his prerogative authority was being usurped, John found that he was now expected to receive into his realm an individual whom he considered 'Frenchified', the creature of his greatest enemy. John thus proclaimed to Innocent that he 'knew nothing [of Langton], save that he had dwelt much among his enemies'.[29] John's concerns were exacerbated by the fact that, as archbishop of Canterbury, Langton would wield authority as one of the greatest barons of the realm, sitting on the king's council as well as fulfilling his core function as a churchman.

For six months (Jan 1207–June 1207) there was an ominous sense of the calm before the storm as Innocent waited in the hope that John would assent to the choice of Langton. John refused him. 'His predecessors', notes D. Carpenter, 'would have done the same.'[30] No other king had failed to obtain an archbishop of his choice. Eventually realizing that he was waiting in vain, Innocent consecrated Langton at Viterbo on 17 June 1207. Three weeks later, John seized the estates of the Canterbury see. Battle had commenced.

Innocent now set about devising the means by which John would be obliged to accept Langton, a mechanism to compel him 'to bow to the divine ordinance'.[31] It is possible to perceive the actions of the papacy as falling into a number of distinct approaches, each increasingly desperate.

First, Innocent resorted to intimidation, an approach which he maintained from August of 1207 until March of the following year. In August he charged the bishops of Ely, London and Worcester to threaten John with the imposition of an interdict, 'permitting no ecclesiastical office save the baptism of infants and the confession of the dying'[32] (see Appendix, Document 10).Then, in November of the same year, a papal letter addressed to the barons implored its readers to save John 'from rejecting the counsel of good men and from walking in the counsel of the ungodly' and concluded that when John 'has taken wiser advice and returned to his senses, he will think you very dear friends for the sincerity of your counsel'.[33] John's response was clever and calculating: he set up the impression that he might be persuaded to accept Langton – he participated in negotiations with Simon Langton (Stephen's brother and representative) whilst at the same time sending the abbot of Beaulieu to Rome to discuss the situation with the pope. This was probably dissimulation to win time during which John could encourage a new sense of community of interest between the Crown and leading elements of the political nation. In fact, the barons were already alert as to how their traditional benefits from ecclesiastical patronage might be infringed if Innocent had his way. As Warren puts it, 'What hope had the barons of getting canonries and bishoprics for their younger sons if the pope were allowed to thrust in outsiders?'[34] John felt thus supported in his stand and on 18 March 1208 announced the appointment of commissioners to confiscate the property of any churchman who might fulfil the commands of an interdict.

Second, the threat having failed, Innocent proceeded actually to proclaim the interdict on 24 March 1208. It was only lifted on 2 July 1214. In theory this banned the celebration of Mass, marriage and denied burials in consecrated land; clergy were permitted only to continue to baptize children and administer confession to the dying. The papal intention was no doubt to instil in the laity in England a sense of resentment against their king, who, held responsible for bringing a sacramental famine on his people, would be placed under increasing pressure from below to accede to papal demands.[35]

This did not transpire. John's immediate response to the interdict was to confiscate church lands – not unreasonable since the clergy were effectively now on strike – returning these upon payment of a fine; and it seems that the vast majority of clergy paid. Historians debate the nature of the impact of the interdict, but the current consensus is that 'much of the Church's business seems to have continued nearly as in normal times' and that 'routine administration of the church did not grind to a halt', even though a number of bishops had now gone into exile.[36] Certainly there were very few clerical refugees – dozens rather than hundreds. Church courts continued to function (though appeals to Rome were forbidden) and religious festivals continued to take place.

Third, the frustrated pope threw another thunderbolt at John: on 8 November 1209 he excommunicated the king. As an excommunicate John was barred from receiving the Mass and other sacraments and thus his soul was in peril if he were to die before he was reconciled to the church. More importantly, this sentence had potentially important political ramifications in that it legitimized any attack by Philip Augustus, who could now claim that an invasion of England amounted to a crusade. As Warren has observed, although the excommunication 'did not require John's subjects to disavow their allegiance…it protected their consciences if they felt unable to follow'.[37] It seems that most did not feel any such sensation. It is true that by 1211 there was only one bishop left in England (Peter des Roches at Winchester, his fellow bishops either having fled to the continent and or died without being replaced) but there was no mass exodus of lesser or regular clergy.[38] In fact, it was not unusual to be excommunicate and John's authority appears to have been little affected by the sentence. Indeed, in the summer of 1211 John felt strong enough to be able to reject the following terms for settlement as put forward by the papal legate Pandulf: Langton should be accepted as archbishop; clerical exiles should be allowed to return and Church property confiscated by John should be returned.

By mid 1212 John was in a less strong position. An ominous letter of July or early August 1212 between Llewellyn, prince of North Wales and Philip Augustus talks of a 'treaty between the kingdom of the French and the principality of North Wales'. Llewellyn proceeds to say that 'I and my heirs, adhering inseparably to you and your heirs, will be friends to your friends and enemies to your enemies'.[39] There is also evidence that Llewellyn had been colluding with disaffected English barons, amongst others Robert Fitz Walter and Eustace de Vesci, and that they were hatching a plot to murder John. Since the king was now travelling with a large retinue and was increasingly precipitate in his use of violence against hostages, we must infer that he sensed that his enemies felt newly emboldened – so much so that John had to call off his planned invasion of France in 1212. Meanwhile, Otto having also been excommunicated, the papacy was now lending its support to the Hohenstaufens, the allies of Philip Augustus – a development which made ever more credible Philip's posturing as a crusader determined to liberate England of its tyrant. Finally, Innocent may have been threatening to issue letters of deposition via Philip Augustus.

The collective effect of all of this was that in the early months of 1213 John sent an embassy to Rome to agree to the terms he had rejected in 1211.

But the pope's position had strengthened sufficiently for him to be able to demand more. Thus, on 15 May 1213 John submitted to terms according to which he placed England and Ireland under apostolic suzerainty, receiving them back as fiefs; agreed that he would render 1,000 marks annually to the papacy and that he would receive Langton as archbishop. Almost two months later, on 9 July, Langton entered England. In a formal ceremony at Winchester, the archbishop absolved the sentence of excommunication. The interdict remained in place, though in June 1214 this too was lifted after John paid some of the compensation due to the clerical exiles.

B) Interpretations

i) What was the Impact of the Interdict and John's Excommunicate Status?

An appreciation of the nature of the impact of the interdict and excommunication upon laity and clergy alike is central to any assessment of John's reign. The older interpretation is that their impact was negative and broadly felt, eventually forcing John's submission in 1213.

Chroniclers such as Gervase of Canterbury and Roger of Wendover exclaim that the religious life in England was devastated by the interdict, not least because this was a land in which clerics were hounded and broken. Wendover, for instance, narrates that John, 'being greatly enraged on account of the interdict, sent his sheriffs and other ministers of iniquity to all quarters of England, giving orders with dreadful threats to all priests…to depart the kingdom immediately… Religious men…when found travelling on the road, were dragged from their horses, robbed and basely ill-treated and no one would do them justice.' Wendover proceeds to tell of a Welshman apprehended for the killing of a priest only to be let free because John asserts that 'he has slain an enemy of mine' (see Appendix, Documents 11 and 12). Yet detailed study of the record evidence casts doubt on such tales by indicating that John apparently sought to uphold the law as established (see Appendix, Document 28 and pages 126–7). Similarly, Wendover's tale of John ordering the killing of Geoffrey, archdeacon of Norwich by having him crushed under a weight of lead in 1209 has not withstood close examination (see Appendix, Document 13). Indeed, it is now generally recognized that this same Geoffrey became bishop of Ely in 1225. W. L. Warren's investigation of this incident led him to conclude that since Wendover 'has the wrong year, the wrong cause, and the wrong man, the odds are heavily against his being right about the leaden cope'.[40] H. G. Richardson considers it 'a stupid fable'.[41] In short, we are reminded to treat with caution the tales that are found in the chronicles.

Nevertheless, we should acknowledge that the interdict did in effect amount to an ecclesiastical strike. In what was an intensely religious age, this must have brought discomfort to many. In the eerie quiet that now enveloped England – the ringing of church bells was forbidden – it does seem as though there were scenes of real horror: bodies were buried in woods or roadside ditches and some sources relate how the dead were placed in coffins and then hung from a tree in a churchyard until they could be given a legitimate burial. With the church doors barred and bolted, sermons were preached in the churchyard. An effect of John's excommunicate status from 1209 was that bishops went into exile. By 1211 only one of the seventeen sees – Winchester – had a bishop and it seems likely that such large-scale absenteeism had a deleterious effect on the religious life of the church. A. L. Poole concludes that 'religiously minded life in these conditions can have been scarcely tolerable'.[42] W. Stubbs, writing in the nineteenth century, lambasted John for exposing 'the country to the shame and horrors of an interdict'.

Over and above the purely religious impact of the quarrel, there are those who are critical of John because it seems as though he took advantage of his argument with Innocent in order to mulct the church. Wendover tells us that John 'ordered all ecclesiastical revenues [of those who refused to perform divine service] to be confiscated' and that the king's agents duly 'converted all the property [of the church] to the king's use'.[43] In fact it was too big an administrative undertaking for such lands to be directly governed by the royal machine and so John let it be known that church property would be returned upon payment of a fine and a promise of payments of a share of future income. In addition to this, John ordered that the mistresses and wives of the clergy be seized, only to be returned upon payment of a fine. Finally, as vacancies occurred, John did not always appoint replacement bishops and leading abbots. Thus, by 1213 seven bishoprics and seventeen abbacies were headless and John, as feudal overlord, received the incomes from their estates.

It has not been easy for historians to calculate how much money John obtained from the church. Painter concluded that 'John's total profits from the struggle with Innocent reached £100,000 and may well have exceeded that sum'.[44] The latest assessment is that John extracted about £11,000 each year – the total ecclesiastical income per annum was about £80,000 – from the church during the six years that the interdict lasted; £66,000 in total.

Although C. R. Cheney has described the 'darkness and contradictions' in the evidence available, the above picture of John as an irreligious despot – careless of the souls of those he governed – is not tenable. Indeed, in a number of respects the king himself appears to have been conventionally religious. In 1212 he gave a large number of gifts to religious houses. In the same year he paid for candles to be placed upon reliquaries. He arranged for relics to accompany him as he travelled. (Indeed, John took a special interest in the relics of St James at Reading.) He founded a new abbey at Beaulieu. He was buried wearing on his head the cowl-like coif of unction he had worn at his coronation. In these ways, notes Cheney, John 'advertised his orthodoxy, though excommunicate'.[45] Clearly, the view put forward by Matthew Paris that John was about to convert to Islam should be discounted![46]

The available evidence does not support the picture presented by Wendover and the 'horrors' spoken of by Stubbs. Indeed it is now generally accepted that the interdict had little impact, in part because of lack of clarity about what the pope intended by the measure. Whenever an interdict was pronounced, clergy in France, England and Italy frequently had to write to the pope for clarification; and even then contradictory instructions might be received. Baptism of babies sometimes took place in church; sometimes at home. This lack of clarity is perhaps part of the explanation for why the ecclesiastical authorities did not shut down religious life in England: organized processions outside churches; observance of fast days; the distribution of ashes on Ash Wednesday; particular treatment of public penitents on Maundy Thursday; the blessing of candles at Candlemas and the visiting of shrines of saints all continued as normal. Then, early in 1209, perhaps uncertain of the impact of his actions, the pope began to soften: he allowed conventual churches (i.e. churches attached to a nunnery) to celebrate Mass once a week behind closed doors; and in the summer of 1212 he permitted the last communion to be given to the dying. We should also note that the financial lifeblood of the lesser clergy did not dry up, allowing them to fulfil many of their normal daily duties. John took the landed revenues from vacant bishoprics but he did not have access to the other ecclesiastical revenues and incomes such as tithe payments. Nor were the activities of the ecclesiastical courts curtailed. 'So far as we can see their work was not interrupted by the interdict', observes Cheney, though appeals to Rome ended.[47] Even vacancies on the Episcopal bench were filled – elections took place in 1209 at Chichester, Exeter, Lichfield and Lincoln – although the bishops elect were not consecrated. Church-building, although not widespread, continued, suggestive of confidence in the future. All of this led to Cheney cautioning that 'the political circumstances [of 1212–13] may conceivably have been due in part to the Interdict, but this cannot be demonstrated'.[48]

After the pronouncement of excommunication in 1209 and the consequent flight of most of the bishops, it seems sensible to speculate that their absence had little impact because absenteeism was nothing new. After all, Hubert Walter's pluralism meant that he had little time for episcopal business. In Henry II's reign, Becket was in exile for six years and yet church life continued as normal, no doubt driven forward by the offices of the archdeacons. It is true that a number of issues coalesced in 1212 to cause John political difficulty and that these issues may have been shaped by the fact that John was excommunicate, but if circumstances had been as Wendover would want us to believe then the evidence offers a deafening silence: John faced no religiously inspired popular rebellion. There was, for example, no equivalent to the Pilgrimage of Grace – the rebellion that nearly toppled Henry VIII in 1536–7 when he began his dissolution of the monasteries – no equivalent of the ominous Northern Rebellion that Elizabeth I had to face down in 1569; no thirteenth-century style 'Gunpowder Plot'. Instead, as a seventeenth-century commentator might have reported, not a dog wagged its tongue.

ii) Why did John's Struggle with the Papacy Last so Long?

A key reason why John's struggle with the Papacy lasted so long is because it seems as though the stance he adopted elicited genuinely popular support. The annalist of Margam Abbey argues that the laity, most of the clergy and even many higher clergy were on the king's side in 1205. Certainly, the laity must have keenly appreciated the implied threat to their own rights of patronage to church livings if John was unable to secure the election of John de Gray. Indeed, if the interdict is seen as a declaration of war by the papacy then John's actions against the church should be understood, not as those of a tyrant expropriating the wealth of the church for his own ends, but as economic sanctions designed to collapse the spirit of his opponent. This is the sense in which Painter has described John's action against the wives of clergy as 'a perfectly magnificent idea. The clergy was harassed, money was extorted from them, and yet no ecclesiastical authority could gracefully protest'.[49]

Similarly, historians ought more readily to acknowledge that John was entirely within his feudal rights to collect landed revenues from vacant sees and royal abbeys. It should also be noticed that it was not unusual for the Crown to procrastinate over making appointments to important church positions. For instance, during the reign of William II (1087–1100) there were eleven vacancies that remained unfilled for more than several months. In fact, two of these, Durham and Canterbury, remained in royal custody for more than three years and four-and-a-half years respectively. The archbishopric of Canterbury was again vacant between 1109 and 1113 and the archbishopric of York was vacant between 1181 and 1191. The chronicler Ralph of Coggeshall condemned Henry II for failing to fill vacant bishoprics promptly.[50] It is true that the vacancies that occurred during the reign of King John were unusually long, but this is understandable given the circumstances.

As a feudal overlord, John was simply doing what any landholder might do, and this therefore is another way in which we can account for the lack of baronial opposition.

iii) Who Won the Struggle, John or Innocent?

The bald terms of the submission have been used to argue that John lost the struggle with Innocent – the image of the king surrendering to the papal nuncio, Pandulf, frequently portrayed as an act of abject humiliation. Matthew Paris, writing in the mid-thirteenth century, calls the charter of May 1213 a '*carta detestabilis*', a thing to be detested for all time.[51] Similarly, the Barnwell annalist tells us that 'to many it seemed ignominious and a heavy yoke of servitude'.[52] Certainly, Innocent must have felt that his prestige was enhanced. He might also have hoped that as overlord he may henceforth be able to manipulate English foreign policy. Moreover, the annual payment of 1,000 marks that John agreed to pay was not insignificant. Posing as exiled martyrs of the church, old enemies returned, amongst whom were, Eustace de Vesci and Robert Fitz Walter, the last two being destined to play a key role in the events of 1215.

Yet in a number of respects a judgement which pronounces John to be the loser in 1213 is at best misleading, and, in the eyes of some Tudor historians, straightforwardly wrong. For these writers John was regarded as a hero figure, a sort of proto-Protestant whose struggle with Pope Innocent foreshadowed the actions of Henry VIII. As the break with Rome unfolded in the 1530s, John was deliberately portrayed as being 'without question…a good man', 'a man both valiant and godly' and 'a most virtuous king'.[53] His subsequent failure – that is, his decision to submit to the papacy in 1213 – is accounted for, not by any weakness or lack of resolution on his behalf, but rather because he was 'forsaken of his own lords, where he would have put a good and godly reformation in his own land'.[54] Thomas Swynnerton, swiping at medieval chroniclers when writing in 1534, asserts that John's reputation had been 'ungodly handled and falsely damned by a malicious sort of traitor of the clergy after his death, and his life and history shamefully interlaced with most abominable lies'.[55] For some, then, John was the winner – albeit only for a while. The very success of the Protestant reformations by the early seventeenth century meant that John's propaganda value had diminished, and 'the need to view John as a hero had for the most part evaporated'.[56]

More particularly, we should take note of the Barnwell chronicler, quoted above, who also asserted that by the submission John 'provided prudently for himself'.[57] Key pieces of evidence support this position. Firstly, it was no disgrace to be a vassal – papal or imperial. For instance, Frederick of Hohenstaufen, the Holy Roman Emperor was himself a papal vassal. John's brother Richard had surrendered England to Emperor Henry VI and had received it back as an imperial fief for £5,000 per annum. Sicily, Sweden, Poland, Denmark, Portugal and Aragon were already fiefs of the Apostolic see. No contemporary recorded the submission as a demeaning surrender. There was no opposition at the time. Though we obviously need to be cautious of its broader purpose, John made this point in a letter he wrote to Innocent, in which he stated that the decision to submit had been encouraged 'by the common counsel of our barons'.[58] Secondly, overnight, John's submission denied the French king the ability to assume the mantle of a crusader, preparing to invade England as a liberator. Thirdly, John could now also expect support from his papal overlord against the English baronage. Indeed, within five months of the submission, Innocent was writing to the English barons to warn them 'not...to move a step against the king until you have consulted the Roman pontiff'.[59] During the momentous events of 1215, Innocent III did all he could to assist his vassal (see page 158), especially since by then John had taken the crusader's vow (4 March 1215). Thus, Innocent expressed his 'amazement and irritation' that some bishops had not provided support against 'the disturbers of the realm' and ordered that they and their supporters be excommunicated. Upon learning of Magna Carta he declared 'we utterly reject and condemn this settlement' and ordered its supporters to be excommunicated.[60] Having by this time fallen out with the king, and believing that Innocent was not fully informed about events, Langton himself fell foul of this pronouncement and suffered excommunication in mid-September 1215 – upon learning this news John must have allowed himself a wry smile. Nor was papal support for John short lived: on 16 December 1215 Innocent excommunicated named rebels; and the same fate befell Prince Louis and his adherents on 29 May 1216. 'John had, in fact,' concluded Kate Norgate writing in 1902, 'at one stroke cut the ground from under the feet of all his enemies both at home and abroad'.[61] Unsurprisingly, recent historical opinion has variously described John's submission as 'a brilliant manoeuvre', 'a diplomatic stroke of genius' and 'prudent and wise'.[62] In short, a masterstroke.

Overall, the evidence that John won a greater amount than the pope is compelling. Notably, he got away without fully compensating the English church for its financial losses. The interdict had remained in place despite the submission of 1213, the reason being that time was needed to work out the financial compensation due to the English church. The king, by playing on the rivalries between Langton, Innocent and Pandulf, successfully negotiated down an initial demand of 100,000 marks to 40,000 marks, payable in six monthly instalments. Of these, there is no evidence that John paid more than a single instalment and yet the interdict was nevertheless lifted on

2 July 1214. As has been seen, John won a valuable papal ally in the civil wars that first broke out in 1215. Above all, John did not concede the principle that had been the root cause of the conflict – the Crown's assertion that to 'gift' high ecclesiastical office was part of the royal prerogative: John's nominees were elected in all of the six elections that took place after the surrender in 1213, despite the fact (as was noted earlier) that his reign coincided with that of a pope whose 'insistence on his rights and duties as God's viceregent, summed up all the efforts of his predecessors'.[63]

Chapter 8

ADMINISTRATION, JUSTICE AND FINANCE

Timeline

1130 Earliest existing Pipe Roll
1156 Date from which Pipe Rolls exist in a continuous series until 1832
1198 Geoffrey Fitz Peter appointed justiciar
1199 Date from which Charter Rolls develop
1200 Date from which Close Rolls develop
1201 Date from which Patent Rolls develop
1203 Levying of the Seventh
1207 Levying of the Thirteenth
1209 Closure of the court of the Bench at Westminster
1213 Peter des Roches succeeds Geoffrey Fitz Peter as justiciar
1214 Hubert de Burgh succeeds Peter des Roches as justiciar

A) Narrative: The Sinews of Government

i) Administration

At the centre of English government was the king. In fact, the government was the king. As such, the texture and tone of any medieval regime was determined by the personality of the monarch. Nothing of importance could be set in motion without his assent. The king was responsible for declaring peace and pronouncing war, for proclaiming economic initiatives and for the smooth functioning of the legal system. He was free to hire and fire men of his choosing to help him in these tasks; and men would want to serve him because of the patronage that he could dispense – usually in the form of land, though titles and privileges were also common. Royal control over inheritances (reliefs), wardships and marriages meant that the king's powers of patronage were immense. As D. Danziger and J. Gillingham observe, 'the king had, in effect, the power to make a trusted servant a millionaire overnight. No head of government in the West today has anything remotely approaching the power of patronage [that was in the hands of King John]'.[1]

Among the most important appointments made by the king were those to the offices of chancellor and justiciar, respectively head of the Chancery (see below) and a sort-of regent – a position that had necessarily evolved because, prior to 1204, kings were frequently absent from England (see page 26). There was no salaried civil service; and since departments of state had barely begun to emerge there were no alternative centres of authority that possessed the wherewithal to initiate alternative policies and programmes. Beyond noble revolt and religious sanctions authorized by the church, there was no check upon the power of the king, and certainly there was as yet no constitutional machinery that might crank into action to restrain ill-received monarchical enthusiasms. Parliament had yet to evolve. If needs be, the monarch could call upon the feudal levy (and latterly, mercenaries) to enforce his authority.

The authority of the monarch was in these ways impressive. But it was, in fact, even more than this – it was supranatural, as was displayed and confirmed in the coronation ceremony. 'Crowned, girded with the sword, holding the rod and sceptre, the new king was presented as judge and war leader. Similarly the image of the king in majesty that appears on the royal seal shows him sitting, enthroned with crown, orb, and drawn sword, a vigorous depiction of majestic and coercive power.'[2] This authority was instituted by God, confirmed by the anointing of the king on his hands, chest and arms with holy oil and on his head with chrism, an especially sacred form of holy oil. In his handbook, *Dialogue of the Exchequer*, Richard Fitz Nigel asserted that royal actions were to be judged or condemned not by mortal men but only by God. Ranulph de Glanville, the lawyer in whose household John had spent some time as he grew up, made use in his legal treatise *De Legibus et Consuetudinibus Angliae* of the famous maxim of Justinian's Institutes: 'What is pleasing to the prince has the force of law'. Little wonder that Richard and John felt no need to issue a coronation charter. Their interpretation of Angevin monarchy did not admit weaknesses. The authority of the monarch was more than impressive: it was awesome.

Despite his power, it was unusual for the king to make decisions on important matters without seeking advice from his political elite and intimates (familiars) – an inchoate and constantly changing core of great officers of state, household servants and feudatories who acted as advisers, administrators and judges. A meeting composed of these elements was known as the *curia regis*, the council of the king. However, the *curia regis* appeared in many forms and, because John rarely stayed in more than one location for more than a few days, in many places. Walter Map, writing of the *curia regis* in the time of Henry II, confessed: 'I speak of the court, but what the court is God alone knows, I do not'.[3] Certainly, the *curia regis* also acted as a judicature in which legal disputes involving barons were dealt with by their fellow barons and the king.

Constantly on the move, the king travelled with his Household. In part, this was composed of his domestic servants: butlers, cooks, grooms and so on. It was also made up of great barons and important officials such as constables and marshals (who were in charge of organizing the household knights) and the head of Chancery, the chancellor. Chancery was the mouthpiece of the king, a secretariat which existed as part of the Household and expressed the king's will in writing. The chancellor was in charge of the royal seal (which, during the reign of John was to become known as the Great Seal), the device used to stamp the king's heraldry onto a wax pendant attached to a parchment, without which no document issued by the Chancery would carry authenticity and thus effect.

Documents issued by Chancery were of three main types: charters, letters close and letters patent. The first of these were used to convey to important persons royal decisions and concessions such as privileges, land and certain immunities (from a particular tax, for example). Letters close – so-called because they were folded and then sealed shut by use of the Seal – were used to convey routine orders. Lastly, letters patent – documents that were not folded but had the Seal affixed – were employed for public matters affecting administrative areas or a number of people such as treaties, diplomatic negotiations, appointments, grants and confirmation of land and office. Letters close and letters patent were generally addressed to royal agents in the localities, often the sheriff. These agents were charged with implementation of the associated matter. Chancery also issued to local agents writs, documents spelling out agents' duties in the name of the king. From 1199 the documents produced by Chancery began to be copied and enrolled, i.e. joined together end-to-end to form a continuous roll. Charter Rolls, Close Rolls and Patent Rolls thus began to exist from 1199, 1200 and 1201 respectively. Other records were being kept also, such as the *Rotuli de Oblatis et finibus*, rolls of offerings for favours undertaken by Chancery. What this means is that 'the reign of John is the first period in English history when political history can be described on a daily basis'.[4]

Another important part of government residing in the Household alongside Chancery was the Chamber, within which was the Wardrobe. Historically, the Chamber and Wardrobe were responsible for the storage of domestic treasure and royal paraphernalia. Over time, and because of the peripatetic nature of the monarchy, the Chamber and Wardrobe strayed from their historic functions and began to serve the political and, more especially, economic needs of the king. The Chamber received monies from royal treasuries based in castles such as Colchester and Chinon and dispensed them according to the will of the king. The growing importance of the Chamber during this period is evidenced by the fact that it guarded a second seal, smaller than that associated with Chancery and latterly known as the Privy Seal. We know of an occasion in May 1208 when King John, frustrated because 'we do not have the Great Seal with us', bypassed Chancery by making use of the Privy Seal. Indeed, this was to become increasingly common: in the last years of the reign it was the case that even letters patent were issued under the Privy Seal. There is also evidence that by the end of John's reign the Wardrobe was fulfilling the same functions as its parent, the Chamber.

The most important governmental machinery outside of the Household was the Exchequer. *The Dialogue of the Exchequer* tells us that twice a year – at Easter and Michaelmas – there was a meeting of the men that the king had appointed as 'barons of the exchequer' with senior officials from the Chancery and Chamber, such as the treasurer. At the Michaelmas meeting, the Exchequer presided over an audit of the accounts of each sheriff. These accounts detailed the monies actually paid to the king and monies yet owing from a wide variety of sources such as the various feudal dues (see pages 121–2) or monies due to the king in return for grants of land or privilege. We know about the workings of the Exchequer because, like the Chancery, it made a record of its audit on membranes of parchment sewn end-to-end and then enrolled to form a single large roll for storage purposes, known as a Pipe Roll. (The Pipe Roll of 1130 is the earliest that survives, but they exist in a continuous series from 1156 until 1832.) Consequently, it was possible for the authorities easily to see from the record if a debt had not been paid. Those that were not were transferred to the roll for the succeeding year, thus ensuring that 'the Exchequer maintained a tenacious grip on what it was owed'.[5] In its fully developed form this was to be the central financial department of royal government but at this time it was almost certainly still operating in the shadow of the Chamber. Some time shortly before 1199 it took up permanent residency in the royal palace at Westminster, allowing some historians to refer to it henceforth as a government 'department'.[6]

The activation, as it were, of this machinery was dependent on the will and initiative of the king. This would obviously be a problem if the king was a minor, incapacitated or absent. Since 1066 the first two circumstances had not been encountered but the last had been a frequent occurrence, even more so when the Anglo-Norman regnum had evolved into the Angevin 'empire'. Thus emerged the office of justiciar, the incumbents of this position acting with authority akin to a regent.

ii) Justice

When Henry II acceded to the throne in 1154 England was still suffering from the effects of the civil war (1136–54) between Matilda and Stephen, years in which, as one chronicler wrote, 'the whole of England was more disturbed than it ever was before, and every evil was in the land'.[7] Many were determined to win back land that they believed had been illegally taken from them during the conflict. Henry realized that if this element sought to redress their grievances through the courts of the barons then this would diminish the authority of the Crown – it would be in tension with the king's duty to see that all men secured justice. Therefore, to this end, Henry instituted a number of legal reforms. These included sending out royal justices on regular kingdom wide visitations – known as eyres – to shire courts, and also developing further the already existing writ system whereby a plaintiff obtained from Chancery a document (the 'writ') empowering the sheriff to 'cause twelve free and lawful men of the neighbourhood…to appear before me or my justices' [to judge the complaint], a process known as novel dissein (see Figure 13, page 118). By intruding royal justice in this way into the courts of barons, Henry II had established a law that was common throughout England – the common law. One authority, perhaps controversially, concludes that these reforms amounted to an 'Angevin leap forward' in legal matters.[8] All historians agree, however, that these legal developments met an incipient demand and put a great deal of pressure on the royal courts that dealt with them. Indeed, prior to John's accession, so great was the number of cases and pleas occurring that a process of departmentalisation seems to have been under way allowing the historian to perceive two distinct royal courts each dealing with the common law. On the one hand there had emerged the justices at the Exchequer at Westminster dealing with pleas in their non-financial capacity. These were sometimes referred to as the justices of the Bench (de banco). They met and transacted business without the king. On the other hand, the justices who travelled with the king and his Household also dispensed justice. When this court met the king would often be present and therefore it was known as coram rege. As we have seen, the king would also be present in a superior court called the curia regis which dealt with issues touching the barons.

Until the loss of Normandy in 1204 John was usually absent from England. Consequently, the process of departmentalisation described above seems to have continued during the absences of the king, when the two royal courts

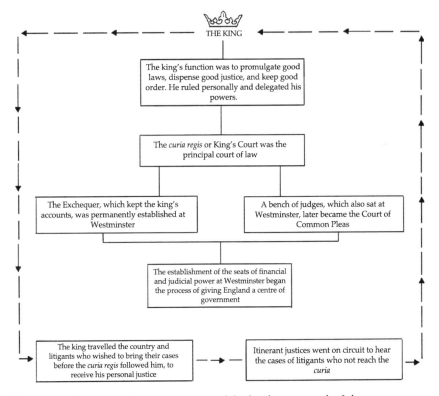

Figure 13. Diagrammatic representation of the legal system under John

responded to directives issued by the justiciar. However, from 1204, with John almost continually present in England, the amount of work finding its way to the Bench at Westminster steadily diminished so that by 1209 it was closed. It came alive again – briefly – when John was abroad in 1214. (For details on justice during this period see Interpretation, pages 129–31.)

iii) Finance

A key method of assessing the efficiency of any government is to examine how successful it is at raising revenues because any such examination gives an insight into the fiscal efficiency (or otherwise) at the heart of that government, and shows to what extent it is able to make its will felt in the localities.

It is first worth saying something about the actual coinage itself. There was only one coin in circulation in England at this time, the silver penny – or 'sterling', as it was also known – minted mostly from silver obtained from Germany. Coins were struck in the king's name and carried a representation of the king on one side and on the other there was nearly always an image based on the cross. After every two or three years the existing pennies would be taken out of circulation and a new one introduced. These were minted by moneyers who had purchased their dies from the Crown. The number of mints gradually declined in this period: there were around 30 in 1158 and only 6 in 1220. Transactions were accounted for not only by references to pennies, but to shillings, marks and pounds. (Twelve pennies amounted to a shilling; 160 pennies made up a mark and 240 composed a pound. Therefore, one mark is two thirds of a pound. Pennies are denoted by the letter 'd', and shillings by the letter 's' e.g. £10.15s.3d.) The number of coins in circulation in this period rose rapidly in number: estimates reckon that in 1086 there were 9 million pennies in circulation; in 1205 that there were some 60 million; and in 1300 that there were 216 million. Most of this increase in supply occurred after 1180, when there were perhaps 24 million pennies in circulation.[9]

John's reign coincided with sharp rises in prices, partly a consequence of the increased money supply but also a result of the growing size of the population. The price of an ox increased by about 125 per cent between the 1190s and 1220s; the price of wheat increased by about 138 per cent between the 1160s and the 1210s. Costs of warfare were not immune from this pattern. Thus, whereas Henry II would have paid a mercenary soldier 8d per day, John had to find 24d – a threefold increase. A consequence of this price inflation was the practical issue of how to transport money around, considering that each penny weighed around 1.45g. For instance, when the city of Lincoln found themselves making a payment to John of £180 i.e. 43,200 pennies – which was by no means unusual – they found themselves facing the task of transporting 138lbs a distance of two hundred miles.

The Crown required large amounts of money for a number of reasons. The most substantial expenditure was warfare and John's campaigns in France, Scotland, Wales and Ireland soaked up significant amounts of money. (Preparations for the campaign of 1205, which never actually took place, cost around £5,000.) Regular expense was also incurred on castle construction and repair, about £1,000 annually during John's reign. Significant expenditure was required to maintain, and indeed, enhance, the dignity of the monarchy. Thus, to run his household in appropriate style, John observed feast days and held banquets; he purchased jewels and fir-trimmed robes, spending £700 on the latter for the Christmas feast of 1205. Moreover, though historians of expenditure in John's reign do not seem to have noticed, John had a queen and a great and growing family from 1207 which must have necessitated some considerable expenditure.[10]

Total royal income evidenced from receipts received at the Exchequer has been averaged at about £18,500 per annum for the decade 1165–74, rising to about £32,000 per annum by the end of John's reign. However, not all royal revenues found their way to the Crown via the Exchequer. Taking account of these 'unseen' revenues, one estimate – controversially – puts John's average income per annum at £60,000.[11] To put this into context, a labourer could not expect to make more than 30s a year and the goods and chattels of an ordinary person were worth only 10s; the annual income of a knight would have been about £20 and the average annual income of a baron around £200.

Revenues came to John from five main sources: the Crown lands (known as the royal demesne); income obtained from feudal rights resulting from overlordship; taxation; profits from justice and, during the reign of John, revenues obtained from the church because of the quarrel with the papacy. The Crown had been the greatest landholder in England since the Conquest, and, despite the impact of the ongoing process of granting land away in return for political favour, this was still the case at the time of King John. Nonetheless, the royal demesne was significantly smaller than it once had been – John had perhaps two thirds of the land that William the Conqueror had held in demesne at the time of the Domesday Book in 1087. The king obtained revenues from his demesne from the produce of his farms, though, lacking the means to do so, this would not be taken directly by the Crown but via his sheriffs. In return for a lump sum payment the sheriff would then manage the king's lands within that county, a process known as 'farming', and the payment made by the sheriff to the Crown known as the 'county farm'. During the course of the twelfth century the annual payment from county farms was in the order of £10,000. However, by the end of Henry I's reign these sums had been fixed, creating a major problem for the Crown during a period of rapid and substantial inflation. To overcome this, John demanded an 'increment', a fixed payment made by the sheriff over-and-above his 'county farm' payment. John also continued the policy advanced by his brother of selling sheriffdoms; and since sheriffs took in much more money than they handed over, there were always those willing to pay. (In 1200 William de Stuteville, for example, offered John £1,000 to be sheriff of Yorkshire.) In order to try and ensure that the Crown was not being overly exploited by the sheriff, in several counties from 1204 John experimented with the appointment of 'custodian sheriffs' – sheriffs who had to account for everything they received from their county, thus ensuring that more went into the royal coffers. This resulted in a 30 per cent increase in payments by the end of 1205; and between 1207 and 1212 sheriffs returned on average an extra £1,400 per annum to the Exchequer. The other source of income that the Crown could obtain from its demesne was an arbitrary payment levied on those vassals – which in John's case included the Jews – living on Crown land, known as a tallage. Money from this source could be significant: one of John's tallages brought in £8,276. In 1207 he demanded a tallage of 4,000 marks from the Jews (having already demanded the same amount in 1200 in return for confirming their Charters of Privilege).

It remains the case that the value of the county farms was seriously below the actual wealth-generating capability of the king's lands. Royal administration was not yet sufficiently sophisticated to grapple with the problem (it took until the late 1230s), and consequently, even with John's reforms of 1204–8, the financial yield was still below that enjoyed by most other landowners from their lands. It was this fundamental structural flaw that forced John to press harder on incidental sources of income to keep afloat, which in turn led directly to increasing disaffection amongst the barons and the road to Runnymede.

As a landowner, like any other lord, the Crown had a right to expect certain payments from its vassals. Significant among these were relief, wardship and control over rights of marriage. The first of these was a payment ('relief') made to the lord when the tenant died and the son of the tenant was to succeed him as holder of the land, or fief; the second was the right of the lord to have custody of minors and unmarried female heirs upon the death of a tenant. These were lucrative sources of income for the Crown. A total of sixty sons succeeded to their father's baronies during the reign of John and the king imposed on them reliefs ranging from 40 to 10,000 marks, an average payment of 600 marks. Obtaining estates as feudal custodies through the process of wardship not only meant that the Crown could benefit from the revenues that these estates ordinarily produced whilst it held them, but that ultimately it could also benefit by selling them off to the highest bidder. For instance, William Briwerre, finding himself in favour with John, purchased six wardships at prices ranging from 10 to 10,000 marks. The Crown steadily racked up what vassals needed to pay in order to secure royal assent to their marriage – the average payment under Henry II was 101 marks; under Richard 174 marks and 314 marks under John. Widows, wanting to avoid a forced marriage, also had to pay. Fifty-nine women in this condition paid King John, including the countess of Aumale – the prospect of a fourth husband proving too much for her, she offered John 5,000 marks in 1212 to remain single. The amounts offered by widows under John increased to an average of 278 marks from an average of 110 marks during the reign of Henry II. It is estimated that John obtained in total over 40,000 marks (about £27,000) from payments made to secure his consent to a marriage or, indeed, to secure royal confirmation that a marriage would not take place.

Another payment that the Crown could demand as a feudal lord was scutage (shield money) – a levy made in place of a vassal providing military service. The tenants of the Crown owed differing numbers of knights according to

the extent of their estates – for example, in the late twelfth century the Earl
of Essex owed sixty and the Earl of Oxford thirty. It was increasingly the
case that the Crown commuted this obligation into a monetary payment,
much preferring to use the money thus obtained to hire the more reliable –
and usually, more effective – services of mercenaries. Under the Angevins
the frequency of scutage levies was increasing: John levied it on eleven
occasions in sixteen years (raising on average £2,020 from each); Richard
on three occasions in eleven years; Henry II had taken it on eight occasions
in thirty four years. John also raised the rate at which scutage was levied:
when requested by Henry it was mostly levied at £1.6s.8d, half the level at
which John raised his last scutage in 1213 (which aroused such strong protest
that J. C. Holt saw it as a *casus belli*, a cause of war). John also demanded
a fine for the personal exemption from military service of the tenant-in-chief,
a practice initiated by Richard. In 1201 a baron had to pay a fine for this
reason levied at 3 or 4 marks for every knight that he owed; by 1210 this had
been increased to 10 marks.

   Alongside the feudal dues which the king took from his vassals he could
also demand taxes from all of his subjects, a principle which had first been
established when Anglo-Saxon kings, responding to assaults from the Vikings,
had levied emergency taxation as a general land tax, known as the *geld*. Having
not been levied since 1162, the *geld* resurfaced in 1194 when the government
was employing all possible means to raise Richard's ransom. By this time it
was known as *carucage* and was levied by John in 1200. When it was collected
in 1220, it produced £3,400 but inflation means that this represents less in
real terms than the £2,400 it had reaped in 1130. Much more worthwhile
was the general tax raised as a percentage levy on income and movable
wealth, mostly corn and animals. A tax of this sort had been raised several
times before 1199 – in 1166, 1185, 1188 (the Saladin Tithe) and 1195 –
and John appreciated that, by demanding that individual property holders
swear to their goods' value in front of special justices sent into the shires, they
produced substantial yields. Thus, in 1203 he instituted the tax known as the
Seventh. Precise records of the revenues that this produced do not survive,
but R. V. Turner reckons that 'an estimate of £7,000 seems reasonable'.[12] Even
more lucrative was the general tax of 1207, known as the Thirteenth because
it demanded one thirteenth of income from rents and moveable property.
This was astonishingly successful, bringing in perhaps more than £60,000.
As he had done in relation to feudal dues, John encouraged developments in
fiscal innovation. Notably, between 1202 and 1207 he imposed customs on
imports and exports, perhaps bringing in £2,500 per annum as a result.

   By 1199 large areas of England – an estimated one third of the country in
total – was known as Royal Forest (see Figure 14). This area did not actually

have to be afforested; nor did it need to be royal demesne but it had its own law, Forest Law. The main purpose of this law was to preserve the beasts of the forest for the royal hunt. This law could be fierce: some offenders who took deer or boar were sometimes executed; others suffered the more gentle punishments of blinding and castration. More commonplace was the levying of fines for lesser offences in the forest, such as clearing woodland, stealing timber or keeping hounds. Fines were high: Henry II's spot check in the form

Figure 14. Areas of Royal Forest in England in the early thirteenth century (courtesy of Yale University Press)

of the Forest eyre which he set forth in 1175 produced £12,000; John's Forest
eyres of 1207 and 1212 obtained fines totalling £11,350.

The royal coffers also benefitted from the dispensation of justice. John was
open to bribes sometimes to fast track a case; sometimes to obstruct or collapse
the legal process, achieved by making a payment known as an oblation.
For example, the king received three horses from one of the parties in a case
in 1207 and we learn that the suit was dismissed because John 'does not wish
that plea to be held'.[13] In another instance William de Briouze offered the
king 300 cows, thirty bulls and ten horses in order to expedite a 1205 plea
challenging his right to the barony of Totnes, Devon.

It was also increasingly easy to get on the wrong side of the authorities for
such things as neglect of public duties, failing to bring a criminal to justice or
stumbling whilst pleading in a case before a court. Those who did such things
were judged in *misericordiam* – that is, at the king's mercy, which might result
in forfeiture of goods unless they made a payment known as an amercement.
Rates were not large but rarely fell below half a mark (6s and 8d), reasonably
substantial when, as we have seen, the annual income of a wage labourer was
no more than 30s a year and the goods and chattels of an ordinary person
were worth on average perhaps 10s. (In 1202 the general eyre in Lincolnshire
produced £633 in amercements whereas the first eyre in 1166 had produced
roughly £250.) Most men could expect to be amerced at least once a year.

We should remind ourselves also, that the quarrel with the papacy
meant that by the spring of 1213 John had some seven bishoprics and over
12 abbacies in his hands, each of which had an income of several hundred
pounds a year. In total, John benefitted to the tune of at least £66,000
because of his difficulties with Innocent (see page 106).

From all of the above, it comes as no surprise to learn that the Barnwell
annalist regarded John as 'a pillager of his subjects', and concluded that
this was one of the reasons why '[his people] forsook him and, ultimately,
little mourned his death'.[14] For a long time this was the generally accepted
interpretation of the impact of John's financial policies: he had pushed too
hard; he was a tyrant. On the eve of the campaign of 1214, bearing in mind the
considerable amounts of money that had by that time been raised and spent,
it is extraordinary that John may have had a war chest of 200,000 marks –
well over 30,000,000 pennies, amounting to perhaps as much as one half of all
the coinage in circulation.[15] Taxation is, of course, never popular but John's
taxes were doubly unpopular because they were levied to fight a cause that
had little emotional purchase on the bulk of the political nation. Against this
background the growing discontent from 1212 seems easily understandable
and the tone of Magna Carta, for the large part, entirely pertinent.

It was not just the amount of money that John had taken that had caused
dissent, but also the methods he used to obtain it. For instance, John took

scutages in 1204, 1205 and 1209 but since these did not accompany military campaigns he was seen to be divorcing his actions from accepted feudal practice. Unlike his predecessors, the king insisted on prompt payments of debt and used the court at the Exchequer to effect this so that it became 'a potent instrument of oppression'.[16] Debtors might suffer imprisonment or loss of their lands (disseized) if they did not pay money they owed. The Crown seized Richmond castle because its constable refused to swear to the value of his wealth and movable goods. The systematic keeping of records made the collection process ominously efficient, the Pipe Rolls showing for the first time accumulated debts, perhaps from one year to the next, lumped together as one. Whereas a baron may previously have hoped that the details of his debt may be lost or forgotten, there was now no real chance of this happening. Another grievance for many was the assessment process for taxes based on moveable goods and wealth. This involved the sending of royal agents into the localities to collect and record up-to-date information in a way which had not been done since the Domesday Book. The fact that people hid their property in monasteries to avoid assessment gives some indication of the thorough nature of the process. The centre was penetrating the periphery.

B) Interpretations

i) The 'Record Revolution'

As described above (see pages 115–16), a distinctive feature of the reign of John is that this is the moment from which the secretariat of government – Chancery – begins to keep a systematic record of its business in the form of charters, letters close and letters patent, all enrolled. Combined with records from the Exchequer – the Pipe Rolls – this material offers us a significantly different perspective on John to that provided by the chronicle evidence. One historian concludes that for this reason '1199 is a real turning point in English history. The materials available to the historian suddenly become more numerous and more exact.'[17] 'There is scarcely a subject connected with the history and government of this country which does not receive illustration from the Patent Rolls', says the editor of the rolls from the reign of King John.[18] The survival of these records means that we are presented with events apparently just as they were, 'intriguingly preserved like flies in amber', says another authority.[19] Through these documents we can see the wheels of government turning: grants of land and office made; payments transacted for services and goods; the royal will transformed into legal warrant. Moreover, because these documents were attested by John, they provide us with a detailed itinerary of the king: on any one day we are aware of where he was (see Appendix, Document 35). In short, this material in effect allows us to hear the voice of John himself – almost literally so, since the vast majority of these instructions and decisions must have received oral assent as he went about other business. For all these reasons the record evidence, says Warren, allows us to get closer to [John] there 'than through any pages of any chronicle'.[20]

A careful study of the record material does serious damage to the John as portrayed in the much of the chronicle evidence. For example, in the immediate aftermath of the sealing of Magna Carta on 15 June 1215, Wendover would have us believe that 'whilst lying sleepless that night in Windsor castle [John's] thoughts alarmed him much and before daylight he fled by stealth to the Isle of Wight, and there in great agony of mind devised plans to be revenged on the barons'[21] (see Appendix, Document 23). Numerous historians have allowed themselves to be seduced by this version of events. J. R. Green, clearly basing his own account on that of Wendover and the palpably dubious Paris (see Appendix, Document 24) imagines John in the immediate aftermath of the sealing of Magna Carta suffering 'a burst of fury, flinging himself on the floor and gnawing sticks and straw in his impotent rage. But the rage soon passed into the subtle policy of which he was master. Some days after he rode from Windsor and lingered for months along the southern shore, the Cinque Ports and the Isle of Wight, [plotting his revenge]'.[22] It makes for a good read but it is unquestionably wrong. The record evidence demonstrates that the king did not then visit the Isle of Wight, nor is there any evidence of his ever having been in that island – except in May and June of 1206 and in February of 1214 – thus casting serious doubt over the whole of Wendover's version of events (see Appendix, Document 35). Close study of the record evidence has actually led some historians to conclude the exact opposite of Wendover. For instance, A. L. Poole was convinced that this evidence demonstrated that 'the government at once set to work to give effect to the settlement [of 1215]'; and that 'evidently the king was seriously trying to make the peace a reality'.[23] In what other ways has Wendover misled his audience?

Another instance whereby damage is done to the credibility of the chronicle material, as we have seen (see page 105), relates to the alleged occasion in 1208 when John orders that a priest killer be freed. Wendover has John say: "He has slain an enemy of mine, release him and let him go" (see Appendix, Document 12). And yet this sits uncomfortably with a Letter Patent, issued at roughly the same time, in which John is clearly concerned that justice should be done (see Appendix, Document 28). Similarly, whereas Wendover asserts that John inflicted harsh treatment on Jews (see Appendix, Document 14), the record evidence suggests that he was at least sometimes pleased to take them under his protection, and that when he did so he clearly intended his will to be enforced with fierce energy (see Appendix, Document 34). Chronicle accounts frequently portray John as impious, Wendover and Paris stating that he often blasphemed by using the phrase 'By the feet of God'. This sits awkwardly with record evidence that shows that John frequently gave to the poor, took a particular interest in St James' relics at Reading and founded Beaulieu Abbey. The record material also straightforwardly contradicts the notion that John was lazy, a key criticism of the chroniclers (see Appendix, Documents 7 and 8). As a whole the record material reveals that John was possessed of energy, drive and vision. Documents 28 to 34 (see Appendix), for instance, show John to have been absolutely involved in the administrative bowels of his regime. It is difficult not to conclude that John was an administrative genius, able to see and understand the broad picture because he was aware of its constituent details. S. B. Chrimes talks of 'a fresh spirit being given to the administration'; Holt asserts that John took a thoroughly intelligent and immensely energetic interest in the running of the country; and Warren concludes that 'It was indeed a *tour de force* of personal monarchy. It required unbounded energy and universal competence. John had it.'[24]

A close study of the record evidence thus results in Bad King John disappearing, to be replaced by an image of a king possessed of terrific energy (he rarely stayed in one place for more than a few days), the wherewithal to deal with events great and small and an aptitude and preparedness to drill down to the details of those events. Consequently, as J. C. Holt asserts, 'It is now recognised that John took a thoroughly intelligent and immensely energetic interest in the running of the country... The total achievement was enormous, fit to stand alongside that of Henry II or Edward I. Together, these two and John represent a standard which was never again equalled in the medieval period.'[25]

Not all historians, however, have been persuaded by this interpretation of the evidence. In particular, J. Gillingham asserts that 'John is the most overrated king in English history' because his reign 'coincides with the beginning of a much more bureaucratic system of record-keeping than had existed hitherto...[and that consequently]...compared with his predecessors, John's days appear to be crowded with business but this, of course, does not mean that he actually worked harder or more effectively than they had... Historians have allowed themselves to give the impression that John was unusually competent'.[26] Yet there remains a question over why records began to be kept from the start of John's reign, rather than an earlier point. It may be that this is explained by the presence of Hubert Walter, the dynamic justiciar of Richard and latterly archbishop of Canterbury from 1198 until his death in 1205. Certainly, Bartlett seems to think this is the case: 'there is every reason to think that he [i.e. Walter] was personally responsible', he asserts.[27] On the other hand, Warren sees it differently, describing John as an 'energetic new broom sweeping vigorously under the guidance of an experienced old hand [i.e. Walter]'.[28] Indeed, an awareness of John's approach in other areas – his resilience in his clash with the papacy or his dedication to winning back Normandy, for example – suggests that it is by no means far-fetched to see the 'record-revolution' as significantly the result of the drive, ambition and sheer attention to detail of John. After all, John had been brought-up in the household of Glanville, from whom he is likely to have been influenced positively about the processes of record keeping and administration. In fact, from the earliest years of John's reign, all sorts of documents were copied and enrolled, not just the charters, letters patent and letters closed. This is highly suggestive of a determination to bring a new precision and efficiency to administration and there seems much to suggest that the driving force in this development was John, a king who, as one historian alleges, took 'perverse delight in the detail of government'.[29]

This record evidence took some time to enter into the public domain, thus giving an explanation for why interpretations based on the testimony of the chroniclers influenced historians for so long. A so-called 'Calendar to the Patent Rolls' (a calendar in this context being a sort-of-guide) was published in 1802 but proved 'most imperfect and unsatisfactory', for instance listing only 23 letters patent for the 5th year of King John whereas 448 exist.[30] Printed transcripts of the original Latin enrolments letters patent for the period 1201–16 were published by the Public Record Office in *Rotuli Litterarum Patentium* in 1835; Latin transcripts which exist for most of the Charter Rolls for King John's reign were published by the same authority in the *Rotuli Chartarum* in 1837. Printed transcriptions of every Pipe Roll until 1224 have been published mainly by the Pipe Roll Society, which was founded in the Public Record Office in 1883 for this purpose. Despite this, eliciting information from record sources is not always straightforward and sometimes not even possible – for instance, there are no Chancery Rolls for the years 1209 – 1212. Some entries are enigmatic. Many historians have put their minds to understanding what we can learn about John from this detail entered on the Fine Roll of 1204–5:

> The wife of Hugh de Neville gives the lord King 200 chickens that she may lie with her husband for one night. Thomas de Sanford stands surety for 100 chickens, and her husband, Hugh, for 100.[31]

What inferences can be made about John from this entry: That he liked chickens? That he had a sense of humour? That he was holding the wife of Hugh de Neville as a sex slave? That he had incarcerated Hugh de Neville? That this was a deliberately mischievous entry made by clerks and since it exists to this day it suggests that John did not see it, which in turn indicates that he did not in fact possess that facility for close attention to detail which in general the record evidence is made to suggest? Any, or all, of these may be correct but all are pure guesswork.

Despite the difficulties encountered in decoding the meaning of the wife of Hugh de Neville's chickens, it is clear that record evidence provides an important corrective to the image of a monstrous John put forward by chroniclers like Wendover and Paris, judged by W. L. Warren to be no more than 'scurrilous gossip-mongers'.[32]

ii) A Contextual View: Judicial Practices and Price Inflation

a) Judicial Practices

Detractors of John explain his closing of the court of the Bench at Westminster in 1209, which forced plaintiffs to proceed in the court over which he presided, as a consequence of his chronic inability to trust others. They assert that, in the context of 1209, when John was facing the prospect of excommunication by the papacy, this was a move to win greater control over a key area of his government so as to ensure that it jumped to his tune. For these commentators, this is a sinister development which sits well with John's reputation as established by the chronicle sources. The explanation for this development is perhaps better understood, however, as being a structural response brought about by the fact that after the loss of Normandy John was almost permanently resident in England. This meant that from 1204 the place for the court of the Bench at Westminster was diminished.

A different explanation is offered by the suggestion that a rift had emerged between John and Geoffrey Fitz Peter, his justiciar, the official who would ordinarily have had much involvement with the court of the Bench at Westminster. However, sources which indicate hostility between the two men date from 1210, which post dates the closure of the Bench in 1209. Moreover, John made no moves against Simon of Pattishall and James of Potterne, two justices with whom he worked, despite the fact that they had strong ties to the justiciar.

The most compelling explanation is probably that John felt a compunction to be directly involved in this most important function of monarchy and that he did not want a separate court fulfilling the same role without his presence. Certainly, the plea rolls and writs show that the king was actively involved. John frequently took a direct role in judgements. Apparently, John advised his justices on uncertain points of law, modified procedures or showed his benevolence. Turner reveals that the records show that John was occasionally 'moved by mercy', and would, for example, pardon those who had committed involuntary homicide. We learn of the case of a woman who came before the king seeking recovery of her land and 'so cried upon the lord king that he gave her possession'.[33] Stenton concluded that 'in the matter of judicial administration King John deserves credit rather than blame' and that 'his interest in legal development, his untiring activity in hearing pleas, and his readiness to admit litigants not only to his court but to his presence must be remembered in his favour'.[34] There is no evidence to suggest that John tried to turn this court into a prerogative court, a conduit to deliver the king's alleged absolutist ambitions.

In all of this there is a strong sense that John was fulfilling a key function of medieval kingship: he was acting as a lawgiver and lawmaker – peace within the kingdom was, after all, the 'king's peace'. The justices themselves recognized this, frequently making a note in documents, *loquendum cum rege* – speak with the king. In this context it is perhaps not surprising, then, to learn that John set forth new judicial initiatives: for instance, in order to try and limit lords' disciplinary power over their tenants he introduced a new common law procedure facilitating tenants' recovery of chattels (goods) distrained (taken) unjustly by their lord. This new writ process was called withername. John also developed the writ for a jury of attaint: by purchasing a writ *de odio et atia* a litigant could empanel a jury of twenty-four to convict an initial jury of having judged by wrongful decision. It proved highly popular. By closing the court of the Bench John ensured that his form of justice could be not only concentrated, but exactly as he wished.

As well as being charged with closing the court of the Bench at Westminster because of an apparent inability to trust others, John has also been accused of using the law for profit – in short, that he openly sold justice. That John was guilty of this cannot be denied, but he was doing little that was new. Henry II, the supposed creator of the common law, saw nothing wrong with accepting a gift in advance of hearing a case: 'Men who wished to obtain a speedy hearing of their lawsuits knew that a good falcon was the gift most acceptable to the king.'[35] We should recognize that it had always been the case that justice was lucrative for those who dispensed it. It follows that the wider and lower the king's jurisdiction spread, the greater the royal income. It is not inconsistent to see John as dramatically fulfilling his role as a dispenser of justice and gaining financially as a consequence. That is the way the system worked. That is only what his predecessors had done. That is what everyone at the time would have expected of the king. Judged against modern legal practice it is hardly surprising that John has been accused of selling justice, though in context we ought to see such payments as court fees. Indeed, a recent authority, commenting on oblations, asserts that the 'the object of these oblations was not the perversion of royal justice, but at most the diversion of its course'.[36]

It is clear that the traditional representation of John as the betrayer of justice must be abandoned. Loyn's judgement that under John 'justice…suffered often from his arbitrary and unscrupulous methods…[and followed]…neither custom nor procedure', is at best misleading and, when viewed in the broader context of the Angevin period, ill-conceived.[37] 'Do nothing', John instructed his justiciar in 1203, 'contrary to the customs of our kingdom.'[38] Complaints articulated in Magna Carta were not new – John's predecessor and father had been accused of the same. Yet this line of argument can perhaps go too far. We can put ourselves into a position of explaining why a baronial revolt should not have taken place. Profits from justice did go up as John prepared for a new invasion of France. Above all, we need to be alert to the fact that the judicial programme advanced by John was not accessible to the baronage. As Turner points out, 'a writ of right could hardly be purchased by magnates whose immediate lord was the king; neither could barons purchase writs of novel disseizin, summoning juries to declare that the king had taken property "unjustly and without judgement".'[39] In short, the king could not summon himself to judgement. Thus, even as the leading barons felt themselves aggrieved and sought alternative means of redressing their grievances, the knights and lesser freeholders made ever increasing use of a judicial system which empowered them to win their suits against their lords. And for this, they had John to thank.

b) Price Inflation

We should alert ourselves to the fact that the Barnwell annalist's judgement of John as a 'pillager of his subjects' was made without appreciating that the king had been dealt a bad economic hand, far worse than that which any of his predecessors had faced. We have noted (see page 119) that the beginning of John's reign coincided with a rapid period of inflation, seemingly more severe in England than was the case on the Continent.[40] The consequence of this was twofold: on the one hand royal revenue from the sources that accounted at the Exchequer was completely failing to keep pace with inflation and, on the other hand, costs were becoming ever greater. By 1214 it was probably around at least three times more expensive for John to wage war than it had been for his father.

The combination of the relative inelasticity of income from core royal sources, and the rapid inflation of prices, meant that John faced severe financial constraints which forced him to resort to squeezing the flexible – but unpopular and more arbitrary – sources of royal revenue. He thus levied taxes like the Thirteenth of 1207, thereby ensuring that the wealth of those who paid it was assessed according to the new economic circumstances. Already unpopular, these demands were imposed upon a country that had recently been subjected to huge taxation during the reign of Richard to pay that king's ransom and to fund his wars. Much goodwill must have already been expended even before John came to the throne. Unsurprisingly, Warren concludes that 'in these circumstances the very continuation of the war [to regain the lost French territories] was a triumph of determination and financial effort [even though] to many Englishmen the triumph was a tyranny'.[41]

For many such Englishman this 'tyranny' was defined especially by John's demand for feudal dues, notably his insistence upon higher reliefs – an area of complaint that features in Magna Carta. Yet Painter remarks that 'I can see no justification for calling John a tyrant in the political or constitutional sense... No effort to obtain for a government its share of increasing profits is ever popular.'[42] This is supported by Turner who considers that John's higher demands may well be considered 'justified'.[43] He points out that barons tended to be exempt from many other dues and that therefore John's requests were reasonable. Moreover, it has been argued that the barons had an obligation to pay for 'the privilege, power [and] social positions their estates afforded them'.[44] Until the time of John, most barons had been able to avoid payment of relief thanks to 'either great leniency or great slovenliness in the work of the officials.'[45] John demanded such huge sums from his barons that he clearly intended to make them indebted to the crown so that if a baron's behaviour caused John to be suspicious of his loyalty then the king could legitimately call in the debt and break the baron. The king engineered these debts to be of such a scale that the barons were thereby provided with a powerful motive for serving faithfully and remaining compliant, a policy that paralleled closely the actions of his successful rival, Philip Augustus. In this way John had developed an existing system so that it anticipated the bonds and recognisances developed by Henry VII, of which many historians have approved.[46]

Although the barons judged many of John's actions as unjustified novelties this was not really the case. When viewed against the bigger picture of Angevin economic governance, John's financial policies do not appear out of place. One authority has judged John's general behaviour toward heavily indebted barons as being 'lawful and traditional.'[47] Painter concludes that John generally remained 'within the framework of custom set by his predecessors even though he strained it at the edges'.[48] And it is worth pointing out that where John strayed outside that framework he trialled some policies that were to become mainstream in royal financial policy in the later medieval period, notably his implementation of customs – judged by Bartlett to be an 'example [of John's] precocious ingenuity in administrative and financial matters'.[49]

Chapter 9

CIVIL WAR: A FALSE START, 1215

Timeline

1213

July	Langton returns to England
August	Langton meets with the barons(?)

1214

May	Baronial dissidents refuse to pay scutage
October	John returns from France; barons meet at Bury St Edmund's Abbey

1215

6 January	Rebel barons meet with John in London; John is perhaps presented with the 'Unknown Charter of Liberties'; John promises to reply to rebel demands on 26 April at Northampton
Jan–April	John and the barons try and elicit support for their respective positions from the Pope
4 March	John takes the Cross i.e. crusading vows
19–26 April	Rebel barons assemble at Stamford
Late April	John having failed to reply to rebel demands, the barons issue the Articles of the Barons; John declines them
3 May	Rebels formally renounce their homage and fealty to John
5 May	Rebels begin their attack on the castle at Northampton
Mid-May	Rebels takes the castle at Bedford
14 May	John begins to grant rebel lands to his supporters
17 May	Rebels take London
27 May	Start of truce
10–23 June	Negotiations between John and rebel barons at Runnymede

10 June	Articles of the Barons emerges as a basis for discussion
15 June	Terms agreed and John appends the Great Seal to Magna Carta
19 June	Rebels renew their oaths of homage

A) Narrative

i) The Emergence of Magna Carta

Ever since 1212 England had been in febrile condition, and the outcome of the encounter at Bouvines was set to make this worse. Military defeat nearly always induces political instability, even when a regime appears robust prior to that eventuality. As John travelled back across the Channel in October 1214, he must have anticipated that his newly weakened position would encourage renewed criticism of his governance and that his critics would be emboldened to take action. Malcontent barons coalesced around a variety of grievances, but these men had grown particularly resentful of John's style of governance and of the moneys he demanded. In the months following John's return, England teetered on the brink of civil war and then finally fell into that condition in May 1215, only to escape from this affliction – albeit temporarily – because of the king's acceptance of Magna Carta, a great charter outlining various liberties appertaining 'to all free men of our kingdom'.

Civil war was not a particularly unusual condition for a medieval regime, and it was certainly far from unusual in the case of England. Indeed, depending upon one's definition of the term, it can be argued that no English king prior to the reign of Edward I (r. 1272–1307) managed to avoid this condition. On previous occasions when tensions had existed in the English polity the malcontents had supported a legitimate alternative figurehead – usually a fellow member of the royal family – which was exactly the reason for Arthur's disappearance. In 1215 there was no such alternative figure: Arthur was dead; John's sons were as yet too young to command political respect and Prince Louis of France, the only possible claimant through his marriage to Blanche, a grand-daughter of Henry II from the union of Eleanor and Alfonso VIII of Castile, was as yet unpalatable to many because he was not only a distant kinsman, but also French. In these circumstances the rebels would have to find a new way forward if they were successfully to redress their grievances.

The manner in which the rebel barons ultimately proceeded was ironically borrowed from the practice of kings. By 1215 it was not unknown for kings to issue lists of promises at the start of their reign as a bid for support, recognized by historians as coronation charters. The most famous of these, and directly pertinent to the gestation of Magna Carta, is the coronation oath of Henry I.

Issued by Henry upon his accession to the throne in 1100, he promised to 'abolish all the evil customs by which the kingdom of England has been unjustly oppressed'.[1] Magna Carta is unique in that for the first time a king was forced to accept a list of terms, a charter of liberties, imposed upon him by the political nation. It was, in a way, the world turned upside down; and when John finally assented to Magna Carta in June 1215 'he was in effect accepting the first written constitution in European history'.[2]

Roger of Wendover would have his readers believe that the seeds of Magna Carta were sown in the summer of 1213, significantly by the actions of Stephen Langton who, from July 1213, was back in England as archbishop of Canterbury following John's submission to the papacy.[3] Perhaps in August of that year, Langton met with the barons and, according to Wendover, told them:

Did you hear how, when I absolved the king at Winchester [i.e. released him from his excommunicate status], I made him swear that he would do away with unjust laws and would recall good laws, such as those of King Edward [the Confessor], and cause them to be observed by all in the kingdom. A charter of Henry I the king of England has just now been found, by which you may, if you wish it, recall your long lost rights and your former condition. [And when the paper had been read the barons] were much pleased with it and all of them...swore that when they saw a fit opportunity they would stand up for their rights, if necessary would die for them. The archbishop faithfully promised them his assistance.[4]

Wendover goes on to say that shortly after John had returned from the continent in October 1214 the 'earls and barons of England' met at St Edmund's Abbey. There, they swore that 'if the king refused to grant these liberties and laws, they themselves would withdraw from their allegiance to him, and make war on him, till he should, by a charter under his own seal, confirm to them everything they required'. They also agreed that at some point after Christmas they would go to the king 'and demand the confirmation of the aforesaid liberties'.[5]

J. C. Holt has done much to modify this picture of the barons being guided by Langton so that the notion that Langton was the driving force in the formation of Magna Carta is now generally discounted. After all, we would expect a chronicler writing in the reign of Henry III, aware of the apparently growing importance of Magna Carta after its reissues in 1216, 1217 and 1225, to place a churchman at the centre of its gestation. Holt acknowledges that 'There can be no doubt that Langton had the intellectual equipment to influence the course of events in 1215 and that he shared in the ideas from which the Great Charter drew its strength', but goes on to conclude that 'the evidence...presents him as a mediator and a moderator, rather than an originator'.[6] The text of Magna Carta (see pages 139–50) reflects the voices of multiple churchmen and barons, many of whom, as Holt points out, 'had been assuming, discussing and applying the principles of Magna Carta long before 1215'.[7]

Although Wendover suggests that the whole of the baronage was united against John, this was clearly not the case – not least because there would have been no possibility of civil war if there had not been two sides, each with the wherewithal to resist the other. Indeed, by the spring of 1215, it has been estimated that of England's 197 baronies only 39 were in active opposition to the king with perhaps the same number acting in his support. Also, despite the fact that the majority of chronicle sources refer to John's baronial opponents as the 'Northerners', historians have perceived that the malcontents were in fact concentrated in three regions. In Essex and East Anglia there was a group of about twelve barons. This element included Robert Fitz Walter; Geoffrey de Mandeville, Earl of Essex; Richard de Clare, Earl of Hertford; Hertford's son, Gilbert; Roger Bigod, Earl of Norfolk and Robert de Vere, Earl of Oxford. In the western shires existed a group of ten rebel barons, including amongst their number Henry de Bohun, Earl of Hereford. Finally, in the north was a group of eighteen barons, including Eustace de Vesci, John de Lacy and William de Mowbray. To contemporaries, it seems that the northern element was by-and-large the driving force of the opposition, perhaps because in 1214 they were most vociferous in their resistance to the scutage levy of 1213. It should also be appreciated, that of the rebels that John faced in 1215 it is possible to discern only thirteen (from a possible twenty-seven) of the 'super' barons. R. V. Turner speculates that 'it seems likely, then, that the majority of the English baronage never defected to the rebels, although perhaps more passively sympathised with the baronial cause than with the royalists'.[8]

On 6 January 1215 an element of rebel barons, probably headed by Robert Fitz Walter and Eustace de Vesci, met John in London. The chronicle evidence for this event is too vague to allow any meaningful reconstruction of what actually took place. Nonetheless, in the developing context we can speculate that the assembled barons demanded that John issue a charter of liberties, though whether this should simply be a reissue of Henry I's coronation oath or a more developed document cannot be determined. Some historians believe that a document referred to as the (undated) 'Unknown charter of liberties' was presented to John on this occasion.[9] Supporters of this hypothesis point to Article 7 – whereby John was to 'grant to my men that they should not serve in the army outside England save in Normandy and Brittany' – and claim that this directly addressed the debate initiated by the northern barons who refused to pay John's most recent demand for scutage on the basis that their tenure did not allow them to serve in Poitou. Other historians, however, are not persuaded and insist that the twelve new clauses contained in the 'Unknown charter' emerged during the negotiations under the truce from 27 May 1215 (see page 138). Regardless, John told the assembly that he needed time to consider how to satisfy both their demands and the dignity of the Crown. He informed them that he would deliver his answer on 26 April.[10]

John had bought time and he used it well: he sent envoys to Rome to elicit the public support of his new overlord, the pope; and he summoned mercenaries under Savary de Mauléon from Poitou (though many diverted to Ireland so that they were close at hand without causing aggravation to the English population). Then, on 4 March, John took the vows as a crusader. 'This was a brilliant move to give himself a protective screen', says Warren; 'a truly masterly move', says Painter.[11] Certainly, it made the rebel barons now appear as though they were hindering the prospects of John's participation on crusade and therefore brought the pope very firmly, and very publicly, onto the king's side.

During the week of 19–26 April, the rebel barons assembled at Stamford in anticipation of John's answer which he had promised in January that he would give on 26 April. John, however provided no such answer, perhaps believing that letters recently received from the papacy spoke for him: the letters urged the barons to abandon conspiracies and any thought of force and 'warned and exhorted' them to satisfy the king's demands in relation to scutage.[12] Stalemate had been reached and the descent into civil war was rapid. The rebels renounced their homage and fealty on 3 May. On the same day they appointed Robert Fitz Walter their leader, in which role he took the curious title of 'Marshal of the Army of God' – undoubtedly an attempt to counter John's new crusader status. Two days later the rebels began their attack on the castle at Northampton but, lacking siege equipment, enjoyed no success. Two weeks after this they moved to Bedford, where the castle, governed by a sympathizer, quickly surrendered. The rebels were no doubt trying to provoke the king into a harsh retaliatory move, sufficient to bring the waverers over to their side. Wise to this, John in fact stayed his hand. Instead, he reached out to the more moderate of his opponents by, for example, issuing letters offering to put all grievances to papal arbitration and he offered to have the reliefs that had been imposed on two of the rebel leaders – the Earl of Essex and the bishop of Hereford for the Mandeville and Briouze inheritances respectively – reviewed by their peers in court. If this part of the king's approach was the carrot, the stick was when, from 14 May, he began granting the lands of the rebels to his own supporters. It was a policy that may well have worked – with time.

On 17 May time ran out. The king's foes took London. With its walls for protection, its finances and the support of its citizens, the rebel barons in London could hold out against the king for some considerable time, perhaps indefinitely. Nevertheless, even though the rebels in London now sent out letters to those barons who appeared to be still faithful to king, threatening their property if they did not come over to them, there was in fact little they could do to coerce them over to their side. Meanwhile, Robert de Bethune and the Earl of Salisbury, loyal to the king, had successfully put down a rising in Devon. Moreover, John still had the vast majority of the royal castles. It was another stalemate, albeit stalemate in the rebels' favour.

John thus instructed Langton to institute a truce from 27 May, during which time negotiations took place. Beginning their meetings on 10 June, the king met leaders of the malcontents at Staines and it seems that over the next few days the Articles of the Barons were discussed as a basis for settlement, with – according to some historians – significant input as to their nature from Stephen Langton.[13] By 15 June the terms in the Articles had been refined and resulted in the charter, later to become known as Magna Carta, to which John duly allowed his Great Seal to be affixed, 'given in the meadow that is called Runnymede between Windsor and Staines'.[14] The rebels formally renewed their oaths of allegiance on 19 June. W. L. Warren concluded that John had 'handled the situation with a sensitivity to its delicate balance and a resourceful ingenuity which, whatever one thinks of him as a man, can only enhance his reputation as a ruler of consumate ability'.[15] It seemed that the civil war was over – for now, at least.

The Magna Carta that John confirmed in June 1215 consists of sixty-three clauses, which can be grouped into five main areas. One area is the church. It is stipulated that 'the English church shall be free' (Clause 1). A second area relates to issues concerning the feudal dues levied by the Crown and demands for military service (see particularly Clauses 2–6, 8, 12, 14–16). A third area deals with administrative issues (see particularly Clauses, 9–11, 17, 19, 25, 44, 47, 48). A fourth area deals with Scotland and Wales (see Clauses 56–9). A fifth area sought to establish general principles of governance and community (see particularly Clauses 12, 14, 20, 21, 28, 30, 31, 39, 40, 52). Perhaps the most famous of all the Clauses in Magna Carta is number 39: 'No free man shall be taken or imprisoned or dispossessed or outlawed or exiled or in any way ruined, nor will we [i.e. the king] go or send against him, except by the lawful judgements of his peers or by the law of the land.'[16]

In 1215 the barons, having agreed a programme, also needed a mechanism for binding the king. Thus, a sixth area of Magna Carta deals with machinery of enforcement (see particularly Clause 61). However, this machinery was so antagonistic to the interests of the Crown that it alone was to ensure that the civil war would restart sooner rather than later.

ii) The Text of Magna Carta

Clauses marked (+) are still valid under the charter of 1225, but with a few minor amendments. Clauses marked (*) were omitted in all later reissues of the charter. In the charter itself the clauses are not numbered, and the text reads continuously. The translation sets out to convey the sense rather than the precise wording of the original Latin.

John, by the grace of God King of England, Lord of Ireland, Duke of Normandy and Aquitaine, and Count of Anjou, to his archbishops, bishops, abbots, earls, barons, justices, foresters, sheriffs, stewards, servants, and to all his officials and loyal subjects, Greeting.

Know that before God, for the health of our soul and those of our ancestors and heirs, to the honour of God, the exaltation of the holy Church, and the better ordering of our kingdom, at the advice of our reverend fathers Stephen, archbishop of Canterbury, primate of all England, and cardinal of the holy Roman Church, Henry archbishop of Dublin, William bishop of London, Peter bishop of Winchester, Jocelin bishop of Bath and Glastonbury, Hugh bishop of Lincoln, Walter bishop of Worcester, William bishop of Coventry, Benedict bishop of Rochester, Master Pandulf subdeacon and member of the papal household, Brother Aymeric master of the knighthood of the Temple in England, William Marshal Earl of Pembroke, William Earl of Salisbury, William Earl of Warren, William Earl of Arundel, Alan de Galloway Constable of Scotland, Warin Fitz Gerald, Peter Fitz Herbert, Hubert de Burgh seneschal of Poitou, Hugh de Neville, Matthew Fitz Herbert, Thomas Basset, Alan Basset, Philip Daubeny, Robert de Roppeley, John Marshal, John Fitz Hugh, and other loyal subjects:

+ (1) First, that we have granted to God, and by this present charter have confirmed for us and our heirs in perpetuity, that the English Church shall be free, and shall have its rights undiminished, and its liberties unimpaired. That we wish this so to be observed, appears from the fact that of our own free will, before the outbreak of the present dispute between us and our barons, we granted and confirmed by charter the freedom of the Church's elections – a right reckoned to be of the greatest necessity and importance to it – and caused this to be confirmed by Pope Innocent III. This freedom we shall observe ourselves, and desire to be observed in good faith by our heirs in perpetuity.

To all free men of our Kingdom we have also granted, for us and our heirs for ever, all the liberties written out below, to have and to keep for them and their heirs, of us and our heirs:

(2) If any earl, baron, or other person that holds lands directly of the Crown, for military service, shall die, and at his death his heir shall be of full age and owe a 'relief',[i] the heir shall have his inheritance on payment of the ancient scale of 'relief'. That is to say, the heir or heirs of an earl shall pay £100 for the entire earl's barony, the heir or heirs of a knight 100s. at most for the entire knight's 'fee',[ii] and any man that owes less shall pay less, in accordance with the ancient usage of 'fees'.

(3) But if the heir of such a person is under age and a ward, when he comes of age he shall have his inheritance without 'relief' or fine.

(4) The guardian of the land of an heir who is under age shall take from it only reasonable revenues, customary dues, and feudal services. He shall do this without destruction or damage to men or property. If we have given the guardianship of the land to a sheriff, or to any person answerable to us for the revenues, and he commits destruction or damage, we will exact compensation from him, and the land shall be entrusted to two worthy and prudent men of the same 'fee', who shall be answerable to us for the revenues, or to the person to whom we have assigned them. If we have given or sold to anyone the guardianship of such land, and he causes destruction or damage, he shall lose the guardianship of it, and it shall be handed over to two worthy and prudent men of the same 'fee', who shall be similarly answerable to us.

(5) For so long as a guardian has guardianship of such land, he shall maintain the houses, parks, fish preserves, ponds, mills, and everything else pertaining to it, from the revenues of the land itself. When the heir comes of age, he shall restore the whole land to him, stocked with plough teams and such implements of husbandry as the season demands and the revenues from the land can reasonably bear.

(6) Heirs may be given in marriage, but not to someone of lower social standing. Before a marriage takes place, it shall be made known to the heir's next-of-kin.

---

i Relief: a succession duty (fine) taken from anyone entering upon an inheritance held by military tenure.

ii Knight's fee (fief): an estate charged with the service of providing one fully equipped knight (or his monetary equivalent).

(7) At her husband's death, a widow may have her marriage portion and inheritance at once and without trouble. She shall pay nothing for her dower, marriage portion,[iii] or any inheritance that she and her husband held jointly on the day of his death. She may remain in her husband's house for forty days after his death, and within this period her dower shall be assigned to her.

(8) No widow shall be compelled to marry, so long as she wishes to remain without a husband. But she must give security that she will not marry without royal consent, if she holds her lands of the Crown, or without the consent of whatever other lord she may hold them of.

(9) Neither we nor our officials will seize any land or rent in payment of a debt, so long as the debtor has movable goods sufficient to discharge the debt. A debtor's sureties shall not be distrained upon so long as the debtor himself can discharge his debt. If, for lack of means, the debtor is unable to discharge his debt, his sureties shall be answerable for it. If they so desire, they may have the debtor's lands and rents until they have received satisfaction for the debt that they paid for him, unless the debtor can show that he has settled his obligations to them.

* (10) If anyone who has borrowed a sum of money from Jews[iv] dies before the debt has been repaid, his heir shall pay no interest on the debt for so long as he remains under age, irrespective of whom he holds his lands. If such a debt falls into the hands of the Crown, it will take nothing except the principal sum specified in the bond.

* (11) If a man dies owing money to Jews, his wife may have her dower and pay nothing towards the debt from it. If he leaves children that are under age, their needs may also be provided for on a scale appropriate to the size of his holding of lands. The debt is to be paid out of the residue, reserving the service due to his feudal lords. Debts owed to persons other than Jews are to be dealt with similarly.

* (12) No 'scutage'[v] or 'aid'[vi] may be levied in our kingdom without its general consent, unless it is for the ransom of our person, to make our eldest son a knight, and (once) to marry our eldest daughter.

---

iii Marriage portion: an endowment in property bestowed on the wife at the time of marriage by her own family.

iv The Jews were the principal moneylenders since the charging of interest – usury – was prohibited by the church.

v Scutage: a payment made to the Crown in lieu of military service. Literally, shield money.

vi Aid: a general money payment.

For these purposes only a reasonable 'aid' may be levied. 'Aids' from the city of London are to be treated similarly.

+ (13) The city of London shall enjoy all its ancient liberties and free customs, both by land and by water. We also will and grant that all other cities, boroughs, towns, and ports shall enjoy all their liberties and free customs.

* (14) To obtain the general consent of the realm for the assessment of an 'aid' – except in the three cases specified above – or a 'scutage', we will cause the archbishops, bishops, abbots, earls, and greater barons to be summoned individually by letter. To those who hold lands directly of us we will cause a general summons to be issued, through the sheriffs and other officials, to come together on a fixed day (of which at least forty days notice shall be given) and at a fixed place. In all letters of summons, the cause of the summons will be stated. When a summons has been issued, the business appointed for the day shall go forward in accordance with the resolution of those present, even if not all those who were summoned have appeared.

* (15) In future we will allow no one to levy an 'aid' from his free men, except to ransom his person, to make his eldest son a knight, and (once) to marry his eldest daughter. For these purposes only a reasonable 'aid' may be levied.

(16) No man shall be forced to perform more service for a knight's 'fee', or other free holding of land, than is due from it.

(17) Ordinary lawsuits shall not follow the royal court around, but shall be held in a fixed place.

(18) Inquests[vii] of *novel disseisin*,[viii] *mort d'ancestor*,[ix] and *darrein presentment*[x] shall be taken only in their proper county court. We ourselves, or in our absence abroad our chief justice, will send two justices to each county four times a year, and these justices, with four knights of the county elected by the county itself, shall hold the assizes[xi] in the county court, on the day and in the place where the court meets.

---

vii Inquests: a legal procedure involving the use of a jury or neighbours initiated by a royal writ obtained from Chancery by the plaintiff.

viii Novel disseisin: an action initiated claiming dispossession of property by force.

ix Mort d'ancestor: an action initiated claiming an individual was being deprived of their rightful inheritance.

x Darrein presentment: an action initiated to enquire who was in fact the last patron to present an ecclesiastical benefice then vacant, of which the plaintiff complained that he was unlawfully deprived by the defendant.

xi Assizes: courts, usually consisting of twelve men.

(19) If any assizes cannot be taken on the day of the county court, as many knights and freeholders shall afterwards remain behind, of those who have attended the court, as will suffice for the administration of justice, having regard to the volume of business to be done.

(20) For a trivial offence, a free man[xii] shall be fined only in proportion to the degree of his offence, and for a serious offence correspondingly, but not so heavily as to deprive him of his livelihood. In the same way, a merchant shall be spared his merchandise, and a villein[xiii] the implements of his husbandry, if they fall upon the mercy of a royal court. None of these fines shall be imposed except by the assessment on oath of reputable men of the neighbourhood.

(21) Earls and barons shall be fined only by their equals, and in proportion to the gravity of their offence.

(22) A fine imposed upon the lay property of a clerk in holy orders shall be assessed upon the same principles, without reference to the value of his ecclesiastical benefice.

(23) No town or person shall be forced to build bridges over rivers except those with an ancient obligation to do so.

(24) No sheriff, constable, coroners, or other royal officials are to hold lawsuits that should be held by the royal justices.

* (25) Every county, hundred,[xiv] wapentake,[xv] and riding[xvi] shall remain at its ancient rent, without increase, except the royal demesne[xvii] manors.

(26) If at the death of a man who holds a lay 'fee' of the Crown, a sheriff or royal official produces royal letters patent of summons for a debt due to the Crown, it shall be lawful for them to seize and list movable goods found in the lay 'fee' of the dead man to the value of the debt, as assessed by worthy men. Nothing shall be removed until the whole debt is paid, when the residue shall be given over to the executors to carry out the dead man's will. If no debt is due to the Crown, all the movable goods shall be regarded

---

xii   Free man: free men made up perhaps 50 per cent of the population of early thirteenth-century England (see Chapter 9, note 16).
xiii Villein: an unfree man, in the sense that he was legally tied to the land he worked on and he owed labour services to his lord.
xiv   Hundred: an administrative subdivision of the county.
xv   Wapentake: the name by which the hundred was known in the counties of Derby, Nottingham, Lincoln, Leicester and parts of Yorkshire.
xvi   Riding: a reference to ancient territorial divisions in Yorkshire. There were three Ridings: East, West, and North.
xvii Royal demesne: lands belonging to the Crown.

as the property of the dead man, except the reasonable shares of his wife and children.

* (27) If a free man dies intestate, his movable goods are to be distributed by his next-of-kin and friends, under the supervision of the church. The rights of his debtors are to be preserved.

(28) No constable or other royal official shall take corn or other movable goods from any man without immediate payment, unless the seller voluntarily offers postponement of this.

(29) No constable may compel a knight to pay money for castle-guard if the knight is willing to undertake the guard in person, or with reasonable excuse to supply some other fit man to do it. A knight taken or sent on military service shall be excused from castle-guard for the period of this service.

(30) No sheriff, royal official, or other person shall take horses or carts for transport from any free man, without his consent.

(31) Neither we nor any royal official will take wood for our castle, or for any other purpose, without the consent of the owner.

(32) We will not keep the lands of people convicted of felony in our hand for longer than a year and a day, after which they shall be returned to the lords of the 'fees' concerned.

(33) All fish-weirs shall be removed from the Thames, the Medway, and throughout the whole of England, except on the sea coast.

(34) The writ called *precipe*[xviii] shall not in future be issued to anyone in respect of any holding of land, if a free man could thereby be deprived of the right of trial in his own lord's court.

(35) There shall be standard measures of wine, ale, and corn (the London quarter), throughout the kingdom. There shall also be a standard width of dyed cloth, russet,[xix] and haberject,[xx] namely two ells[xxi] within the selvedges.[xxii] Weights are to be standardised similarly.

(36) In future nothing shall be paid or accepted for the issue of a writ of inquisition of life or limbs. It shall be given gratis, and not refused.

(37) If a man holds land of the Crown by 'fee-farm', 'socage', or 'burgage',[xxiii] and also holds land of someone else for knight's service,

---

xviii Writ precipe: a writ instructing the sheriff to command the defendant to restore property of which the plaintiff claimed he was being wrongfully deprived, or to appear in court before royal justices to explain reasons for not doing so.

xix Russet: a coarse cloth.

xx Haberject: a type of cloth.

xxi Ell: a measurement approximating the length of a man's arm from the elbow to the tip of the middle finger.

xxii Selvedge: a particularly woven edge to a piece of fabric to keep it from fraying.

xxiii Fee-farm; socage; burgage: types of non-military tenure, usually involving money rent.

we will not have guardianship of his heir, nor of the land that belongs to the other person's 'fee', by virtue of the 'fee-farm', 'socage', or 'burgage', unless the 'fee-farm' owes knight's service. We will not have the guardianship of a man's heir, or of land that he holds of someone else, by reason of any small property that he may hold of the Crown for a service of knives, arrows, or the like.

(38) In future no official shall place a man on trial upon his own unsupported statement, without producing credible witnesses to the truth of it.

+ (39) No free man shall be seized or imprisoned, or stripped of his rights or possessions, or outlawed or exiled, or deprived of his standing in any other way, nor will we proceed with force against him, or send others to do so, except by the lawful judgement of his equals or by the law of the land.

+ (40) To no one will we sell, to no one deny or delay right or justice.

(41) All merchants may enter or leave England unharmed and without fear, and may stay or travel within it, by land or water, for purposes of trade, free from all illegal exactions, in accordance with ancient and lawful customs. This, however, does not apply in time of war to merchants from a country that is at war with us. Any such merchants found in our country at the outbreak of war shall be detained without injury to their persons or property, until we or our chief justice have discovered how our own merchants are being treated in the country at war with us. If our own merchants are safe they shall be safe too.

* (42) In future it shall be lawful for any man to leave and return to our kingdom unharmed and without fear, by land or water, preserving his allegiance to us, except in time of war, for some short period, for the common benefit of the realm. People that have been imprisoned or outlawed in accordance with the law of the land, people from a country that is at war with us, and merchants – who shall be dealt with as stated above – are excepted from this provision.

(43) If a man holds lands of any 'escheat'[xxiv] such as the 'honour'[xxv] of Wallingford, Nottingham, Boulogne, Lancaster, or of other 'escheats' in our hand that are baronies, at his death his heir shall give us only the 'relief' and service that he would have made to the baron, had the barony been in the baron's hand. We will hold the 'escheat' in the same manner as the baron held it.

---

xxiv Escheat: an estate that has reverted to the overlord for such reasons as lack of an heir or forfeiture upon having committed a felony.

xxv Honour: a substantial lordship, composed of a large number of manors.

(44) People who live outside the forest need not in future appear before the royal justices of the forest in answer to general summonses, unless they are actually involved in proceedings or are sureties for someone who has been seized for a forest offence.

* (45) We will appoint as justices, constables, sheriffs, or other officials, only men that know the law of the realm and are minded to keep it well.

(46) All barons who have founded abbeys, and have charters of English kings or ancient tenure as evidence of this, may have guardianship of them when there is no abbot, as is their due.

(47) All forests that have been created in our reign shall at once be disafforested. River-banks that have been enclosed in our reign shall be treated similarly.

* (48) All evil customs relating to forests and warrens, foresters, warreners, sheriffs and their servants, or river-banks and their wardens, are at once to be investigated in every county by twelve sworn knights of the county, and within forty days of their enquiry the evil customs are to be abolished completely and irrevocably. But we, or our chief justice if we are not in England, are first to be informed.

* (49) We will at once return all hostages and charters delivered up to us by Englishmen as security for peace or for loyal service.

* (50) We will remove completely from their offices the kinsmen of Gerard d'Athée, and in future they shall hold no offices in England. The people in question are Engelard de Cigogné, Peter, Guy, and Andrew de Chanceaux, Guy de Cigogné, Geoffrey de Martigny and his brothers, Philip Marc and his brothers, with Geoffrey his nephew, and all their followers.

* (51) As soon as peace is restored, we will remove from the kingdom all the foreign knights, bowmen, their attendants, and the mercenaries that have come to it, to its harm, with horses and arms.

* (52) To any man whom we have deprived or dispossessed of lands, castles, liberties, or rights, without the lawful judgement of his equals, we will at once restore these. In cases of dispute the matter shall be resolved by the judgement of the twenty-five barons referred to below in the clause for securing the peace. In cases, however, where a man was deprived or dispossessed of something without the lawful judgement of his equals by our father King Henry or our brother King Richard, and it remains in our hands or is held by others under our warranty, we shall have respite for the period commonly allowed to Crusaders, unless a lawsuit had been begun, or an enquiry had been made at our order, before we took the Cross as a Crusader.

On our return from the Crusade, or if we abandon it, we will at once render justice in full.

* (53) We shall have similar respite in rendering justice in connexion with forests that are to be disafforested, or to remain forests, when these were first afforested by our father Henry or our brother Richard; with the guardianship of lands in another person's 'fee', when we have hitherto had this by virtue of a 'fee' held of us for knight's service by a third party; and with abbeys founded in another person's 'fee', in which the lord of the 'fee' claims to own a right. On our return from the Crusade, or if we abandon it, we will at once do full justice to complaints about these matters.

(54) No one shall be arrested or imprisoned on the appeal of a woman for the death of any person except her husband.

* (55) All fines that have been given to us unjustly and against the law of the land, and all fines that we have exacted unjustly, shall be entirely remitted or the matter decided by a majority judgement of the twenty-five barons referred to below in the clause for securing the peace together with Stephen, archbishop of Canterbury, if he can be present, and such others as he wishes to bring with him. If the archbishop cannot be present, proceedings shall continue without him, provided that if any of the twenty-five barons has been involved in a similar suit himself, his judgement shall be set aside, and someone else chosen and sworn in his place, as a substitute for the single occasion, by the rest of the twenty-five.

(56) If we have deprived or dispossessed any Welshmen of lands, liberties, or anything else in England or in Wales, without the lawful judgement of their equals, these are at once to be returned to them. A dispute on this point shall be determined in the Marches by the judgement of equals. English law shall apply to holdings of land in England, Welsh law to those in Wales, and the law of the Marches to those in the Marches. The Welsh shall treat us and ours in the same way.

* (57) In cases where a Welshman was deprived or dispossessed of anything, without the lawful judgement of his equals, by our father King Henry or our brother King Richard, and it remains in our hands or is held by others under our warranty, we shall have respite for the period commonly allowed to Crusaders, unless a lawsuit had been begun, or an enquiry had been made at our order, before we took the Cross as a Crusader. But on our return from the Crusade, or if we abandon it, we will at once do full justice according to the laws of Wales and the said regions.

* (58) We will at once return the son of Llywelyn, all Welsh hostages, and the charters delivered to us as security for the peace.

* (59) With regard to the return of the sisters and hostages of Alexander, king of Scotland, his liberties and his rights, we will treat him in the same way as our other barons of England, unless it appears from the charters that we hold from his father William, formerly king of Scotland, that he should be treated otherwise. This matter shall be resolved by the judgement of his equals in our court.

(60) All these customs and liberties that we have granted shall be observed in our kingdom in so far as concerns our own relations with our subjects. Let all men of our kingdom, whether clergy or laymen, observe them similarly in their relations with their own men.

* (61) Since we have granted all these things for God, for the better ordering of our kingdom, and to allay the discord that has arisen between us and our barons, and since we desire that they shall be enjoyed in their entirety, with lasting strength, for ever, we give and grant to the barons the following security:

The barons shall elect twenty-five of their number to keep, and cause to be observed with all their might, the peace and liberties granted and confirmed to them by this charter.

If we, our chief justice, our officials, or any of our servants offend in any respect against any man, or transgress any of the clauses of the peace or of this security, and the offence is made known to four of the said twenty-five barons, they shall come to us – or in our absence from the kingdom to the chief justice – to declare it and claim immediate redress. If we, or in our absence abroad the chief justice, make no redress within forty days, reckoning from the day on which the offence was declared to us or to him, the four barons shall refer the matter to the rest of the twenty-five barons, who may distrain upon and assail us in every way possible, with the support of the whole community of the land, by seizing our castles, lands, possessions, or anything else saving only our own person and those of the queen and our children, until they have secured such redress as they have determined upon. Having secured the redress, they may then resume their normal obedience to us.

Any man who so desires may take an oath to obey the commands of the twenty-five barons for the achievement of these ends, and to join with them in assailing us to the utmost of his power. We give public and free permission to take this oath to any man who so desires, and at no time will we prohibit any man from taking it. Indeed, we will compel any of our subjects who are unwilling to take it to swear it at our command.

If one of the twenty-five barons dies or leaves the country, or is prevented in any other way from discharging his duties, the rest of them shall choose another baron in his place, at their discretion, who shall be duly sworn in as they were.

In the event of disagreement among the twenty-five barons on any matter referred to them for decision, the verdict of the majority present shall have the same validity as a unanimous verdict of the whole twenty-five, whether these were all present or some of those summoned were unwilling or unable to appear.

The twenty-five barons shall swear to obey all the above clauses faithfully, and shall cause them to be obeyed by others to the best of their power.

We will not seek to procure from anyone, either by our own efforts or those of a third party, anything by which any part of these concessions or liberties might be revoked or diminished. Should such a thing be procured, it shall be null and void and we will at no time make use of it, either ourselves or through a third party.

* (62) We have remitted and pardoned fully to all men any ill-will, hurt, or grudges that have arisen between us and our subjects, whether clergy or laymen, since the beginning of the dispute. We have in addition remitted fully, and for our own part have also pardoned, to all clergy and laymen any offences committed as a result of the said dispute between Easter in the sixteenth year of our reign (i.e. 1215) and the restoration of peace.

In addition we have caused letters patent to be made for the barons, bearing witness to this security and to the concessions set out above, over the seals of Stephen archbishop of Canterbury, Henry archbishop of Dublin, the other bishops named above, and Master Pandulf.

* (63) It is accordingly our wish and command that the English Church shall be free, and that men in our kingdom shall have and keep all these liberties, rights, and concessions, well and peaceably in their fullness and entirety for them and their heirs, of us and our heirs, in all things and all places for ever.

Both we and the barons have sworn that all this shall be observed in good faith and without deceit. Witness the above-mentioned people and many others.

Given by our hand in the meadow that is called Runnymede, between Windsor and Staines, on the fifteenth day of June in the

seventeenth year of our reign (i.e. 1215: the new regnal year began on
28 May).[17]

B) Interpretations

i) Why Magna Carta?

Careful examination of Magna Carta has encouraged the conclusion that it
came about as the inevitable consequence of an 'Angevin despotism'. After
all, many of the 'liberties' it asserts were first compromised by Henry II, and
then more determinedly so by his successors. As E. Miller puts it, 'rebellion
and the charter...were a commentary on the whole system of Angevin
government, and not merely upon John's particular version of it'.[18] However,
whilst there may be validity in such a proposition, it does not explain either
the timing of Magna Carta nor its nature – a negotiated document to which
the king put his Great Seal. The fact that it occurred towards the end of
John's reign suggests that its appearance had much to do with that monarch.
  John's fundamental ambition from 1204 was to win back the lost French
territories. Nearly everything that he did after that time – and perhaps,
indeed, the way he did things – can be explained by this ultimate goal.
Moreover, from that time John, unlike his predecessors, was almost
constantly present in England. However – for reasons outlined in Chapter 3 –
the royal ambition was little shared by the majority of the political elite
in England who had increasingly scant interest in preserving the Angevin
'empire'. What appeared to be an equal and opposite force was at work: the
harder John pressed to achieve his aim, the more the political elite protested
against it. Polarization was taking place, a necessary condition for civil war.
Baronial recalcitrance began to manifest itself from an early moment in the
guise of passive resistance, notably by a refusal to support John's proposed
continental campaigns in 1205, 1212 and 1213. In May 1214, when John
sought to collect scutage from those barons who baulked at participating
in the expedition of that year, he met with a widespread refusal to pay in
Essex, Hertfordshire, Lancashire and Yorkshire. Coupled with the fact that
this resistance was principled – the barons, particularly the 'Northerners',
asserted that their tenure did not oblige them to do military service in
Poitou – it seemed that an issue had been raised of sufficient significance
to induce civil war. However, S. Painter has cautioned against seeing
this as a fundamental reason for the baronial revolt in 1215. 'Altogether
too much has been made of the expedition to Poitou [in 1214] and the
scutage connected with it as one of the reasons for the baronial revolt',
says Painter.[19] He points out that the barons' 'argument was a feeble one'.

(Other historians go further and assert that feudal law and long-standing practice contradicted the baronial position.) Above all, casting doubt on how far this principle mattered to the barons, Painter describes how 'a third of the English earls took part in the campaign [of 1214] in person, another third performed their service through deputies, and only a third abstained altogether'.[20] Nonetheless, it remains true that baronial reluctance to participate in Poitou contributed to the postponement of John's intended campaigns in 1212 and 1213 and the issue can only have done harm to John's relations with the baronage. Indeed, in 1213, the king was on the point of marching north to bring his recalcitrant northern barons into line when Stephen Langton persuaded him otherwise.

All historians are agreed that growing financial pressures were generally feeding baronial discontent, and that these pressures reached new levels during the reign of John. On the eve of the 1214 campaign John had amassed a war chest of some 200,000 marks, more than five times the size of average royal revenue per annum between 1199–1202.[21] As we have seen, John raised money by a variety of devices (see pages 120–25). Empowered in his position as overlord, he demanded immense sums of money from feudal incidents such as reliefs, wardships and rights to marriage. Fines (bribes) to purchase royal favour or forgiveness (*benevolentia regis*) and amercements (a monetary charge incurred because of some political offence) were also being levied to new extents and with great energy. Some of the heaviest financial demands made by John occurred in the months prior to the 1214 campaign: for instance, William Fitz Alan offered 10,000 marks for a succession; John de Lacy, offered 7,000 marks for a succession and Geoffrey de Mandeville offered 20,000 marks for marriage to Isabella, John's one-time queen. Baronial indebtedness had become so widespread that a study of the financial condition of the king's opponents in 1215 led Holt to conclude that the rising 'was a rebellion of the king's debtors'.[22] Although R. V. Turner cautions that this is an 'overstatement' he admits that 'over half the barons at any one time were in debt to the king'.[23] But it is the extent of the indebtedness which really matters because so huge were the sums involved that they could not easily be paid off, meaning the king had a stick with which to beat barons whom he considered had fallen out of favour. A baron who fell foul of the king would be expected immediately to pay his debts, but necessarily being unable to do so would thereby provide the king with reason to seize his chattels and land until he paid up – which, of course, he would then never be able to do. By these means the king could destroy a baron – as he had done in the case of William de Briouze (see pages 86–91). The king asserted that royal actions concerning debt collection were 'according to the custom of our kingdom and by our law of the exchequer'.[24] Technically, he was probably correct;

but from the point of view of the baronage 'the law of the exchequer did not [now] constitute government *per judicium* [i.e. by due process] but simply ratified arbitrary royal will'.[25] Moreover, the barons' argument in this respect was made more robust by the fact that elements within the church also began to place an emphasis upon government *per judicium*. In the judgement of D. Danziger and J. Gillingham, 'King John was now paying the price for having reduced the time-honoured bond of good lordship and faithful service to nothing more than a calculation of profit and loss.'[26]

Alongside concerns that John was breeching feudal precedent and enmeshing many barons in financial difficulties which could more easily allow the king to effect their destruction, some barons appear to have had more personal grievances against the king. For instance, Giles de Briouze, who was in the rebel camp by 1215, was perhaps seeking revenge for the fate of his brother and sister-in-law. Others asserted that their wives or daughters had been the victims of John's lust (see Appendix, Documents 15 and 22). Robert Fitz Walter claimed that John had stolen his daughter to have her 'a force a amie'; Eustace de Vesci stated that he had only saved his wife from John by substituting her for a prostitute whilst she lay in bed; and one source says that John seduced the wife of his half-brother, William Longespée, Earl of Salisbury. These are stories told by the chroniclers and we need therefore to be suspicious of their veracity, not least because lustfulness was a common criticism set forth by such pens. Moreover, as J. Bradbury points out, 'even the harshest contemporary comment is of [John as] a rake rather than a pervert'.[27] In the broader context, it was not unusual – it was perhaps even expected – that medieval kings should take mistresses. Henry I produced twenty-five acknowledged bastards, for example. (John seems to have managed five.) Nevertheless, the taking of a noblewomen as a mistress had political ramifications in that it directly affected a monarch's personal relations with his political elite. C. J. Tyerman's view is that 'whether or not John was a smutty-minded groper, it does seem that many thought him personally unsavoury. In a world where private relationships were the stuff of high politics, that was a distinct problem.'[28]

There was not just baronial resentment of what John did; there was also resentment of how he did it. John tended to use foreigners – aliens – to implement his will, men like Gerard d'Athée, Falkes de Breauté, Savary de Mauléon, Engelard de Cigogné, Geoffrey de Martigny and Peter des Roches. For the large part these men were ruthless mercenaries who, because they demonstrated a loyalty which John discovered to be lacking in much of the English baronage, found themselves on the receiving end of royal patronage. For instance, as part of the crackdown on questionable border areas during the years 1209–12, Falkes de Breauté was appointed as bailiff of Glamorgan and Gerard d'Athée as sheriff of both Gloucester and Hereford; when Gerard died at some point in 1213 he was replaced as sheriff of Gloucester by Engelard de Cigogné. Then, upon the death of Geoffrey Fitz Peter on 14 October 1213, Peter des Roches was appointed justiciar, 'amidst murmurings from the magnates of the entire realm that an alien had been advanced over them'.[29] W. L. Warren judged that by 1215 des Roches 'had emphasised the most unbearable features of Angevin despotism', a conclusion now slightly softened by the recent work of N. Vincent.[30] The Barnwell annalist, perhaps the most reliable of the chroniclers, felt certain that the favour that John showed to these men was a key explanation for the king's poor relations with many of his barons. Since many of John's agents were low born and seen to be usurping positions which the baronage felt rightfully to be theirs, he was surely correct. Indeed, offices, wardships control over rich heiresses and such-like had for long been elements and opportunities which men of substance expected to find available for competition, but they were now monopolised by a group of royal familiares, some of whom were aliens. E. Miller suggests that 'this feature of John's government after 1204 made the movement against him a movement of "outs", just as intense financial exploitation made it a movement in which his debtors bulked large. The king's enemies were first and foremost concerned to eject the familiares from their positions of power and profit rather than to reshape the government of the kingdom.'[31] Unsurprisingly, then, Clause 50 of the Magna Carta stipulated that aliens and their associates be 'removed completely'.

The appointment of such men begs an important question: why was John unable to trust the English baronage? Certainly, he had suffered some bad experiences. When Robert Fitz Walter opened the gates of the vital stronghold of Vaudreuil to the French in 1203, Philip Augustus advertised that he thought 'such men were like torches, to be used and then thrown in the cesspool'.[32] Even though William Marshal remained loyal after he had paid homage to Philip in 1205, John remained constantly suspicious. Perhaps then, one explanation is that the barons, or some of them at least, were simply not trustworthy. Another explanation is that the barons' lack of trust was instilled by the duplicitous nature of the king. Certainly John's dealings with William de Mowbray, for example, did not encourage confidence in the word of the king: having led Mowbray to believe that a fine of 2,000 marks would assist in the defence of his barony against a claim by William de Stuteville, John nevertheless allowed his court to judge against Mowbray. In fact, each explanation has validity, giving motion to a vicious circle of ever decreasing trust between the king and his barons.

ii) Magna Carta Out of Context

Any historian seeking to provide an assessment of King John must of course offer an evaluation of the significance of Magna Carta. In this respect, John's reputation has suffered immense damage because of the way that Magna Carta has come to be perceived by the general public as a talisman of freedom, a buttress against tyranny; in short, the cornerstone of English liberties. If this is the essence of Magna Carta, then it follows that John must have been despotic, inestimably so since he went on to ignore it altogether. Arguably, however, this amounts to a serious misunderstanding of the document to which John gave his assent in June 1215, a misunderstanding that has developed because of the later history of Magna Carta.

In the years immediately after John's death, Magna Carta was reissued in 1216, 1217 and again in 1225, each with revisions to the 1215 version (substantial in the case of the 1225 issue). As J. C. Holt points out, 'those who wrote during Henry III's minority [i.e. 1216–27] were at work in a period in which the battles of John's reign were still being fought [but before long] these battles were won by the old opposition to the king…[Consequently] the rebellion of 1215 was astonishingly successful viewed from a standpoint ten years later…The reissues and confirmations of [Magna Carta in 1216, 1217 and 1225] made it far easier to assume that John's rule had been especially burdensome and contrary to custom.'[33] Thereafter Magna Carta continued to evolve to the detriment of John's reputation. During the later Middle Ages Magna Carta was confirmed about thirty times, 'each reissue', notes Turner, 'required re-interpretation of its clauses to fit changing circumstances, and this enabled the document to grow and take on new meaning'.[34] For instance, as Turner points out, under Edward III in 1354 Article 39 was altered from 'no free man' to be denied due process of law to 'no man, of what Estate or condition that he be'.[35] Then, in 1368, it was declared that Magna Carta was the fundamental law of the land. Thereafter, interest in Magna Carta falls away under the Yorkists and the Tudors – it does not even get a mention in Shakespeare's play 'King John'. Interest in Magna Carta was revived in the seventeenth century and used as a means of justifying resistance to the allegedly absolutist intentions of Charles I. 'Magna Carta', said the lawyer Sir Edward Coke, 'is such a fellow that he will have no sovereign'.[36] In the Petition of Right in 1628, opposition MPs made direct reference to Magna Carta on three occasions, the stark inference being that Charles was as bad a king as John had been. Since Charles went on to be defeated in the civil war of the 1640s and then suffered execution in the last year of that decade, this was a perception that deepened in the popular mind. Then, as America began to be colonized, the founding charters of Massachusetts (1629), Maryland (1623),

Maine (1639), Connecticut (1662) and Rhode Island (1663) all asserted that they had the right to the 'Liberties' conferred in Magna Carta. 'By this time', says G. Hindley 'the very words "Magna Carta" and "Great Charter" had acquired an almost mystic incantatory quality'.[37] A hundred-or-so years later, the American revolutionaries who raised the cry 'No taxation without representation' justified their resistance by invoking Magna Carta, even though the notion of 'parliament' was foreign to John and his barons. The final part of the process of Magna Carta becoming a symbol of the concept of the sovereign power of the people able to impose their will on the government was when it was again invoked in the making of the United States Bill of Rights, 1789. Yet this was not the Magna Carta to which John gave his assent in 1215.

When viewed in the context of the early thirteenth century, once the layers of myth obtained through anachronistic interpretations have been removed, Magna Carta of 1215 can be viewed for what it was: a set of peace terms between an element of malcontented barons and a particular king, not a device espousing new constitutional principles. As a peace settlement it was always destined to be short lived because Clause 61, empowering the barons to select twenty-five of their number who, if the king should 'offend in any respect…[will proceed to]…distrain and assail [John] in every way possible…by seizing castles, lands [and] possessions' was at odds with monarchical government. No king could have submitted to this for any length of time. There were too many concerns: who would the twenty-five be? Why was there no arbitrating machinery to decide if and how the king had offended? Why were the twenty-five empowered to establish themselves as a self-perpetuating oligarchy? In short, Clause 61 meant that 'the barons had created a political monstrosity, a constitution that could not possibly survive'.[38] In effect, they had destroyed the sovereignty of the Crown. They had turned John into an unreal king.

No doubt there is something in the claim made by detractors of John that the barons were pushed to these extremes because of the untrustworthiness of the king. A yet different interpretation is obtained if the barons – or at least the leading faction amongst them – are seen, not as forward-thinking visionaries seeking a great assertion of principle, but as feudal reactionaries hankering after office and privilege like their predecessors in the reign of King Stephen.[39] From this perspective, the rebels of 1215 can be perceived as desperately trying to halt a progressive government which, by its very nature, was encroaching upon their traditional privileges and liberties by transforming a feudal structure in which their baronial interests were entrenched.[40] Certainly the rebel leadership seems to have been populated by second and third-raters – none appears in the corridors of power once

Henry III is wearing the crown. Wendover, usually an adherent of whoever is an enemy of the king, calls them 'promoters of pestilence'.[41] K. Norgate and S. Painter ultimately 'dismissed Robert Fitz Walter "as a haughty, selfish, but ultimately cowardly, feudal grandee, ready to obstruct justice by private warfare and to cloak treason with a series of makeshift justifications"'.[42] He was no doubt fiery and fractious, quick to resort to violence in support of his claims. With qualities such as these, it does not seem that Fitz Walter was readily equipped to provide firm leadership as a bold defender of English liberties; but he fits well our notion of a vicious, narrow-minded, feudal reactionary whose interests would be well served by the security clauses. Adding support to the interpretation that it was the rebel barons who were fomenters of discord is the fact that John had already begun to implement substantial concessions in 1212–13, indicative of a new tone in royal policy and winning the sympathy of the Barnwell chronicler (see Appendix Document 21).

Chapter 10

CIVIL WAR RENEWED, 1215–1216

Timeline

1215
19 June	John begins to make restorations
24 August	Innocent annuls Magna Carta
September	Rebels occupy Rochester castle
13 October	John begins his siege of Rochester castle
October?	Rebels offer throne to Louis
30 November	Rochester surrenders to John

1216
January–February	Louis transports troops to England
January–March	John harries the east and north
January	Alexander II reaches Newcastle
Mid-May	John's fleet destroyed by storms
21 May	Louis lands in England
2 June	Louis enters London
8 August	Alexander II takes Carlisle
19 October	John dies
28 October	Henry crowned
11 November	Magna Carta reissued

1217
20 May	Battle of Lincoln
24 August	Sea battle off Sandwich
12 September	Louis makes peace in the Treaty of Lambeth

A) Narrative

i) Civil War Renewed

Three main conditions are necessary for civil war: the existence of 'sides' of roughly equal strength; an issue over which to fight, usually ideological in nature; and the absence or failure of any persons or processes by, or through, which such differences might be resolved. In the summer of 1215 each of these conditions came into existence with remarkable, if not entirely unexpected, rapidity.

In the immediate aftermath of the sealing of Magna Carta John moved to bolster his support in two main ways, by apparently responding to the baronial grievances expressed in Magna Carta and by eliciting the support of his new feudal overlord, Pope Innocent III. D. A. Carpenter says that 'the reversal of John's arbitrary fines and disseisins commenced at once'.[1] Amongst those who enjoyed concessions and restorations were Eustace de Vesci and Robert Fitz Walter, the latter regaining Hertford castle that had been taken from him as a result of his alleged involvement in the plot against John in 1212. The suspicion that the concessions made by John were designed to win support to restart the war rather than to establish a lasting settlement is confirmed by the fact that, as these restorations were occurring, he was simultaneously appealing for support from the pope. It worked. As revealed in his letter of 24 August, Innocent had been persuaded of two things in particular. First, that John had not assented to Magna Carta of his own free will but that 'he was forced to accept an agreement which is not only shameful and demeaning but also illegal and unjust'. As such, it followed that Magna Carta was not binding. Second, because Magna Carta impaired the king's 'royal rights and dignity...the whole plan [for John's participation in] a crusade [was] seriously endangered...and therefore we utterly reject and condemn this settlement [i.e. Magna Carta] and under threat of excommunication we order that the king should not dare to observe it and that the barons and their associates should not require it to be observed. The Charter...we declare to be null and void of all validity for ever.'[2] Then, on 5 September, letters were issued with papal backing attacking the baron's whole programme for 'despoiling the king of his royal dignity'.[3] W. L. Warren considers John's actions to have been 'double-dealing of the most contemptible kind'.[4] Duplicity, however, is often a necessary tool in political affairs and it is difficult not to conclude that John used it well here.

It seems likely that John won support not only because of his own actions but also because of the actions of the barons. In particular, despite a promise that they would relinquish their possession of London by 15 August, the barons continued to hold the city thus erecting a major impediment to a lasting settlement whatever the nature of Magna Carta. Robert Fitz Walter let it be known 'how useful it is for us [i.e. the barons] to hold the city of London, which is our refuge, and how damaging it would be to us to lose it'.[5] (Meanwhile, 'extremist' barons who had slipped away from Runnymede and therefore did not consider Magna Carta binding, were busy fortifying their castles.) We can also speculate that John must have won at least sympathy if not demonstrable support from the fact that when nominating the twenty-five to the committee established by Clause 61, the barons did not choose from amongst their number a single moderate such as Stephen Langton or William Marshal. In fact, the security clause in Magna Carta establishing the baronial committee of twenty-five and empowering it to act against the king when it judged him to breaking the terms of Magna Carta was destructive to monarchy. In short, it refashioned John as a mere 'phantom of a king', as Charles I said of the Nineteen Propositions in 1642. As such, Magna Carta in this way provided John with an ideological engine to restart the war. He had shown himself to be tolerant of the moderate clauses of Magna Carta – he had even acted quickly upon some of them – but he could not tolerate the intolerable.

As both sides began to mobilize in August it was not yet inevitable that war would restart, for there was still a chance that reconciliation could be effected by negotiation. The figure apparently most associated with the gestation of Magna Carta, Stephen Langton archbishop of Canterbury, was also thus best equipped to facilitate any such negotiation. Indeed, he and the bishops tried to bring the two parties together at Oxford on 16 August and then again at Staines on 28 August. Neither was successful. Nor was any further attempt made to negotiate an exit from the crisis because Langton simultaneously fell from favour with both John and Innocent. Relations between John and the archbishop – which had always been strained – now became impossible because Langton refused to concede to John the castle at Rochester, which was traditionally under the control of the archbishopric of Canterbury. Unsurprisingly, John considered Langton to be 'a notorious and barefaced traitor to us'.[6] Then, when Langton refused to implement the papal instruction to excommunicate all 'disturbers of the king and kingdom' – presumably on the ground that the pope lacked full knowledge of the facts – he was suspended by papal authority in mid-September.[7] Langton now made his way to Rome, not to reappear in England until 1218. In this way, in one of the great ironies of the reign, John emerged triumphant in his long-running battle against Langton.

ii) The Nature of the Sides

In the war that was now about to unfold, the royalist cause had a number of advantages. First, as we have seen, by skilfully playing upon his position as a papal vassal John had elicited the strong support of the pope and most of the bishops – indeed, of these, only Giles de Briouze sided openly with the baronial malcontents. Second, of the barons who supported John, a number of them, such as William Marshal and Ranulf of Chester, could mobilize significant feudal forces, particularly important since the royal coffers had been depleted by the costs of the continental campaign of 1214. Nonetheless, it seems that John's finances were sufficiently robust to pay for large numbers of foreign mercenaries, a key feature of this war (S. Painter points out that throughout the war John controlled 'the most profitable of English industries – the tin mines of Devon and Cornwall').[8] Other important royalist barons such as the Earl of Arundel, Earl of Warenne and the Earl of Salisbury possessed strategically located castles and territories. Overall, of the 209 castles that S. Painter has estimated were in use during the civil war, 149 were held by John and his men against 60 held by his foes.[9] Moreover, it seems that some fifty of these royalist castles were of the greatest strength – such as Dover, Windsor and Lincoln – whereas the rebels held only twenty fortresses of like quality. Finally, in John, the royalists had a distinct leader, one who was bloodied in the experiences of war in ways which probably none of his opponents were, certainly not their leader Robert Fitz Walter. Above all, John was the appointed and crowned king of England, ruling by God's authority.

The rebels' main advantage was their possession of London. With its wealth, population, traditions and accompanying status it was clear that John would have to force the surrender of that city in order to win the war; and considering London's substantive fortifications this was going to be no easy task. A particular difficulty for the rebels was that they needed to find an apparently legitimate way of going beyond Magna Carta – after all, the king had already demonstrated that he would not be bound by words. The logical outcome of this line of thought was to seek to replace John altogether. Thus, in the autumn of 1215 the rebels offered the crown to Prince Louis, the son of Philip Augustus. The chronicles reported an expectation that Louis would 'prevent the realm being pillaged by aliens'.[10]

In 1216 Louis was twenty-eight. His claim to the throne was through his wife, Blanche, a grand-daughter of Henry II, whom he had married in 1200. It was by no means a strong claim. (Indeed, if an alternative monarch was sought then Eleanor, the elder sister of Arthur of Brittany, at the time a prisoner at Corfe castle, had a far stronger claim.) No doubt, also, there were some who had misgivings at the idea that a monarch might be 'elected' in this way, hence the necessity for justifying the deposition of John. It was thus alleged that John had lost his right to the throne when he betrayed Richard in 1193–4; that he had been convicted by the French court of murdering Arthur and that he should have sought baronial consent before surrendering his kingdom to the papacy. Not one of these was particularly convincing, though collectively they seem to have been sufficient to have appeased those rebels who were nervous of inviting Louis. Henceforth they could allow themselves to believe that the throne was vacant. Louis duly landed in England on 21 May 1216 and shortly thereafter entered London where he was proclaimed king, though not crowned.

iii) The Course of the War

Before the arrival of Louis, John had all but defeated his opponents. Upon learning of the surrender in October 1215 of the castle at Rochester to the 'Army of God', John moved immediately to assault it. Robert Fitz Walter had installed a garrison in the castle under William d'Albini, Lord of Belvoir, one of the most capable of the rebel commanders. John personally supervised the siege which lasted for seven weeks, initially attempting to break the castle with massive siege engines and then successfully bringing down one of the towers by undermining. As the tunnels were dug under the walls they were shored with wooden beams. 'When everything was ready', says S. Painter 'a herd of pigs to which had been tied burning torches was released [into the tunnels] to set fire to the shoring'.[11] After a seven week siege, the castle surrendered on 30 November. In typical fashion, Wendover asserts that John had to be restrained from hanging all the inmates; in the end, only one of the garrison suffered this fate (see Appendix, Documents 25 and 26). By any standards it was an extraordinary victory, one that is demonstrative of John's ability in this aspect of warfare. The Barnwell annalist recorded that after the siege of Rochester 'there were few who would put their trust in castles'.[12]

Dividing his army so that part of it under the Earl of Salisbury, Falkes de Breauté and Savary de Mauléon prevented the rebels from leaving London, John and the rest of the army headed north where, over the course of three months January–March 1216, he perpetrated a 'harrying' which seems to have been akin in its extent and impact to that of William the Conqueror's expedition into that region in 1069 (see Appendix, Document 27 and Figure 15). Having mobilized resources from his supporters, John's army was composed of mercenary elements whom Wendover described as being like 'locusts, who assembled…to blot out everything from the face of the earth; for, running about with drawn swords and knives, they ransacked towns, houses, cemeteries, and churches, robbing everyone, sparing neither women nor children.'[13] It is likely that the chroniclers' imagination has heightened the depravations of this army, but whatever the actual nature of John's expedition it had tremendous success. Fearful of incurring royal wrath, towns and castles opened their gates to him; and the royal coffers benefitted from the fines he demanded for recovery of his good will – York offered a thousand pounds. Alexander II, king of Scotland, having travelled as far south as Newcastle to see how he could profit from things, scurried back over the border. Eustace de Vesci sued for peace. Probably the only rebel stronghold left in the north was Robert de Ros' stronghold of Helmsley. And the outcome was the same when John took his force through East Anglia. 'In three months', says W. L. Warren, '[John] had knocked the heart out of resistance everywhere save in London.'[14]

John no doubt had London as his next objective in the early months of 1216. In fact, with its hinterlands now in his possession, the king could simply undertake a siege and wait for the city to surrender. However, he was distracted from such an undertaking because of the news that Prince Louis was about to embark for England. John thus spent April and May gathering an army in Kent and preparing his navy to thwart the invasion. But in a moment of desperate ill-fortune like that which afflicted the Spanish Armada in 1588, a huge storm in mid-May destroyed much of the royal fleet and dispersed the rest. Perhaps concerned about the loyalty of his (French) mercenaries if he put them into battle against Louis, John decided that he could not risk an all-or-nothing battle on the beaches and so withdrew westwards with the intention of fighting another day. Louis was therefore able to land unopposed on 21 May.

Louis' arrival galvanized the rebels and provoked some serious defections, including the Earl of Arundel, the Earl of Surrey and even the king's half-brother and victor at Damme, William Longespée, Earl of Salisbury. Then, in September, Alexander of Scotland marched to Dover where he paid homage to Louis. Meanwhile, Llywelyn the Great was on the move again, already having taken Carmarthen before the end of 1215. These were devastating developments for John, though he could take some comfort from the fact that the arrival of Louis had also revealed that the royalist cause had a substantial irreducible core of support. Perhaps two thirds of the barons had gone over to Louis, but at that level the haemorrhaging stopped. The important castles of Windsor, Barnard and Dover – the last, despite suffering a siege led by Louis from July to October 1216 – remained loyal; the Cinque ports continued to harry French shipping; William Marshal and Ranulf of Chester kept the west midlands and the Marches loyal; Ireland was royalist; and Llywelyn's ambitions remained fairly localized. By the end of the summer there is a sense that John's sails were beginning to billow once more, perhaps a consequence of growing disquiet at the prospect of a French overlord. Some important figures, such the Earl of Salisbury came back to John. The annalist of Dunstable says that 'day by day the adherents of the Frenchman dwindled'.[15]

With typical energy, John thus renewed his efforts in the autumn of 1216. Proceeding into East Anglia he retook Cambridge and several

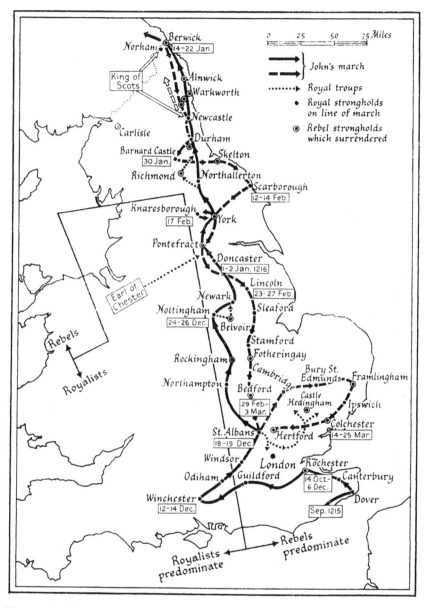

Figure 15. John's itinerary during the civil war, 1215 to March 1216 (courtesy of Yale University Press)

castles in Essex, sufficient success to draw off the rebels from their siege of Windsor. Having relieved pressure on the castle at Lincoln – held on his behalf by the remarkable Nichola de la Haye – John then proceeded to King's Lynn, a major trading port from which he knew he could obtain supplies. His intention now was probably to cut off Alexander as he headed back north. However, he suffered a set-back when travelling through the marshy territory between Wisbech and Swineshead Abbey, for it was somewhere on this journey that John's baggage train became trapped in quicksand and was duly lost. The king was also ill, weakened by dysentery contracted whilst he was at King's Lynn.

By 16 October John was at Newark and, aware that he was dying, he dictated a will. He asserted his wish that his leading counsellors should 'render assistance to my sons for the recovery and defence of their inheritance', reward 'those who have served us faithfully', and that alms should be distributed 'to the poor and to religious houses for the salvation of my soul'. Last, he expressed his desire 'that my body be buried in the church of the Blessed Virgin and St Wulfstan at Worcester'. He died on 19 October.

John's death resolved the crisis afflicting England. On 28 October the king's son, nine-year-old Henry, was crowned and William Marshal agreed to act as regent. On 11 November Magna Carta was reissued, with some of its more problematic clauses removed. 'It is a supreme irony', says Warren, 'that after being demanded by rebels and killed by the pope, [Magna Carta] should have been brought back to life as a royalist manifesto'.[16] This appeased many rebels; the remaining element was extinguished when Louis' forces were defeated by troops led by William Marshal and Falkes de Breauté at Lincoln on 20 May 1217. Finally, any remaining hopes that Louis might have had evaporated completely when his reinforcements were destroyed in a naval encounter off Sandwich on 24 August. Peace was established on 12 September. The civil war was over.

B) Interpretations: How Good a Soldier was John?

One of the main criteria by which medieval chroniclers judged their subjects was according to the prowess, or otherwise, that they exhibited in war. Consequently, because John presided over the loss of the Angevin 'empire', and then failed to win it back, his reputation has suffered significantly in this respect. John, they say, was 'Softsword'.[17]

The structural weaknesses of the Angevin 'empire' (see Chapter 3), or the role played by what R. V. Turner describes as the 'the legendary faithlessness and fickleness of the Poitevin nobles', do not receive monastic contemplation when those authors sought to explain John's difficulties.[18] Instead, for the chroniclers, John's military failures were largely a consequence of cowardice. 'My brother John is not the man to conquer a country if there is a single person able to make the slightest resistance to his attempts', asserts Richard according to Howden.[19] As we have seen, Wendover accuses John of 'incorrigible idleness', of preferring to linger in bed enjoying the pleasures of his young queen rather than face the rigours of war.[20] 'I will stay in a safe place with my dog', John is made to say by the pen of William the Breton.[21] And chronicle opinion has been accepted by some modern authorities who argue that John fully deserves his reputation for 'military incapacity and incredible lethargy'.[22] W. L. Warren, generally sympathetic to John, nevertheless frequently portrays him as pusillanimous, particularly when compared to his predecessor. In 1204, says Warren in a flight of counter-factual speculation, 'Richard would have been on the heights above Les Andelys; [he] would have been urging the citizens of Rouen to arms...[whereas]...John stayed in England biting his nails.'[23] Commenting on the unopposed French landings in May 1216, John Gillingham writes 'this time it was on the beaches of England that John chose not to fight'.[24] 'The litany of John's military failures is tedious', says F. McLynn.[25] Then, on those occasions when John did choose to fight, his detractors say that he was frequently guilty of atrocities: of killing prisoners taken at Mirebeau; of killing Welsh hostages in 1212; of harrying the north of England in 1216 so fiercely that 'scenes of atrocity such as events in the reign of Stephen alone in English history afford a parallel'.[26] 'Such was John's lust for slaughter and mayhem', asserts F. McLynn – here borrowing from Wendover – about events in 1216 'that even when his men were exhausted by the day's burning, looting and raping, he sent out parties at night to fire all the hedges and villages within a ten-mile radius'.[27] Finally, John has also been accused of having little sense of strategy. For instance, J. T. Appleby, when describing John's continental campaign of 1206, says 'it is difficult to detect any strategy underlying this apparently random attacking, defending and seizing of castles'.[28]

The above amounts to an apparently substantive and damaging criticism of John. However, a number of correctives can be offered, alongside a reminder that chronicle opinion has to be treated cautiously.

John's military achievement has frequently been assessed out of the context of medieval warfare. This was an age in which pitched battles were rare. All leaders deliberately avoided them. Philip Augustus shied away from a set-piece battle at least as frequently as his protagonist. 'Like all contemporary commanders', says Bradbury, 'Philip generally avoided battle'.[29] As R. V. Turner notes, 'John's supposed lack of boldness merely reflects a medieval commander's caution'.[30] Thus, for example, John's decision not to engage with Louis in May 1216 was far more likely to have been a result of his concern that the French mercenaries in Angevin pay would perhaps simply change sides. It was, after all, a real possibility and as such it was far better to retreat to fight another day. Similarly, John's decision not to assault London in 1215 before the arrival of Louis can be justified on the basis that a siege – the only way to try and collapse resistance by the city – would have been difficult and prolonged. A more realistic option was to isolate London by forcing the rest of the country to submit after experiencing plundering raids.

Indeed, plundering raids and sieges of castles and towns – perhaps best epitomized by each of the three crusades that had taken place by the reign of John, 1095–9, 1147 and 1189–91 – were the key features of warfare at this time. By their very nature such raids tend to appear as no more than vague wanderings, a series of disconnected coming and goings. In practice, to have an effect they need to be fierce, to impoverish. If these were the requirements of such raids then those perpetrated by John were of a high order, as seen by the ready offering of fines for royal forgiveness by rebel barons in the north of England in 1216. But even from an early stage in his reign it is arguable that John had won an effective reputation in this respect, the peace with Philip in 1200 perhaps being obtained as a result of John threatening force without seriously using it. Moreover, a war fought with mercenaries was always likely to be a war that featured plunder – soldiers of this nature sought to obtain what they could from the missions upon which they were engaged. John had no reason to restrain these 'locusts' because without any such restraint their impact was all the greater. Consequently, civilians were legitimate casualties of warfare in this age as much as they were in World War II.

John was frequently at the centre of events, demonstrating the sort of energy and determination that in this context is usually only spoken of in reference to Richard and Henry II. There is no doubt that he understood that castles were the 'bones of the kingdom', as William of Newburgh described them.[31] Thus, we see him, for example, razing the walls and castle of Le Mans in 1200, assaulting the forces besieging Mirebeau in 1202 (having covered a distance of eighty miles in forty-eight hours), marching upon Montauban in 1206, taking the Lusignans castles of Mervent and Vouvant in 1214 and pressing the siege of Rochester castle in 1215, an event which the leading authority of castles and castle warfare in this period considers was 'the greatest operation in England up to that time'.[32] Clearly, John was well equipped to meet the administrative challenges of an effective siege, keeping his troops supplied with food, clothing and arms sometimes for weeks on end. In short, in this era there were few who were more accomplished at siegecraft than John.

Accusations that John lacked strategic ability and vision must also be dismissed. There is little doubt that John could conceive the strategy for a grand campaign, as well as mobilize the necessary allies and resources. Thus, for example, we see him establishing an anti-Capetian coalition which by 1214 was composed of Otto of Brunswick, the Counts of Flanders and Boulogne and several Rhineland princes, designed to strike at Philip as one half of a pincer, the other part being led by himself. The main purpose of the scheme was to divide the Capetian forces, and this it achieved. Similarly, John's plan to relieve the siege of Chateau-Gaillard in 1203 by arranging a simultaneous assault from land and amphibious forces has been described as 'a masterpiece of ingenuity'.[33] In Ireland in 1210, John demonstrated an ability to prosecute a siege effectively by land and sea: having placed the main body of his army across Carlingford Lough by means of a bridge of boats, he denied his enemy (Lacy) the shelter of the Mourne Mountains. John's organization of a defensive line along the Touques River in 1203, thus preventing Philip from accomplishing a straightforward march across the northern part of Normandy, was similarly accomplished.

John also saw the need to create an alternative to the old feudal levy (achieved by the employment of mercenaries) and appreciated the requirement of founding a 'standing' navy. The 'standing' navy during John's reign has a claim to be the first manifestation of the royal navy. Most historians recognize that John enjoyed significant success at sea, the destruction of the French fleet off Damme in 1213 being particularly noteworthy. However, few accounts give sufficient mention to two sea battles that took place in 1217, known as the Battle of Dover and the Battle of Sandwich. In the former occurred perhaps the first formal tactics of battle at sea when the English commander, Hubert de Burgh, attacking from upwind, launched a shower of crossbolts into the French who were simultaneously blinded by quicklime dust. These two battles put a decisive end to Louis' attempts to win England. Although these engagements took place a year after John's death, it is difficult to imagine that the English ships would have been as prepared, or would have achieved as much, without John's earlier contributions. It was not until 1744 that the French attempted another seaborne invasion.

Finally, we perhaps ought to recall the Barnwell annalist's view that John 'was indeed a great prince but less than successful [and that]…he met with both kinds of luck'.[34] It is arguably in military events that John was most unlucky. Counter-factual history has its detractors, but it is worth considering how different John's reputation would have been from his own day onwards if any one of these events had not happened: if Eleanor had not died in April 1204; if his Poitevan allies had not melted away outside the walls of Roch-au-Moine in 1214; if a storm had not blown up during the night of 18 May 1216 and scattered the armada he had prepared to thwart the landing of Louis; and above all, if his allies had won at Bouvines. If this last scenario had in fact transpired, then John's harsh rule and hated money raising devices would have been vindicated and the Angevin 'empire' would have been recreated. John would have been dominant in Europe. There would have been no Magna Carta. No civil war. No French invasion. John may even have become Good King John.

Chapter 11

CONCLUSION:
WILL THE REAL KING JOHN
PLEASE STAND UP?

The quest to determine the nature and attributes of any historical personality is never straightforward. Such personalities frequently appear chameleon-like, sometimes because they are assessed out of context and sometimes because existing evidence is newly interpreted and/or new evidence becomes available. As we have seen, an unusually complex evidential base, composed of record evidence and chronicle material, has encouraged mutually antagonistic representations of John, ranging from on the one hand the reckless monarch who 'does nothing great' (as described by W. Stubbs) to, on the other hand, the monarch whose 'total achievement was enormous' (as described by J. C. Holt).[1] In addition, King John is particularly difficult to perceive because he does indeed seem to have been by nature 'a curiously twisted and enigmatic figure'.[2] There is little doubt that he was capricious. Unsurprisingly, therefore, A. L. Poole hedged his bets when he came to summarize his thoughts about King John. 'Almost any epithet', concluded Poole, 'might appropriately be applied to him in one or other of his many and versatile moods. He was cruel and ruthless, violent and passionate, greedy and self-indulgent, genial and repellent, arbitrary and judicious, clever and capable, original and impulsive.'[3] What is certain, is that John was not the literally diabolical character as described by Matthew Paris at the start of this book.

This book has employed a variety of approaches in an attempt to avoid the equivocation of Poole's judgement and to present generally a much more positive picture of John. First, it has argued that Richard's legacy – and more broadly, the Angevin legacy in 1199 – amounted to a *damnosa hereditas* and that the Angevin 'empire' was already tottering by the time John acceded, its inherent structural weaknesses, combined with the fact that Philip

Augustus was adept at exploiting his position as suzerain over John, having induced inexorable fissures in the whole. Second, it has insisted that John be evaluated in the context of his own time. 'John was harsh and cruel, certainly', writes J. C. Holt, 'but a [medieval] king was more likely to suffer disaster through kindness than through cruelty'.[4] Third, it has demonstrated that Bad King John is substantially the John of the chronicle accounts, of which Stubbs – a churchman as well as an historian – knew thoroughly. Yet these accounts, written by clergymen are necessarily antagonistic to John for bringing an interdict upon the country and perpetrating privations upon the clergy. Moreover, most of the key stories of John's alleged inadequacy – his perfidy, cruelty, indolence and recklessness – can be traced to one authority: Roger of Wendover, the St Albans chronicler who wrote several years after John's death and whose unreliability V. H. Galbraith long ago demonstrated. In Warren's words, 'so many of [Wendover's] stories...are utterly without foundation, or are so palpably inaccurate and confused that it is almost impossible to place any credence in the picture of John that emerges from his chronicle'.[5] Finally, it has been shown that not only is much chronicle material dangerously prejudiced but also the Bad King John found therein is contradicted by what can be gleamed from the record evidence. 'No chronicler should be believed who is not strictly contemporary, and is not supported by record evidence when he makes extravagant statements about the King's evil deeds', warned Lady Stenton as long ago as 1951.[6]

All of this begs the question of why the Stubbsian historiographical framework persisted for as long as it did. In part, the explanation is that a negative view of John suited an overall interpretation of medieval England that emphasized the barons' pursuit of liberties, culminating in the later rise of Parliament. This Whiggish interpretation of the past, presenting events as an inexorable progression towards ever greater liberty and enlightenment, must have seemed compelling to the Stubbs generation witnessing, as it did, strides towards personal freedoms such as the Reform Act of 1832. Developments of such big proportions demanded equally big, deep-rooted explanations. However, as the twentieth century progressed Parliament as a national institution lessened in authority and esteem. This encouraged historians to become critical of Whiggish interpretations of the past, a development which in turn removed any methodological necessity to see John in a negative light. The explanation for why the Stubbsian explanation prevailed for so long is in part also that only latterly have historians made significant use of the record evidence, largely ignored by Stubbs and the earlier generations of writers. This material has allowed historians to perceive a monarch who was at once inquisitive and insightful, driven and determined, capable and clever. Moreover, since the record material upon which these judgements are based is composed of 'facts' they are regarded as presenting a truer picture of their subject – though we have seen, for example, how disagreement over what the financial records actually reveal has led to the contrasting interpretations put forward by Gillingham on the one hand, and Holt *et al* on the other.

Yet it would be wrong to ignore the chronicle material altogether, sweeping it aside on the basis that it represents little more than hearsay. After all, Wendover was writing only a little while after the reign of John and, based at St Albans, he was in a good place to pick up the received wisdom of the day. Indeed, it seems likely that Wendover was reporting the anecdotes of men who had direct personal experience of John, and in a sense it may be averred that what matters is what the political nation *thought* John was like. Predisposed to be hostile to John, Wendover undoubtedly exaggerated the anecdotes he heard and no doubt added some of his own, but it seems probable that John was commonly regarded at the time as having been indolent, feckless and irresponsible – in short, an impediment to effective governance. Why was this the nature of John's reputation in the early thirteenth century when the record evidence apparently shows it to be false? A key explanation is that the timing and circumstance of John's death in 1216 meant that contemporaries could blame him with impunity for England's recent sufferings. Indeed, particular developments in 1216 created conditions in which recent traumas could safely be attributed entirely to John: the dead king's successor – his son Henry – was a minor; William Marshal was elevated into the office of regent and Magna Carta was reissued with revisions so that it enjoyed success where its first incarnation had suffered failure. Though the barons had won by default, they had nevertheless won – and it is the winners who write the history.

Of course, the evidence clearly does not allow for an interpretation which presents John as blame-free for the troubles that England suffered in the early thirteenth century. Yet his actions, and the atmosphere in which he governed, are only really to be understood once it is acknowledged that very few of the political elite in England felt the same way about the Angevin 'empire' as their king. In particular, few in England had any reason either to fight to retain Normandy or, after its loss in 1204, to fight for its recovery; and yet the king could not contemplate its irredeemable loss. There was too much at stake, not least his place in history. There was a great and growing tension in this respect. After 1216 it was in the interests of the barons to encourage a collective belief that John's failures were a result of his inadequate leadership rather than in any way a consequence of their own recalcitrance. Yet, arguably it was their obstinacy, such as the baronial 'strike' of 1205, that atrophied the proposed continental campaign of that year, which in turn fomented in John a chronic suspicion of his barons that led him to promote aliens such as Gerard d'Athée, Engelard de Cigogné and Falkes de Breauté in their place – the sort of men whom Wendover asserts 'thirsted for nothing more than human blood'.[7] Whatever the truth about Wendover's remark, the elevation of aliens – many of whom were low-born – thwarted the ambitions of members of the political nation. Their promotion caused resentment and induced an equal and opposite effect, ensuring ever greater dissonance in relations between John and his political elite. In other words, there was in motion a circular process which became increasingly vigorous and dynamic after 1204 because from that time John was almost permanently resident in England. As John pressed harder, so too did elements of the barons protest more loudly, such as in the conspiracy of 1212 and ultimately, of course, in Magna Carta and civil war. Despite this great and growing disconnect, and in increasingly difficult circumstances, John very nearly achieved his goals. Underrated indeed.

APPENDIX

A) Chronicle and Record Material

i) Examples of Chronicle Evidence

Document 1: From *The Chronicle of Richard Of Devizes of the Time of King Richard the First*. Observations on the conflict between John and Longchamp, 1191. Edited and translated by J. T. Appleby (London and New York: Thomas Nelson and Sons Ltd, 1963), 32.

> [The archbishop i.e. Walter Coutances, archbishop of Rouen] advised that the count [i.e. John] and the chancellor [i.e. Longchamp] should come to a conference and that they should put an end to their differences by committing them to arbitrators. The count, more than angry at the presumption of the chancellor's orders, became unrecognisable in all his body. Wrath cut furrows across his forehead; his burning eyes shot sparks; rage darkened the ruddy colour of his face. I know what he would have done to the chancellor if in that hour of fury he had fallen like an apple into the hands of the raging count. Indignation so swelled in his closed breast that it had either to burst or to vomit forth its venom somewhere.

Document 2: From the *History of William the Marshal*. The author describes the meeting between John and Richard, 1194. Edited by J. A. Holden, translated by S. Gregory with notes by D. Crouch, vol 2 (London: Anglo-Norman Text Society, 2002–6), 21.

> Trembling with fear, John came before the king [i.e. Richard] and fell at his feet. It did not turn out badly for him at all, for the king

lifted him up by the hand and kissed him, saying: "John, have no fear. You are a child, and you had bad men looking after you. Those who thought to give you bad advice will get their deserts! Get up and go and eat… It is always right that kindness and generosity should come out when they are implanted in a man's heart. But this much I tell you, in a word, that from the heart of a bad man no good can come."

Document 3: From *Concerning the Instruction of Princes* by Gerald of Wales. Translated by J. Stevenson in *English Historical Documents II* (London: Seeley, 1858; reprinted 1991), 103–4.

John, who far more atrociously than all other tyrants, during his own days, by confounding right and wrong, presumed with a rashness well meriting vengeance, to be mad and to rage not only against the priesthood but the English kingdom. For the said John…could not equal his illustrious brothers and his parents in good qualities for, as he was younger in years, so being far worse in moroseness of his disposition and in the depravity of his actions, he not only surpassed them in bad qualities but even eclipsed all vicious men in his enormities.

Document 4: Ralph of Coggeshall narrates John's conflict with the Cistercians in 1200. From *The Plantagenet Chronicles*, edited by E. Hallam (London: Guild Publishing Ltd, 1986), 263.

King John, coming to the province of York, demanded money from certain Cistercian abbots who met him there, and from other abbots of the order. He wished to oppress the order with the obligations of the tax, since until now it had been held free from payments of that kind… The abbots replied that they never paid any money without the common consent of the general chapter. The king was greatly irritated by their response. In anger and fury he ordered his sheriffs that they should injure the men of that order by whatever means they could. They should persecute them, show them no justice in their injuries and law-suits and not help them in their disputes, but refer everything to the king. At this harsh edict those men of virtue were not a little sorrowful and fearful, and referred the king's mandate to Hubert, archbishop of Canterbury, begging him to meet the king to discuss this cruel command and to soften his animosity in any way possible… Hubert reproached the king openly for his great harshness, pronouncing him a persecutor of the Holy Church who presumed to impose such great and so many injustices on these most worthy sons of the Church... King John favoured the arguments of the archbishop at the time, and in irritation recalled the priors with new letters but he did not rid his mind of the animosity he bore towards them. As the king was about to cross the sea, the archbishop, to please him, promised 1,000 marks of silver on behalf of the order, on condition that he confirmed the liberties granted to them by King Richard. The king completely rejected this offering because it was so small. Then he crossed the sea, breathing threats and slanders against the disciples of Christ.

Document 5: Ralph of Coggeshall describes the outbreak of the war with Philip in 1202. From *The Plantagenet Chronicles*, edited by E. Hallam (London: Guild Publishing Ltd, 1986), 272.

King Philip had many times ordered John to desist from harassing his men and to make a peace settlement with them. But as he refused to comply with Philip's orders and requests, the king of England, as count of Aquitaine and Anjou, was summoned by the nobles of the kingdom of France to come to the court of his lord, the king of France, at Paris. He was to submit to its judgement, answer for his wrongs and comply with the law, as determined by his peers. The king of England, however, replied that he was the duke of Normandy and was in no way obliged to attend a court at Paris. He would only confer with the king on the subject of the frontier between the kingdom and the duchy. This had been agreed in ancient times between the duke and the king and confirmed in genuine documents. King Philip, however, argued that it was not at all just that, because the same man was count of Aquitaine and duke of Normandy, he should lose his rights over Aquitaine. The argument dragged on... Gradually animosity increased on both sides, with the addition of cruel threats. At length, the French court assembled and judged that the king of England should be deprived of all the lands which he and his predecessors had held from the French king, because they had scarcely any service owed for a long time, and had refused to obey their lord. King Philip, therefore, gladly accepted and approved of the judgement of his court. He gathered an army and immediately attacked the castle of Boutavant... Then he seized all the land of Hugh de Gournay and all the nearby castles. He took the county and castle of Aumale, the county of Eu and the whole of that land as far as Arques and met with no resistance.

Document 6: Ralph of Coggeshall describes the rebellion of Arthur and his ultimate fate. From *The Plantagenet Chronicles*, edited by E. Hallam (London: Guild Publishing Ltd, 1986), 274, 276 and 278.

At the age of sixteen Arthur, King John's nephew was knighted by King Philip and betrothed to his small daughter. At the importune suggestion of some, he rebelled against his uncle and, following evil and rash advice, set out with Hugh the Brown and Geoffrey of Lusignan and two hundred and fifty soldiers to besiege the castle of Mirebeau, where his grandmother, Queen Eleanor, was staying with her men. The queen, fearing capture, ordered her son John to bring aid as soon as possible...The counsellors of John, realising that the Bretons were causing much destruction and sedition everywhere on behalf of their lord Arthur, and that nor firm peace could be made while Arthur lived, suggested to the king that Arthur be blinded and castrated thus rendering him incapable of rule, so that the opposition would cease from their insane programme of destruction and submit themselves to the king. Enraged by the ceaseless acts of his enemies, hurt by their threats and misdeeds, at length in a rage and fury, King John ordered three of his servants to go to Falaise and perform this detestable act. Two of the servants, hating to do so evil a deed on such a noble young man, fled from the king's court. The third, however, took the king's order to Hubert de Burgh, who was guarding the royal youth. Great grief and sorrow arose among those guarding him and they were moved with great pity for the noble youth... Hubert, having regard for the king's honesty and reputation and expecting his forgiveness, kept Arthur unharmed. He thought that the king would immediately repent of such an order and that ever afterwards would hate anyone who presumed to obey such a cruel mandate, which Humbert believed was the result more of a sudden anger than a calm consideration. Wishing to mollify King John's anger and at the same time stop the savagery of the Bretons, Hubert had it announced through the castle and the whole region that the sentence had been carried out and that Arthur had died from a broken heart and from the bitter pain of his wounds... It was also announced that Arthur's body had been taken to the Cistercian abbey of St Andre-en-Gouffern, in Normandy, and buried there... [In fact, in 1203] Arthur was taken from Falaise to Rouen and shut up in the castle, under the keeping of Robert de Vieuxpont. King Philip of France, with the Bretons, instantly ordered King John of England to release Arthur to them... When John refused,

Philip again attacked the castles of Normandy... [Thereafter] King Philip would make a peace settlement only if Arthur were released to him alive. For if Arthur were now discovered to be dead, Philip hoped to marry his sister and thus to gain all her continental possessions... King Philip always raged about the death of Arthur, whom he had heard had been drowned in the Seine. Therefore he swore that he would never desist from making war on John until he had derived him of his entire kingdom.

Document 7: Wendover on John's response to Philip's military progress in Normandy 1203–4. From *Flowers of History*, translated by J. A. Giles, 2 vols (London: Bohn, 1869), 206–7.

A.D. 1203. King John spent Christmas at Caen in Normandy, where, laying aside all thoughts of war, he feasted sumptuously with his queen daily, and prolonged his sleep in the morning till breakfast time. But after the solemnities of Easter had been observed, the French king, having collected a large army, took several castles belonging to the king of England, some of which he levelled to the ground, but the stronger ones he kept entire. At length, messengers came to King John with the news, saying, the king of the French has entered your territories as an enemy, has taken such and such castles, carries off the governors of them ignominiously bound to their horses' tails, and disposes of your property at will, without anyone gainsaying him. In reply to this news, king John said, "Let him do so; whatever he now seizes on I will one day recover." And neither these messengers, nor others who brought him the like news, could obtain any other answer. But the earls and barons, and other nobles of the kingdom of England, who had till that time firmly adhered to him, when they heard his words and saw his incorrigible idleness, obtained his permission and returned home, pretending that they would come back to him, and so left the king with only a few soldiers in Normandy.

Document 8: Matthew Paris describes the king's reaction to the fall of Chateau Gaillard (1204). From *Flowers of History*, translated by C. D. Yonge, 2 vols (London: Bohn, 1853), 100–101.

A.D. 1204. In those days, the castle of Chateau Gaillard was besieged for nearly a year, and though the besiegers repeatedly requested aid from king John, none came to them... [Eventually Chateau Gaillard] fell into the power of the French king. And when the garrisons of other cities and castles in Normandy on the side of king John saw this, they informed him in what a strait they were placed, and that, unless they received more prompt and effectual assistance, they must go over to the French king, whether they would or no. To which he replied, that each of them must provide for himself as appeared to him to be most for his advantage. In the mean time, King John went on, wretched indeed, but undeserving of any one's pity, indulging his gluttony and luxury with his wanton queen, while lying in whose bosom he thought that he was in possession of every joy, relying on the money which he had sworn to extort from England.

Document 9: Ralph of Coggeshall describes John's failed expedition of 1205. From *The Plantagenet Chronicles*, edited by E. Hallam (London: Guild Publishing Ltd, 1986), 281–2 and 284.

King John, who was very worried although he appeared to hide his sorrow, decided to cross the sea with a large army to recover his lost lands... So, after Easter, having held a council at Northampton, King John made for the sea at Portchester with a great and noble army. He was joined there by a great multitude of ships from many ports. When the ships [had been made ready]...behold, the archbishop of Canterbury and Earl William Marshal, who had just returned from overseas, came to the king to persuade him at all costs to abandon the expedition. They put forward the many dangers which could come from his crossing: that it would be very dangerous to land troops amongst the enemy without a secure base; that the French king could lead a much greater army against him... that it was not safe to rely on the guile and fickleness of the Poitevins who were always planning something deceitful against their princes; that the count of Boulogne with his accomplices would quickly invade England if he heard it was empty of its leaders and famous army; that it was greatly to be feared that he would lose what he held in trying to recover what he had lost, especially since he left behind him no obvious heir to the kingdom... Although he heard these and other arguments the king could not be persuaded to give up his plan of going overseas. The archbishop and Earl William, seizing him by the knees, clung on to him lest he should escape from them, insisting that if he would not listen to their entreaties, they would detain him by force lest the whole kingdom be thrown into confusion by his departure... At length the king was reluctantly persuaded to stay and told his lords and knights to return home... These men cursed the archbishop and other counsellors who had given the king such bad advice...for they said that never had so many ships sailed to an English port for crossing and that never had a bigger army of strong knights assembled in England... The king set out for Winchester with great sadness. He was touched by such a great sorrow and heaviness of heart that the next day he immediately returned to the coast. He rowed to the Isle of Wight and sailed here and there for two days, while his friends tried to dissuade him from crossing the sea without the army which he had disbanded.

Document 10: Wendover describes attempts in 1208 by the bishops of London, Ely and Winchester to get John to accept Langton. From *Flowers of History*, translated by J. A. Giles, 2 vols (London: Bohn, 1869), 245–6.

A.D. 1208. The bishops of London, Ely and Winchester...went to King John and...entreated him humbly and with tears, that he, having God in his sight, would recall the archbishop and the monks of Canterbury to their church... And they informed him that thus he would avoid the shame of an interdict... When the said bishops wished, out of regard to the king, to prolong the discourse, the king became nearly mad with rage, and broke forth in words of blasphemy against the pope and his cardinals, swearing by God's teeth, that, if they or any other priests soever presumptuously dared to lay his dominions under an interdict, he would immediately send all the prelates of England, clerks as well as ordained persons, to the pope, and confiscate all their property. He added moreover, that all the clerks of Rome or of the pope himself who could be found in England or in his other territories, he would send to Rome with their eyes plucked out, and their noses slit, that by these marks they might be known there from other people. In addition to this he plainly ordered the bishops to take themselves quickly from his sight if they wished to keep their bodies free from harm. The bishops then, not finding any repentance in the king, departed, and, in the Lent following, fearlessly fulfilled the duty required of them by the pope and accordingly...on 23 March they laid a general interdict on the whole of England.

Document 11: Gervase of Canterbury describes the impact of the Interdict, 1208. From *The Plantagenet Chronicles*, edited by E. Hallam (London: Guild Publishing Ltd, 1986), 290.

On 24 March [1208] by papal mandate, divine services were suspended throughout England. Great sorrow and anxiety spread throughout the country. Neither Good Friday nor Easter could be celebrated, but an unheard-of silence was imposed on all the clergy and monks by laymen. The bodies of the dead, whether of the ordinary fold or the religious, could not be buried in consecrated cemeteries but only in vile and profane places. The king ordered the few monks who remained at Canterbury, the blind and the crippled, also to be expelled, and the monks to be regarded as public enemies. Some fled from England, some were imprisoned, some were saved by money, others suffered many afflictions – their woods were cut down and their men were fined and taxed heavily. The whole of England suffered this burden. The people were forced to pay at first a quarter of their money, then a third, then a half. Even the rents of the cardinals and whatever they had in England were taken away from them and Peter's Pence, which the Roman Church had had since the time of Cnut, was withheld by the king. He especially imposed great afflictions on this occasion on the men of the Cinque Ports who defended the coast against hostile invasion. For he hanged some of them and put others to the sword; he imprisoned many, bound them in irons and at length released them only in return for pledges and money. Therefore the rich and poor left England, countless men and women. Theirs was a thankless pilgrimage to avoid the enormous cruelty of the king rather than a devoted one. John even imprisoned the queen, his wife, in strict custody at Corfe castle.

Document 12: Wendover describes an occasion in 1208 when John orders a priest killer to be released. From *Flowers of History*, translated by J. A. Giles, 2 vols (London: Bohn, 1869), 246–7.

A.D. 1208. The King of England being greatly enraged on account of the interdict, sent his sheriffs and other ministers of iniquity to all quarters of England, giving order with dreadful threats to all priests…to depart the kingdom immediately… Religious men and other persons ordained of any kind, when found travelling on the road, were dragged from their horses, robbed and basely ill-treated by the king's men. About that time the servants of a certain sheriff on the confines of Wales came to the king bringing in their custody a robber with his hands tied behind him, who had robbed and murdered a priest on the road; and on their asking the king what it was his pleasure should be done to the robber in such a case, the king immediately answered, "He has slain an enemy of mine, release him and let him go." The relations, too, of the archbishop and bishops, who had laid England under an interdict, wherever they could be found, were by the king's orders taken, robbed of all their property, and thrown into prison.

Document 13: Wendover describes the fate of Geoffrey, archdeacon of Norwich. From *Flowers of History*, translated by J. A. Giles, 2 vols (London: Bohn, 1869), 251.

> A.D. 1209. In a short time the decree [i.e. of excommunication] became known to all in the roads and streets...it afforded a subject of secret conversation to all. Amongst others, as Geoffrey archdeacon of Norwich was one day sitting in the Exchequer at Westminster, attending to the king's business, he began to talk privately with his companions who sat with him, of the decree which was sent forth against the king, and said that it was not safe for beneficed persons to remain any longer in their allegiance to an excommunicated king. After saying which, he went to his own house without asking the king's permission. This event coming soon after to the knowledge of the king, he was not a little annoyed, and sent William Talbot a knight, with some soldiers, to seize the archdeacon, and they, after he was taken, bound him in chains and threw him into prison. After he had been there a few days, by command of the said king a cap of lead was put on him, and at length, being overcome by want of food as well as by the weight of the leaden cup, he departed to the Lord.

Document 14: Wendover describes torture of the Jews, 1210. From *Flowers of History*, translated by J. A. Giles, 2 vols (London: Bohn, 1869), 252–3.

> A.D. 1210. By the king's order, all the Jews, throughout England, of both sexes, were seized, imprisoned and tortured severely, in order to do the king's will with their money. Some of them then after being tortured gave up all they had and promised more, that they might thus escape. One of this sect at Bristol, even after being dreadfully tortured, still refused to ransom himself or to put an end to his sufferings, upon which the king ordered his agents to knock out one of his cheek-teeth daily until he paid ten thousand marks of silver to him. After they had for seven days knocked out a tooth each day with great agony to the Jew, reluctant as he was to provide the money required, [he] gave the said sum to save his eighth tooth, although he had already lost seven.

Document 15: Wendover accuses John of lasciviousness, 1210. From *Flowers of History*, translated by J. A. Giles, 2 vols (London: Bohn, 1869), 259.

> There were at this time in the kingdom of England many nobles, whose wives and daughters the king had violated to the indignation

of their husbands and fathers; others whom he had by unjust exactions reduced to the extreme of poverty; some whose parents and kindred he had exiled, converting their inheritances to his own uses. Thus the said king's enemies were as numerous as his nobles.

Document 16: Gervase of Canterbury describes John's invasion of Ireland, 1210. From *The Plantagenet Chronicles*, edited by E. Hallam (London: Guild Publishing Ltd, 1986), 293.

John did not exclude the clergy from his search for money. When the Cistercian abbots met together he asked them to help him not with their prayers but with their money. When his request was rejected quite humbly, he left enraged and he led the army and the fleet, which it is believed he had prepared to go to Poitou, into Ireland and quickly subdued [that place] either by force or fraud. There, though many opposed it, they could not resist; he instituted English laws and customs and ordered them to be observed and then he returned to England. Many hoped that because of this victory the king would make amends for the bad deeds he had done towards the Church of God and would correct his errors. But a new anger inflamed him, especially towards the Cistercians, from whom he could exact no money either by force or prayer, so that, dispersed through various churches in England, they were forced to beg for food.

Document 17: Gervase of Canterbury describes John's British achievement, 1210. From *The Plantagenet Chronicles*, edited by E. Hallam (London: Guild Publishing Ltd, 1986), 293.

The king sent a great army into Wales under William [Longespée, Earl of Salisbury], his brother, and the Earl of Chester, who laid waste that land all around and killed many different men. And many said that Merlin's prophecy had come about saying: 'the sixth shall pull down the walls of Ireland' and 'his beginning shall succumb to his own unstable nature'. William I, William II, Henry I, Henry II, afterwards Richard. The sixth is John who acquired Ireland but in all other things was vain and useless.

Document 18: The Barnwell Chronicle describes the conspiracy against John in 1212. From *The Plantagenet Chronicles*, edited by E. Hallam (London: Guild Publishing Ltd, 1986), 263.

The Welsh princes, encouraged by the pope...attacked the English king in return for the interdict being relaxed throughout their lands. King John, stirred up to violent anger, hanged the hostages and gathered an army against them from all parts of the kingdom. And then, when he had gathered such a multitude as had never before been seen in our times, God put his forces to flight. Then King John's heart was troubled, since it was being said, without authority, that rumours had been heard that the barons who had gathered together were conspiring against him, and that in many ears there were tales of letters absolving the barons from John's allegiance. It was said that another king should be elected in his place and that John should be expelled from the kingdom. If on the other hand the king captured them, they would suffer death or perpetual imprisonment.

Document 19: The Barnwell Chronicle describes Philip's plans for an invasion, 1213. From *The Plantagenet Chronicles*, edited by E. Hallam (London: Guild Publishing Ltd, 1986), 300.

The English bishops who were in exile in France petitioned the pope on behalf of the English Church. Moved by their pleas, he agreed to bring about an end to the evil. For he wrote to Philip, the king of France, and to the princes of those parts that unless the king of England capitulated, they should liberate England from his rule with a strong army... The French king himself awaited the gathering of the ships not far from the sea. Having assessed the size of his army it was believed that it comprised no less than fifteen thousand men. Every day ships converged on the ports and knights on the castles. The king of England heard this and had a large fleet gathered from all the English ports, and he appointed strong men skilled in arms to his galleys. With a large force they resisted the enemy's attack, and with great endeavour opposed them and injured the enemy's cause.

Document 20: The Barnwell Chronicle describes the execution of Peter Wakefield and his son, 1213. From *The Plantagenet Chronicles*, edited by E. Hallam (London: Guild Publishing Ltd, 1986), 304.

It was suggested to the king that Peter had disturbed the land, spread alarm and despondency among the people and had encouraged the king's enemies. For his words had even been carried to the farthest part of France and had been regarded as an incitement for the invasion of England. All this enraged the king so that he ordered that Peter should be hanged and furthermore that his son, who was imprisoned with him, should also be hanged in case he was either a participant in, or the author of, his father's prophecies.

Document 21: The Barnwell Chronicle comments on the concessions John made in February 1213 to the barons. Quoted in J. C. Holt, *Magna Carta* (Cambridge: Cambridge University Press, 1969), 128.

Amid so many hazards [John] did something which should be remembered to his honour. For the foresters were levying novel and burdensome exactions on almost all England, and the king showed pity for those affected and completely remitted them. There were others who by reason that they were keepers of the ports were molesting burgesses and travellers and merchants, and these too he restrained and had their exactions remitted. He is also said to have acted with more kindness towards widows and to have shown considerable energy in maintaining the peace, at least in temporal matters... He began to destroy evil customs and to restrain the violence and greed of the sheriffs and their agents, who were a sore affliction on the people, since they held their shrievalties and lesser offices at an annual charge and sought only this, namely how to exact money from the people in their charge. And he removed such men from office and substituted others who would treat the people justly and take the advice of prudent men and would seek the peace and quiet of their charges rather than the emptying of their purses. And he began a searching enquiry into these matters so that he should know who had received such extortions while in office. But it was not carried through to a conclusion because there intervened that time of terror and tumult when all were called to arms for fear of the French.

Document 22: Matthew Paris comments upon the personality of the king. From *Flowers of History*, translated by C. D. Yonge, 2 vols (London: Bohn, 1853), 108–9.

In the meantime the king kept on oppressing one or other of the nobles of the kingdom, either by extorting money from them unjustly, or by stripping them of their privileges or properties. Of some he seduced the wives, or deflowered the daughters, so that he became manifestly and notoriously odious and detestable both to God and man. Moreover, that his insatiable avarice and unappeasable gluttony and licentiousness might be concealed from no one, he prohibited all fowling and taking winged game, and prevented the nobles from hunting, by which measures he not only lost the affections of all men, but incurred their inextinguishable hatred so that even his own wife detested and loathed him – whom he, though an adulterer himself, accused of adultery, and he put to an ignominious death those whom he suspected of familiarities with her. He also ordered the queen herself to be kept in close custody. And, among other flagitious crimes, he, like a second Herod, ordered a great many innocent boys, who were hostages at Nottingham, to be hanged on a gallows – on which account, all his subjects, both English and foreigners, wishing to shake off the intolerable yoke of such a tyrant began seriously to consider what prince there was in whose bosom they might find a refuge.

Document 23: Wendover describes John's actions in the immediate aftermath of the events at Runnymede, June 1215. From *Flowers of History*, translated by J. A. Giles, 2 vols, (London: Bohn, 1869), 325.

After the barons, as has been stated, had gone from the conference, the king was left with scarcely seven knights out of his proper body of attendants. Whilst lying sleepless that night in Windsor castle, his thoughts alarmed him much, and before daylight he fled by stealth to the Isle of Wight, and there in great agony of mind devised plans to be revenged on the barons.

Document 24: Matthew Paris describes John's resolve to ignore Magna Carta. Quoted in *Flowers of History*, translated by J. A. Giles, 2 vols (London: Bohn, 1869), 326–7.

The king then, deeply sighing, conceived the greatest indignation, and began to pine away, giving vent to lamentations and complaints. "Why," said he, "did my mother bring me forth, unhappy and shameless woman that she was? Why was I nursed on her knees, or suckled at her breast? Would that I had been slain rather than suffered to grow to manhood." He then commenced gnashing his teeth, scowling with his eyes, and seizing sticks and limbs of trees, began to gnaw them, and after gnawing them to break them, and with increasingly extraordinary gestures to show the grief or rather the rage he felt. And on that very night he at once secretly prepared letters and sent to Philip Marc constable of the castle of Nottingham, a native of Poitou, and to all his foreign-born subjects, in whom his soul most confided, ordering them to supply their castles with provisions, surround them with trenches, garrison them, and to prepare cross-bows and engines, and to make arrows – telling them, however, to do this cautiously and without open blustering, lest the barons should happen to find it out and prevent the anger of the king from proceeding further. But as there is nothing done in secret which is not discovered…[some leading nobles pondered to themselves] "Woe to us, yea to all England, since it has not a true king, but is oppressed by a tyrant who endeavours to make his people miserable. He has already placed us in subjection to Rome and the Roman court, that we might obtain protection from it; it is to be feared that we shall find the assistance from that place injurious to our posterity. We never heard of any king who was unwilling to withdraw his neck from slavery; but this one willingly succumbs to it."

Document 25: Wendover describes John's actions after the siege of Rochester castle, 1215. From *Flowers of History*, translated by J. A. Giles, 2 vols (London: Bohn, 1869), 339.

This siege had lasted almost three months, and the king, on account of the number of his troops slain, as well as the money he had spent on the siege, was greatly enraged, and in his anger ordered all the nobles to be hung on the gibber. But the noble Savaric de Mauléon standing up before the king said to him, "My lord king, our war is not yet over, therefore you ought carefully to consider how the fortunes of war may turn. For if you now order us to hang these men, the barons our enemies, will perhaps by a like event take me or other nobles of your army, and, following your example, hang us. Therefore, do not let this happen, for in such a case no one will fight in your cause." The king then, although unwillingly, listened to his advice and that of other prudent men.

Document 26: The Barnwell chronicle describes John's actions after the siege of Rochester castle in 1215. From *The Plantagenet Chronicles*, edited by E. Hallam (London: Guild Publishing Ltd, 1986), 316.

[After the siege] came to an end some were sent out from the castle who seemed less warlike, the king causing their hands and feet to be cut off. Not along afterwards all were taken into captivity and were thrown into chains, with the exception of those who proved themselves to be clerics. The king kept the knights and nobles for himself but gave the less important prisoners into the hands of others. Only one did he order to be hanged, a crossbowman whom he had nurtured since childhood – although it was thought that all would die on account of the king's bitter rage. Hearing of the outcome of the siege the rest of the barons were dismayed and with rising panic gathered in London or stayed in religious houses. There were few indeed who felt secure behind fortifications.

Document 27: Matthew Paris describes the impact of the civil war in 1215. From *Flowers of History*, translated by C. D. Yonge, 2 vols (London: Bohn, 1853), 122–3.

[After he had taken Rochester castle] the king became a perfect tyrant, and a destroyer of his own kingdom, hiring, as his soldiers, a band of foreigners… And then there arose unheard-of confusion in the kingdom, of so fierce a character that sons were seen to rise in a hostile manner against the fathers, and fathers against their sons. Accordingly, king John, accompanied by that detestable troop of foreigners, whose leader was Falkes de Breauté, a man of ignoble birth and a bastard, and carried away by his fury, began to lay waste the northern parts of England, to destroy the castles of the barons, or compel them to submit to his own order, to burn without mercy all the palaces and towns which belonged to the barons, to oppress the inhabitants of the country by carefully devised tortures, in order to extort money from them, so that the lord of the country seemed in his madness to be angry with his people and to hate his own inheritance. Everywhere there was grief and misery.

ii) Examples of the Record Evidence

Document 28: T. D. Hardy (ed.), *Rotuli Litterarum Patentium 1201–1216* (London: Record Commission, 1835), vii.

The King to all his justices and faithful people, greeting. We strictly prohibit any one charged with homicide from being bailed, or committed to custody, or placed in hostage, unless by our special command [and order that they] be safely kept in gaol, until after his trial before our justices. Witness the Lord John Bishop of Norwich, at Woodstock, on the 8th day of November in the 9th year of our reign.

Document 29: T. D. Hardy (ed.), *Rotuli Litterarum Patentium 1201–1216* (London: Record Commission, 1835), xvii.

The King to Geoffrey Fitz Peter and others. We had lost the precious stones and jewels which we were accustomed to wear around our neck.

Berchal, the bearer of this letter found them and liberally and faithfully brought them unto us. And for this service we have given to him twenty shillings-worth of rent at Berkhamstead, where he was born. And we therefore command you to assign unto him without delay such rent of twenty shillings. Witness ourself at Mortain in Normandy, on the 12th day of November in the third year of our reign.

Document 30: T. D. Hardy (ed.), *Rotuli Litterarum Patentium 1201–1216* (London: Record Commission, 1835), xviii.

The King to his sheriffs and burgesses of Gloucester and to all other his faithful subjects. Know ye, that it is ordained by our command, and by the advice of our barons, that every year when lampreys are first caught they shall not be sold for more than two shillings each, until after February, when they are to be sold at a lower price. We therefore prohibit you under pain of forfeiture and amercement from acting herein contrary to our commandment. Witness Geoffrey Fitz Peter, Reading on 12th day of January in the 8th year of our reign.

Document 31: T. D. Hardy (ed.), *Rotuli Litterarum Patentium 1201–1216* (London: Record Commission, 1835), xviii.

The King to all his bailiffs and faithful subjects. We command you that if any damsel shall pass through your bailiwicks in coming from Portugal to the Count de Nemours, ye are not to arrest her, nor suffer her in any way to be molested but to treat her honourably and permit her to pass freely. Witness Geoffrey Fitz Peter at Westminster on the 26th day of March.

Document 32: T. D. Hardy (ed.), *Rotuli Litterarum Patentium 1201–1216* (London: Record Commission, 1835), xxiv.

The King to all. We command you to allow the men of Calais to fish, and safely to go and return by sea, and throughout our land, wherever they please, until Christmas day, in the 6th year of our reign. Witness Hubert Archbishop of Canterbury, at Merton, on the 16th day of June in the 6th year of our reign.

Document 33: Issued to remove from particular individuals who had been mutilated the suspicion that their misfortune was the punishment of crime.

T. D. Hardy (ed.), *Rotuli Litterarum Patentium 1201–1216* (London: Record Commission, 1835), xxviii.

The king to all. Know ye, that Robert the son of Robert the mercer lost his ear at Chateaux-neuf-sur-Sart in our service, and not on account of felony. And this we certify to you, that you may know it. Witness ourself at Montfort, the 23rd day of July 1203.

Document 34: T. D. Hardy (ed.), *Rotuli Litterarum Patentium 1201–1216* (London: Record Commission, 1835), xvii.

The king to the mayor and barons of London. We have always loved you much, and have caused your rights and liberties to be well observed… But, when you know that the Jews are under our special protection, we indeed marvel that you have allowed mischief to be done to the Jews dwelling in the city of London, such being manifestly against the peace and tranquility of our realm. And we are so much the more astonished and concerned thereat, because the other Jews throughout England, wheresoever they dwell, excepting those in your city, are in perfect peace. Nor do we notice this on account of the Jews only, but also for our own quiet, because if we had granted our protection to a dog, it ought to be inviolably observed. Henceforth, however, we commit the Jews to your custody, and if any one shall attempt to harm them, you may always defend and assist them. For in future, at you hands will we require their blood, if perchance, by your default, any evil happen to them, which Heaven forfend for we well know that things of this sort do occur through the foolish people of the town. Witness ourself at Montfort on 29 day of July [see itinerary for date].

iii) *Itinerary as Shown by Record Evidence*

Document 35:

Itinerary of King John – June 1208–16

June	A.D. 1208 A.R. 10	A.D. 1209 A.R. 11	A.D. 1210 A.R. 12	A.D. 1211 A.R. 13	A.D. 1212 A.R. 14	A.D. 1213 A.R. 15	A.D. 1214 A.R. 16	A.D. 1215 A.R. 17	A.D. 1216 A.R. 18
1	o.E ' ' '	M. Knep-Castle.	Tu. ' ' '	W. ' ' '	Fr. Chertsey. Ditton.	Sa. Wingham.	C ' ' '	M. Windsor.	W. Winchester.
2	M. ' ' '	Tu. ' ' '	W. ' ' '	pTh. ' ' '	Sa. Tower of London.	n F Wingham.	M. Spina.	Tu. Windsor.	Th. Winchester.
3	Tu. Ludgershall.	W. Bexley.	Th. Cross-on-the-Sea.	Fr. ' ' '	G Tower of London.	M. Wingham. Chilham.	Tu. Spina.	W. Windsor.	Fr. Winchester.
4	W. ' ' '	Th. ' ' '	Fr. Cross-on-the-Sea.	Sa. ' ' '	M. Tower of London. Hertford.	Tu. Chilham.	W. Spina.	Th. Odiham.	Sa. Winchester.
5	pTh. Marlborough.	Fr. ' ' '	Sa. Cross-on-the-Sea.	B ' ' '	Tu. ' ' '	W. Ospring.	Th. Pilem.	Fr. Winchester.	o B Winchester. Ludgershall.
6	Fr. ' ' '	Sa. ' ' '	n C Cross-on-the-Sea.	M. ' ' '	W. ' ' '	Th. Ospring. Rochester.	Fr. Pilem.	Sa. Winchester.	M. Ludgershall.
7	Sa. ' ' '	D Rochester.	M. Cross-on-the-Sea.	Tu. ' ' '	Th. Sleaford.	Fr. Rochester.	Sa. Chezelles.	n D Winchester.	Tu. Ludgershall. Devizes.
8	E Winchester.	M. Rochester.	Tu. Cross-on-the-Sea.	W. ' ' '	Fr. Kingshaugh.	Sa. Rochester.	C ' ' '	M. Winchester. Merton.	W. Devizes.
9	M. Winchester.	Tu. Orsett.	W. Cross-on-the-Sea.	Th. ' ' '	Sa. Kingshaugh.	o F Rochester.	M. ' ' '	Tu. Odiham.	pTh. Devizes. Wilton.
10	Tu. Winchester.	W. Chelmsford. Maldon.	Th. Cross-on-the-Sea.	Fr. ' ' '	G Kingshaugh.	M. Ospring.	Tu. Spina.	W. Windsor.	Fr. Wilton.

#									
11	W. ' ' '	Th. ' ' '	Fr. Cross-on-the-Sea.	Sa. ' ' '	M. ' ' '	Tu. Chilham.	W. Spina. Ancenis.	Th. Windsor.	Sa. Wilton.
12	Th. ' ' '	Fr. Colchester.	Sa. Cross-on-the-Sea.	B ' ' '	Tu. Tickhill. Doncaster. Rothwell.	W. Chilham.	Th. Ancenis. Rochefort. St. Florent.	Fr. Windsor.	B Wilton.
13	Fr. ' ' '	Sa. ' ' '	o C Cross-on-the-Sea.	M. ' ' '	W. Rothwell. Knaresborough.	pTh. Battle. Aldingbourn.	Fr. ' ' '	Sa. Windsor.	M. Wilton. Salisbury.
14	Sa. Winchester.	D Havering.	M. Cross-on-the-Sea.	Tu. ' ' '	Th. Knaresborough.	Fr. Aldingbourn.	Sa. Blaison.	o D Windsor.	Tu. Wilton.
15	E ' ' '	M. Havering.	Tu. Cross-on-the-Sea.	W. ' ' '	Fr. Richmond.	Sa. Aldingbourn. Bedhampton.	C Blaison. Ancenis.	M. Windsor. Runnemead.	W. Sturminster.
16	M. ' ' '	Tu. ' ' '	W. Cross-on-the-Sea.	Th. ' ' '	Sa. Bowes.	F Porchester.	M. ' ' '	Tu. Windsor.	Th. Sturminster.
17	Tu. Melksham.	W. Havering.	pTh. ' ' '	Fr. ' ' '	G Aappleby.	M. Bishop's Stoke.	Tu. Angers.	W. Windsor.	Fr. Blandford.
18	W. ' ' '	Th. ' ' '	Fr. ' ' '	Sa. ' ' '	M. Appleby. Kirkoswald.	Tu. Bishop's Stoke.	W. Angers.	pTh. Windsor. Runnemead.	Sa. Wareham.
19	Th. Bristol.	Fr. London.	Sa. ' ' '	B ' ' '	Tu. Kirkoswald. Plumpton.	W. Bishop's Stoke.	Th. Roche-aux-Moins.	Fr. Runnemead. Windsor.	B Wareham. Beer-Regis.
20	Fr. Winterbourne.	Sa. Westminster.	C Crook, near Waterford.	M. ' ' '	W. Caldbeck, in Allerdale.	Th. Bishop's Stoke.	Fr. Roche-aux-Moins.	Sa. Runnemead.	M. Beer-Regis. Wareham.
21	Sa. ' ' '	D Westminster.	M. Crook. Newbridge.	Tu. ' ' '	Th. Wigton.	Fr. Corfe.	Sa. Roche-aux-Moins.	D Windsor. Runnemead.	Tu. Wareham.
22	E ' ' '	M. Westminster. Chertsey.	Tu. Thomastown.	W. ' ' '	Fr. Wigton.	Sa. Corfe.	C Roche-aux-Moins.	M. Windsor. Runnemead.	W. Wareham.
23	M. ' ' '	Tu. ' ' '	W. Kilkenny.	Th. ' ' '	Sa. Carlisle.	F Corfe.	M. Roche-aux-Moins.	Tu. Runnemead. Windsor.	Th. Corfe.

(Continued)

Continued

June	A.D. 1208. A.R. 10.	A.D. 1209. A.R. 11.	A.D. 1210. A.R. 12.	A.D. 1211. A.R. 13.	A.D. 1212. A.R. 14.	A.D. 1213. A.R. 15.	A.D. 1214. A.R. 16.	A.D. 1215. A.R. 17.	A.D. 1216. A.R. 18.
24	Tu. ' ' '	W. Odiham. Freemantle.	Th. Kilkenny. Naas.	Fr. ' ' '	G Carlisle.	M. Corfe.	Tu. Roche-aux-Moins.	W. Windsor.	Fr. Corfe.
25	W. ' ' '	Th. Freemantle.	Fr. ' ' '	Sa. ' ' '	M. Carlisle.	Tu. Canford.	W. Roche-aux-Moins.	Th. Windsor.	Sa. Corfe.
26	Th. Hereford.	Fr. Ashley.	Sa. Naas.	B ' ' '	Tu. Carlisle.	W. Canford. Beer-Regis.	Th. Roche-aux-Moins.	Fr. Odiham. Winchester.	B Corfe.
27	Fr. ' ' '	Sa. Clarendon.	C ' ' '	M. ' ' '	W. Hexham.	Th. Beer-Regis.	Fr. Roche-aux-Moins.	Sa. Winchester.	M. Corfe.
28	Sa. ' ' '	D Downton.	M. Dublin.	Tu. ' ' '	Th. Durham.	Fr. ' ' '	Sa. Roche-aux-Moins.	D Winchester.	Tu. Corfe.
29	E ' ' '	M. Cranborne.	Tu. ' ' '	W. ' ' '	Fr. Allerton.	Sa. Corfe. Bishop's Stoke.	C Roche-aux-Moins.	M. Winchester.	W. Corfe.
30	M. ' ' '	Tu. ' ' '	W. Dublin. Grenoge.	Th. ' ' '	Sa. Easingwould.	F Bishop's Stoke.	M Roche-aux-Moins.	Tu. Winchester.	Th. Corfe.

B) Examples of the Judgements of Stubbs and Green

Document 36: Stubbs in *Historical Introductions to the Rolls Series*, ed. A. Hassall (New York: Haskell House Publishers Ltd, 1902), 239, 442–3, 487.

There is not one moment, not one of the many crises of [John's] reign, in which we feel the slightest movement towards sympathy. Edward III may have been as unprincipled, but he is a more graceful sinner; William Rufus as savage, but he is a more magnificent and stronger-willed villain; Ethelred the Unready as weak, false and worthless, but he sins for, and suffers with, his people. John has neither grace nor splendor, strength nor patriotism... John, then, was a mean reproduction of all the vices and of the few pettinesses of his family... He never repents, even it be only to sin again; he has no remorse, even for his failures. He condemns both the spirit and the form of the law. Of religion he has none... He neither fears God nor cares for the souls of his people, but he is amenable to the superstitions that his father would have spurned... He heaps neglect on insult, and scatters scorn on the dead, whose chief fault has been that they have served him too well... His recklessness in running into danger is only equalled by the shamelessness with which he retreats before the evils that he has provoked. Of himself he does nothing great, and what is done for him by others he undoes by alienating or insulting them... For John even in the abject humiliation of his end we have no word of pity as we have had none of sympathy. He has deserved none.

Document 37: J. R. Green, *Short History of the English People* (London: Folio Society, 1992), 122.

John was the worst outcome of the Angevins. He united into one mass of wickedness their insolence, their selfishness, their unbridled lust, their cruelty and tyranny, their shamelessness, their superstition, their cynical indifference to honour or truth... He had abandoned one wife and was faithless to another. His punishments were refinements of cruelty, the starvation of children, the crushing of old men under copes of lead. His court was a brothel where no woman was safe from the royal lust... He was as craven in his superstitions as he was daring in his impiety. He scoffed at priests and turned his back on the mass, even amidst the solemnities of his coronation, but he never stirred on a journey without hanging relics round his neck. [It should be noted that Green proceeds to call John the 'ablest and most ruthless of the Angevins'.]

NOTES

1. Outline of the Reign

1 Quoted in Wendover, *Flowers of History*, 379.
2 Kings John, Richard and Henry II are known as Angevins, a term derived from their association with the county of Anjou in France. The term 'Angevin empire' was first coined by K. Norgate in 1902. It appears in speech marks because it is by no means accepted by all historians. Chapter 3 discusses the difficulties associated with this term.
3 Tyerman, *Who's Who*, 309.
4 Quoted in Holt, *King John*, 19.
5 Quoted in Gransden, *Historical Writing in England 550c.–1307 vol. 1*, 327.
6 Quoted in Holt, *King John*, 21.
7 Quoted in ibid., 12.
8 Gransden, *Historical Writing*, 348–9.
9 Quoted in Gransden, *Historical Writing*, 343.
10 Warren, *King John*, 14.
11 Stubbs in A. Hassal (ed.), *Historical Introductions to the Rolls Series*, 239, 442–3, 487.
12 Green, *A Short History of the English People*, 122.
13 Norgate, *John Lackland*, 286. Ramsey, *Angevin Empire*, 502.
14 Harvey, *The Plantagenets*, 78.
15 http://www.imdb.com/title/tt0063227/usercomments (accessed 21 April 2011).
16 Montefiore, *Monsters: History's Most Evil Men and Women* (London: Quercus, 2008).
17 *BBC History Magazine*, June 2010.
18 Hollister, 'King John and the Historians', 16.
19 Warren, *King John*, 259.
20 Turner, *King John England's Evil King?*, 199.
21 Warren, *King John*, 13.
22 Galbraith, *Roger Wendover and Matthew Paris*, 17–18, 35, 36. Compare this to Stubbs' approach: 'there is no reason to suppose that that historian [i.e. Paris] uttered more than the intelligent opinion of his own time justified' (Stubbs in A. Hassal (ed.) *Historical Introductions*, 239, 442–3, 487). Stubbs was Regius Professor of Modern History at Oxford (1866–84) and latterly a bishop, in which role he espoused the morality of the Victorian age writ large.

23 Crouch, *William Marshal*, 6.
24 Hardy (ed.), *Rottuli Litterarum*, xxx.
25 Galbraith, *Roger Wendover and Matthew Paris*, 16. Warren, *King John*, 13.
26 Turner, *King John*, 199.
27 Appleby, *John King of England*, 274–5.
28 Latimer, 'Early Thirteenth-Century Prices', in Church (ed.), *King John New Interpretations*, 54.
29 Warren, *King John*, 99.

2. John in the Shadows, 1167–1199

1 Fontevrault Abbey, near Chinon in Anjou was patronized by the Plantagenets. This is where Henry II, Eleanor of Aquitaine, Richard I and Isabella of Angoulême, second wife of John, are buried.
2 Quoted in Warren, *King John*, 24.
3 Eleanor was held prisoner for at least ten years after 1174.
4 It is interesting that Geoffrey was never promised more than this, perhaps because he was seen as being too close to Philip Augustus who, apparently, was so distraught at the death of Geoffrey that he had to be restrained from throwing himself into the latter's grave.
5 K. Norgate asserts that it was Henry II who gave John this name. The author of the *Estoire de la guerre sainte* was a contemporary of John's and refers to him as Jean sans Terre. Norgate, *John Lackland*, 1.
6 Norgate, *John Lackland*, 6.
7 Warren, 'John in Ireland, 1185', in Bossy and Jupp (eds), *Essays Presented to Michael Roberts*, 14.
8 Gerald of Wales quoted in Duffy, 'John and Ireland: The Origins of England's Irish Problem', in Church (ed.), *King John*, 229.
9 Warren, *King John*, 36.
10 Roger of Howden quoted in Duffy, 'John and Ireland: The Origins of England's Irish Problem', in Church (ed.), *King John*, 232.
11 Norgate, *John Lackland*, 18.
12 Duffy, 'John and Ireland: The Origins of England's Irish Problem', in Church (ed.), *King John*, 224.
13 Warren, *King John*, 37.
14 Quoted in Norgate, *John Lackland*, 23.
15 Gerald of Wales, *Concerning the Instruction of Princes*, 384.
16 Jerusalem had fallen to Saladin in 1187.
17 Norgate, *John Lackland*, 28.
18 For instance, by the autumn of 1191 a dozen counties had new sheriffs selected by the chancellor, and among them were two of his brothers.
19 William of Newburgh quoted in Warren, *King John*, 41; in R.V. Turner, *Oxford DNB* entry on William Longchamp, http://www.oxforddnb.com/view/article/16980?docPos=2 (accessed 14 May 2012).
20 Richard married Berengaria of Navarre on 12 May 1191. He had for some time been betrothed to Alice, the sister of Philip Augustus.
21 An illegitimate son of Henry II. He was born around 1151. Archbishop of York 1191–1212.

22 Coutances acted as justiciar until 1194 when he was replaced by Hubert Walter.
23 Roger of Howden quoted in Warren, *King John*, 45. Richard was freed on 4 February 1194 and landed in England on 13 March.
24 *History of William the Marshal* quoted in Warren, *King John*, 46.
25 Turner, *King John*, 27.
26 Ibid., 22.
27 Petit-Dutaillis, *Feudal Monarchy*, 215.
28 See chapter 7 in Eysench, *Decline and Fall*.
29 Duffy, 'John and Ireland: The Origins of England's Irish Problem', in Church (ed.), *King John*, 232.
30 Warren, 'John in Ireland, 1185', in Bossy and Jupp (eds), *Essays Presented to Michael Roberts*, 19.
31 Ibid., 18.
32 Ibid., 21.
33 Duffy, 'John and Ireland: The Origins of England's Irish Problem', in Church (ed.), *King John*, 233.
34 M. T. Flannagan, *Oxford DNB* entry on Hugh de Lacy, www.oxforddnb.com/view/article/15852/?back=,15853(accessed 12 June 2012).
35 Warren, *King John*, 36.
36 Turner, *King John*, 30.
37 R. Bartlett, *Oxford DNB* entry for Gerald of Wales. Gerald asserts that Henry II 'deserved to be punished for his grave excesses and irregularities through his own offspring…and even his last breath should be disturbed with anxiety'. Gerard of Wales, *Concerning the Instruction of Princes*, 381–2.
38 William of Newburgh, *History of English Affairs*, book V, chapter 5.
39 See Norgate, *John Lackland*, 53. Explanations for John's recovery of Évreux in 1194 have proved controversial.
40 Warren, *King John*, 46.
41 Appleby, *England without Richard*, 36–7.
42 Carpenter, *Coggeshall's Account*, 1225.
43 Howden quoted in Gillingham, *Richard I*, 117.
44 Gillingham, *Richard I*, 118.
45 William of Newburgh, *History*, book 4.
46 Gillingham, *Richard I*, 120.
47 Green, *Short History*, 112.

3. An 'Imperial' Inheritance?

1 Barlow, *Feudal Kingdom*, 160.
2 It is worth noting that Eustace had a younger brother, William. He was aged around eighteen in 1153 and there is a significant 'what might have been' here. But, as Warren put it, 'the death of Eustace seems to have robbed him of resolution' (Warren, *King John*, 51). Moreover, the death of Stephen so soon after the formation of the Treaty of Winchester probably encouraged the political elite to abide by its terms.
3 In 1166 Henry II betrothed his son, Geoffrey, to Constance of Brittany. The marriage took place in 1181. This union produced Arthur.
4 Gerald of Wales, *Topography of Ireland*, quoted in Aurell, *Plantagenet Empire 1154–1224*, 1.

5 Gillingham, *The Angevin Empire*, 1.
6 This is discussed more fully in Section B (ii), Chapter 3.
7 Warren, *King John*, 90, 99.
8 Gillingham, *Angevin Empire*, 100.
9 Le Patourel, *Norman Empire*, 195.
10 Orderic Vitalis quoted in Carpenter, *Struggle for Mastery*, 126.
11 Orderic Vitalis, *Ecclesiastical History*, VI, 455.
12 D. Crouch, 'Normans and Anglo Normans: A divided aristocracy?', in Bates and Curry (eds), *England and Normandy*, 52.
13 E. Tabuteau has established that a great many of the Anglo-Norman French families had fallen into a continental and insular branch long before 1135. See Tabuteau, 'The Role of Law'.
14 D. Crouch, 'Normans and Anglo Normans: A divided aristocracy?' in Bates and Curry (eds), *England and Normandy*, 63.
15 Ibid., 45.
16 See Green, 'Unity and Disunity', *Historical Research*, 131–2.
17 D. Crouch, 'Normans and Anglo Normans: A divided aristocracy?' in Bates and Curry (eds), *England and Normandy*, 62.
18 Ibid., 67.
19 Aurell, *Plantagenet Empire, 1154–1224*, 3.
20 Hollister, *Monarchy, Magnates and Institutions*, 56.
21 Gillingham, *Richard the Lionheart*, 281. Holt, 'End of the Anglo-Norman Realm', *Proceedings of the British Academy*, 240. Vincent, *Peter des Roches*, 43. Richardson, review of Boussard, 'Le Governement d'Henri II', 660.
22 Warren, *Henry II*, 627.
23 R. V. Turner, *King John*, 49.
24 Gillingham, *Angevin Empire*, 32.
25 Davies, *Domination and Conquest*, 46.
26 There has been considerable debate as to what Count Fulk and Henry I did in fact intend by this marriage. Whereas Hollister and Keefe ('Making of the Angevin Empire') have doubted whether Henry sought to make Geoffrey his heir, Gillingham is of the opinion that 'there seems no good reason to doubt' it (*The Angevin Empire*, 11).
27 This was to cause John problems after the death of his mother in 1204.
28 Holt, 'End of the Anglo-Norman Realm', 241–2.
29 Turner and Heiser, *Richard Lionheart*, 33.
30 Ibid., 34.
31 Ibid., 35.
32 Ibid., 54.
33 Aurell believes that Henry II and his sons rendered homage on perhaps twelve occasions in total (Aurell, *Plantagenet Empire*).
34 Everard and Hallam, *Capetian France*, 218.
35 Gervase of Canterbury quoted in Gillingham, 'Doing Homage to the King of France', in Harper-Bill and Vincent (eds), *New Interpretations*, 80.
36 According to Bradbury, *Philip Augustus*, 253.
37 Turner and Heiser, *Richard Lionheart*, 41–2.
38 Bradbury, *Philip Augustus*, 333.
39 Charlemagne expanded the Frankish kingdom into a Frankish empire that incorporated much of Western and Central Europe.
40 See Hallam and Everard, *Capetian France*, 239–45 for a useful summary of this.

41 Turner and Heiser, *Richard Lionheart*, 49.
42 Hollister, 'Normandy, France and the Anglo-Norman Regnum', 202–42.
43 Turner and Heiser, *Richard Lionheart*, 53.
44 Carpenter, *Struggle for Mastery*, 193.
45 Holt, 'The End of the Anglo-Norman Realm', 254.
46 Aurrell, *The Plantagenet Empire*, 10.
47 Gillingham, 'Doing Homage to the King of France', in Harper-Bill and Vincent (eds), *New Interpretations*, 67.
48 Ibid., 83.
49 Gillingham, *Angevin Empire*, 125.

4. War of Succession and the Loss of Continental Territories, 1199–1204

1 Quoted in Bradbury, *Philip Augustus*, 130.
2 Richardson and Sayles, *Governance*, 323.
3 Painter, *King John*, 8.
4 Quoted in Warren, *King John*, 49.
5 Warren, *King John*, 48.
6 Holt, 'Alienor d'Aquitaine', 97.
7 Philip had insisted that John surrender the Vexin and that Poitou, Anjou and Touraine and Maine be transferred to Arthur. Norgate, *John Lackland*, 68.
8 Roger Howden quoted in Norgate, *John Lackland*, 69.
9 Warren, *King John*, 53.
10 Indeed, it was during one of these campaigns that Richard lost his life.
11 Turner, *King John*, 89.
12 Wendover, *Flowers of History*, vol. 2, 188.
13 Warren, *King John*, 67.
14 'Isabella was very much more than an innocent provincial heiress. The descendant of kings, she was close kinswoman to most of the ruling houses of Christendom.' Vincent in Church (ed.), *New Interpretations*, 179.
15 Warren, *King John*, 74.
16 Powicke, *Loss of Normandy*, 148.
17 Warren, *King John*, 77.
18 Quoted in Warren, *King John*, 79.
19 Warren, *King John*, 79.
20 Powicke, *Loss of Normandy*, 153.
21 Warren, *King John*, 80.
22 McLynn, *Lionheart and Lackland*, 304.
23 Quoted in Warren, *King John*, 81.
24 Twenty-two of the twenty-five prisoners held in Corfe castle were starved to death after an attempted break-out.
25 Quoted in Warren, *King John*, 82–3.
26 Appleby, *King John*, 129.
27 Holt, *King John*, 18.
28 Quoted in Holt, *King John*, 18.
29 Quoted in Bradbury, *Philip Augustus*, 147.
30 Warren, *King John*, 88.

31 Quoted in Warren, *King John*, 88.
32 Warren, *King John*, 97.
33 Wendover, *Flowers of History*, 207.
34 Holt, *King John*, 17.
35 Quoted in Warren, *King John*, 133.
36 Warren, *King John*, 99.
37 Turner, 'King John's military reputation reconsidered', 171.
38 Norgate, *John Lackland*, 96.
39 Turner, *King John*, 50.
40 Warren, *King John*, 57.
41 Warren, *King John*, 63. Not all historians agree with this interpretation. See the next section of this chapter.
42 Hallam and Everard, *Capetian France*, 183. Baldwin, *Government of Philip Augustus*, 97.
43 Bartlett, *Norman and Angevin Kings*, 27. Carpenter, *Struggle for Mastery*, 264.
44 Norgate, *John Lackland*. 74.
45 Holt, 'King John and Arthur of Brittany', 90.
46 Humbert Humbert is the middle-aged male protagonist who becomes obsessed and sexually involved with a twelve-year-old girl in Vladimir Nabokov's novel *Lolita*.
47 Coggeshall says that in 1200 she appeared about 12.
48 N. Vincent, 'Isabella of Angoulême: John's Jezebel', in Church (ed.), *New Interpretations*, 175.
49 This point is strengthened by an appreciation of the fecundity of Isabella: she had five children to John and nine to her second husband, Hugh, the son of her intended husband in 1200.
50 Richardson and Sayles, *Governance*, 325.
51 Bradbury, *Philip Augustus*, 141, referring to the work of Duby and Petit-Dutaillis.
52 Quoted in Powicke, *Loss of Normandy*, 149.
53 Ibid.
54 Norgate, *John Lackland*, 77.
55 Powicke, *Loss of Normandy*, 142.
56 Painter, *King John*, 27.
57 Turner, *King John*, 94.
58 *History of William the Marshal*, quoted in Turner, *King John*, 93.
59 Bradbury, *Philip Augustus*, 161.
60 *History of William the Marshal*, quoted in Warren, *King John*, 91.
61 *Howden. Chron.*, IV, 66, quoted in Gillingham, *Richard I*, 342.
62 Coggeshall quoted in Gillingham, *Richard I*, 332.
63 Turner and Heiser, *Richard Lionheart*, 44.
64 See Holt, 'The Loss of Normandy', in Holt and Gillingham (eds), *War and Government*, 93–105.
65 Moss, 'Norman Fiscal Revolution 1191–1198' in Ormrod, Bonney and Bonney (eds), *Essays in European Fiscal History*, 41–61.
66 Ibid., 115.
67 Turner, *King John*, 71.
68 Turner and Heiser, *Richard Lionheart*, 43.
69 Holt, 'The Loss of Normandy', in Holt and Gillingham (eds), *War and Government*, 92–105.
70 N. Barratt, 'The Revenues of John and Philip Augustus Revisited' in Church (ed.), *New Interpretations*, 75–100.

71 Bradbury, *Philip Augustus*, 267.
72 Moss quoted in Turner and Heiser, *Richard Lionheart*, 47–8.
73 From an unpublished paper by Moss, quoted in Turner and Heiser, *Richard Lionheart*, 44.
74 Southern, 'England's first Entry into Europe', *Medieval Humanism*, 152.
75 Gillingham, *Richard I*, 338.
76 The figure of £134,000 is suggested by J. Ramsay, *A History of the Revenue of the Kings of England 1066–1399*, vol. 1, (Oxford: Clarendon Press, 1938), 236–8. He based his estimate on the Thirteenth of 1207, which he reckoned to have raised in England over £57,000. Gillingham, *Angevin Empire*, 99.
77 Gillingham, *Angevin Empire*, 100. Figures produced by N. Barratt suggest an average English revenue 1210–1212 of £63,838 p.a.
78 Gillingham, *Richard I*, 342.
79 Gillingham, *Angevin Empire*, 60–61.
80 Gillingham, *Richard the Lionheart*, 304.
81 Ibid.
82 Quoted in Gillingham, *Richard I*, 341.
83 What follows in this paragraph is a summary of what can be found in Gillingham, *Richard the Lionheart*, 303–4; Gillingham, *Angevin Empire*, 95–100; and Gillingham, *Richard I*, 338–46.
84 Gillingham, *Angevin Empire*, 100.
85 Gillingham, *Richard the Lionheart*, 303.
86 Gillingham, *Angevin Empire*, 98.
87 Gillingham, *Richard I*, 340.
88 For a summary of the key problems with the evidence see Barratt, 'Revenues of John and Philip Augustus Revisited', in Church (ed.), *New Interpretations*, 76.
89 Gillingham, *Richard I*, 339. Holt, *Loss of Normandy*, 99.
90 Turner and Heiser, *Richard Lionheart*, 47.

5. Efforts to Regain the French Territories, 1205–1214

 1 Warren, *King John*, 102.
 2 Quoted in Warren, *King John*, 111.
 3 Hundred: a local unit of civil administration in England, a subdivision of the county.
 4 Turner, *King John*, 96.
 5 Warren, *King John*, 100–101.
 6 Wendover, *Flowers of History*, 214.
 7 Turner, *King John*, 96. Gillingham has challenged this view, preferring instead to give the credit for the founding of the British navy to Richard (see Gillingham, 'Richard I, Galley-Warfare and Portsmouth: The Beginnings of a Royal Navy' in Prestwich, Britnell and Frame (eds), *Proceedings of the Durham Conference 1995*, 1–15).
 8 McLynn, *Lionheart and Lackland*, 331.
 9 Warren, *King John*, 112.
10 Painter, *William Marshal*, 140.
11 *History of William the Marshal*, quoted in Warren, *King John*, 114.
12 Wendover, *Flowers of History*, 219.
13 Turner, *King John*, 98.

14 Baldwin, *Philip Augustus*, 204.
15 Fryde, 'King John and the Empire', in Church (ed.), *New Interpretations*, 345.
16 Warren, *King John*, 218.
17 Ibid., 125.
18 Coggeshall, quoted in Warren, *King John*, 218.
19 Warren, *King John*, 222.
20 Wendover, *Flowers of History*, 298.
21 Bradbury, *Philip Augustus*, 304.
22 Baldwin, *Philip Augustus*, 218.
23 From an account of Bouvines known as *The Relatio Marchianesis de Pugna Bouvini*. http://www.deremilitari.org/RESOURCES/SOURCES/bouvines1.htm (accessed 25 October 2010).
24 Ullmann, *Short History of the Papacy*, 212.
25 Bradbury, *Philip Augustus*, 312.

6. The British Perspective: Scotland, Ireland and Wales, 1199–1214

1 Carpenter, *Struggle for Mastery*, 277.
2 Quoted in Carpenter, *Struggle for Mastery*, 284.
3 Warren, *King John*, 192.
4 Carpenter, *Struggle for Mastery*, 277.
5 Duncan, 'John King of England and Kings of Scots', in Church (ed.), *New Interpretations*, 252.
6 The fact that Philip was already married was not an insuperable issue.
7 W. W. Scott, *Oxford DNB* entry on William the Lion, http://www.oxforddnb.com/view/article/29452?docPos=1 (accessed 14 May 2012).
8 Warren, *King John*, 194.
9 Norgate, *John Lackland*, 138.
10 Duffy, 'John and Ireland: The Origins of England's Irish Problem', in Church (ed.), *New Interpretations*, 235.
11 Carpenter, *Struggle for Mastery*, 278.
12 Ibid., 281.
13 Wendover, *Flowers of History*, 254.
14 Warren, 'The Historian as a "Private Eye"', 14.
15 The figure 700 is from Turner, *King John*, 107.
16 Carpenter, *Struggle for Mastery*, 280.
17 Warren, *King John*, 196.
18 Turner, *King John*, 108.
19 Martin, 'John, lord of Ireland', in Cosgrove (ed.), *A New History of Ireland*, 142.
20 Quoted in Poole, *Domesday Book to Magna Carta*, 317.
21 Martin, 'John, lord of Ireland', in Cosgrove (ed.), *A New History of Ireland*, 132.
22 Warren's remarks appear, respectively, in Warren, *King John*, 196 and Warren, 'The Historian as a "Private Eye"', 16. Curtis, *A History of medieval Ireland*, 111–14. Lydon, *The Lordship of Ireland*, 65.
23 Duffy, 'King John's Expedition to Ireland: The Evidence Reconsidered', 2.
24 Ibid., 10.
25 Wendover, *Flowers of History*, 263.
26 I. W. Rowlands, 'King John and Wales', in Church (ed.), *New Interpretations*, 276.

27 Quoted in Turner, *King John*, 103.

28 I. W. Rowlands, 'King John and Wales', in Church (ed.), *New Interpretations*, 274.

29 Davies, *Domination and Conquest*, 79.

30 Carpenter, *Struggle for Mastery*, 282.

31 I. W. Rowlands, 'King John and Wales', in Church (ed.), *New Interpretations*, 279.

32 A. D. Carr, 'Anglo-Welsh relations 1066–1282', in Jones and Vale (eds), *England and Her Neighbours*, 128.

33 In light of John's difficulties with Llywelyn the Great after 1212, I. W. Rowlands argues that 'it was not the case that he had gone too far but rather that he had not gone far enough'. In Church (ed.), *New Interpretations*, 286.

34 There was particular resentment of their building of castles.

35 Chroniclers differ over the number of hostages executed.

36 Barnwell Annalist quoted in Warren, *King John*, 200.

37 Painter, *King John*, 249–50.

38 R. V. Turner, *Oxford DNB* entry on de Briouze. http://www.oxforddnb.com/view/article/3283?docPos=4 (accessed 22 February 2012).

39 Wendover, *Flowers of History*, 247–8. Turner, in his *Oxford DNB* entry on William de Briouze (http://www.oxforddnb.com/view/article/3283, accessed 12 June 2012), says that he was almost certainly with John at Rouen when Arthur's disappeared in early April 1203, and he may even have encouraged John to end the boy's life. Two sources for young Arthur's death, the annals of Margam Abbey in Glamorgan and the *Philippide* of Guillaume le Breton, reflect information supplied to the authors by William de Briouze; he had close ties to Margam Abbey, and its annals supply the fullest account of any chronicle of Arthur's death.

40 The Annals of Dunstable and of Oseney simply say that they 'died in prison'.

41 Holden, 'King John, the Briouzes and the Celtic Fringe', 1.

42 Carpenter, *Struggle for Mastery*, 280.

43 Poole, *Domesday Book to Magna Carta*, 315.

44 McLynn, *Lionheart and Lackland*, 347. A Moloch is an ancient Semitic god to whom children were sacrificed.

45 Martin, 'John, lord of Ireland', in Cosgrove (ed.), *A New History of Ireland*, 134.

46 Quoted from Old Irish Lawcodes in Bartlett, *Norman and Angevin Kings*, 49.

47 Quoted in Bartlett, *Angevin Kings*, 50.

48 Holt, *The Barons and the Great Charter*, 3.

49 Wendover, *Flowers of History*, 248.

50 Jones, *King John*, 27.

51 Quoted in Norgate, *John Lackland*, 287–8.

52 Holden, 'King John, the Briouzes and the Celtic Fringe', 9.

53 Norgate, *John Lackland*, 287.

7. *Sacerdotium* and *Regnum*, 1199–1214

1 Cheney and Semple (eds), *Selected Letters*, x.

2 Ibid., xi.

3 Turner, *King John*, 109.

4 Christopher Harper-Bill, 'John and the Church of Rome', in Church (ed.), *New Interpretations*, 295.

5 Some single acts of patronage could be substantial. William, Count of Mortain founded a religious house at Montacute in 1100 and bestowed upon it each of the following: Montacute parish church; the borough and market and the castle and castle chapel of Montacute; his demense orchards and vineyard, the manor and mill at Montacute; the manors and churches of Tintinhull, Creech St Michael, East Chinnock, Closworth and West Mudford and lands and churches in Somerset, Doreset, Devon and Cornwall. Walter de Spec gave 1,000 acres to Rievaulx.

6 Saul, *Medieval England*, 59.

7 Quoted in Bartlett, *Norman and Angevin Kings*, 386.

8 Gerald of Wales in Daniel, 151.

9 Bartlett, *Norman and Angevin Kings*, 395.

10 For instance: in 1101, with the prospect of an invasion by Robert Curthose, Duke of Normandy, the chronicler Eadmer records that had it not been for the actions of Archbishop Anselm, 'King Henry would at that time have lost the English throne'; and in 1138 it was Archbishop Thurstan of York who led the victorious English army against the Scots at the Battle of the Standard.

11 See Douglas and Greenaway (eds), *English Historical Documents II*, 903–6.

12 On average, a bishop appointed during the period 1066–1216 'could expect to preside over his diocese for well over a decade and might survive much longer'. Bartlett, *Norman and Angevin Kings*, 395.

13 See Douglas and Greenaway (eds), *English Historical Documents II*, 718–22.

14 Warren, *King John*, 160.

15 Turner, 'Richard Lionheart and English Episcopal Elections', 3.

16 Philip Augustus had married Ingeborg of Denmark in 1193. He sought a divorce on the grounds of consanguinity, though the papacy stated the marriage to be valid. Despite the fact that he was still married, he took another wife in June 1196, Agnes. The papacy thus pronounced an interdict on France. When Agnes died in 1201 Ingeborg was restored and the interdict was lifted.

17 Peter des Roches was consecrated on 25 September 1205.

18 Quoted in Harper-Bill, 'John and the Church of Rome', in Church (ed.) *New Interpretations*, 303.

19 Turner, *King John*, 112.

20 Cheney, *Innocent III*, 99–100.

21 Harper-Bill, 'John and the Church of Rome', in Church (ed.), *New Interpretations*, 301.

22 Quoted in Norgate, *John Lackland*, 113.

23 Painter, *King John*, 155.

24 Wendover, *Flowers of History*, 238.

25 Barlow, *Feudal Kingdom*, 332.

26 Wendover, *Flowers of History*, 240.

27 Ibid.

28 Painter, *King John*, 170.

29 Quoted in Norgate, *John Lackland*, 127.

30 Carpenter, *Struggle for Mastery*, 275.

31 Quoted in Warren, *King John*, 164.

32 Ibid.

33 Quoted in Warren, *King John*, 165.

34 Warren, *King John*, 166.

35 Philip Augustus had ended his adulterous affair within a few months of an interdict being pronounced. See note 16.
36 Turner, *King John*, 119. Harper-Bill, 'John and the Church of Rome', in Church (ed.), *New Interpretations*, 307.
37 Warren, *King John*, 169.
38 John de Gray remained as bishop of Norwich. He was justiciar in Ireland, 1209–11.
39 Rothwell (ed.) *English Historical Documents 1189–1327*, 306–7.
40 Warren, *King John*, 13.
41 H. G. Richardson, quoted in Painter, *King John*, 270.
42 Poole, *Domesday Book to Magna Carta*, 446.
43 Wendover, *Flowers of History*, 246 and 247.
44 Painter, *King John*, 184.
45 Cheney, 'King John and the Papal Interdict', in *Papacy and England*, 307.
46 The story is reproduced in Warren, *King John*, 14–15.
47 Cheney, 'King John and the Papal Interdict', in *Papacy and England*, 308.
48 Ibid., 317.
49 Painter, *King John*, 176.
50 Turner, 'Richard Lionheart and English Episcopal Elections', 2.
51 Quoted in Warren, *King John*, 210.
52 Quoted in Norgate, *John Lackland*, 183.
53 Thomas Swynnerton, *A Muster of Schismatic Bishops of Rome 1534*, quoted in Levine, *Propaganda in the English Reformation*, 81 and 90.
54 William Tyndale, *The Obedience of a Christian Man 1527/8*, quoted in Levine, *Propaganda in the English Reformation*, 61.
55 Thomas Swynnerton, *A Muster of Schismatic Bishops of Rome 1534*, quoted in Levine, *Propaganda in the English Reformation*, 61.
56 Levine, *Propaganda in the English Reformation*, 130.
57 Quoted in ibid., 183.
58 Quoted in Turner, *King John*, 123.
59 Cheney and Semple (eds), *Selected Letters*, 163.
60 Quoted in Warren, *King John*, 245–6.
61 Norgate, *John Lackland*, 184.
62 Painter, *King John*, 194. Cheney, *Innocent III*, 335. Poole, *Domesday Book to Magna Carta*, 458.
63 Cheney and Semple (eds), *Selected Letters*, X.

8. Administration, Justice and Finance

1 Danziger and Gillingham, *The Year of Magna Carta*, 177.
2 Bartlett, *Norman and Angevin Kings*, 126.
3 Quoted in Warren, *Henry II*, 301.
4 Bartlett, *Norman and Angevin Kings*, 200.
5 Ibid., 198.
6 So great had the press of business become that by 1200 a 'Michaelmas' session of the Exchequer might go on until the following March and an 'Easter' session until the beginning of August. Warren, *The Governance of Norman and Angevin England*, 129.

7 Swanton (ed.), *Anglo-Saxon Chronicles*, 266.
8 Stenton, *English Justice*, chapter 2.
9 These figures are obtained from Carpenter, *Struggle for Mastery*. The figures which are used in the rest of this section are taken from the following sources: Bartlett, *Norman and Angevin Kings*; Turner, *King John*; Church (ed.), *New Interpretations*; Warren, *King John*; J. A. P. Jones, *King John*.
10 John had five children between 1207 and 1215.
11 Bartlett, *Norman and Angevin Kings*, 177.
12 Turner, *King John*, 85.
13 Quoted in Turner, *King John*, 161.
14 Barnwell Annalist quoted in Warren, *King John*, 150.
15 This is the estimate of Turner, *King John*, 75.
16 Turner, *King John*, 80.
17 Barlow, *Feudal Kingdom of England*, 328.
18 Hardy (ed.), *Rotuli Litterarum Patentium*, i.
19 Clancy, *England 1066–1272*, 137.
20 Warren, *King John*, 126.
21 Wendover, *Flowers of History*, vol. 2, 325.
22 Green, *A Short History*, 129–30.
23 Poole, *Domesday Book to Magna Carta*, 477.
24 Chrimes, 'An Introduction to the Administrative History of Medieval England', 72. Warren, *King John*, 132. Holt, *King John*, 13.
25 Holt, *King John*, 13–14.
26 Gillingham, *Richard the Lionheart*, 278–9.
27 Bartlett, *Norman and Angevin Kings*, 200.
28 Warren, *King John*, 134.
29 Lyon, *Constitutional and Legal History*, 253.
30 Hardy (ed.), *Rotuli Litterarum Patentium*, ix.
31 Quoted in Holt, *King John*, 6.
32 Warren, *King John*, 5.
33 Turner, *King John*, 160.
34 Stenton, *English Justice*, 113–14.
35 Barber, *Henry Plantagenet*, 60.
36 Flower, *Introduction to curia Regis rolls*, 495–6.
37 Loyn, *Constitutional and Legal History*, 281.
38 Quoted in Jones, *King John*, 78.
39 Turner, 'John and Justice', in Church (ed.), *New Interpretations*, 320.
40 See Harvey, 'English Inflation'.
41 Warren, *King John*, 150.
42 Painter, *King John*, 238.
43 Turner, *King John*, 77.
44 Keefe, *Feudal Assessments*, 128–9.
45 Poole, *Obligations of Society*, 107.
46 See R. Lockyer, *Henry VII*, 3rd ed. (London: Longman, 1997); S. Cunningham, *Henry VII* (London: Routledge, 2007).
47 Holt, *The Barons and the Great Charter*, 14 and 17.
48 Painter, *King John*, 223.
49 Bartlett, *Norman and Angevin Kings*, 168.

9. Civil War: A False Start, 1215

1 Douglas and Greenaway (eds) *English Historical Documents II*, 400–401.
2 Danziger and Gillingham, *1215*, 261.
3 Historians cannot agree on the veracity or otherwise of Wendover's account. J. C. Holt asserts that 'there is no supporting evidence for it' (Holt, *Magna Carta*, 137); Clanchy, however, believes that Holt 'is over critical of Wendover's account' (Clanchy, *England and its Rulers*, 138).
4 Wendover, *Flowers of History*, 276–8.
5 Ibid., 303.
6 Holt, *Magna Carta*, 188.
7 Ibid., 200.
8 Turner, *King John*, 171.
9 Rothwell (ed.), *English Historical Documents III*, 310–11.
10 Wendover, *Flowers of History*, 305.
11 Warren, *King John*, 233. Painter, *King John*, 300.
12 Quoted in Norgate, *John Lackland*, 226.
13 See Rothwell (ed.), *English Historical Documents III*, 311–16.
14 See note 17.
15 Warren, *King John*, 232.
16 Free men made up perhaps 50 per cent of the population of early thirteenth century England, though their geographical distribution varied. In contrast to an unfree villein, a free man, amongst other things, was able to buy and sell land, leave his manor, own goods and chattels and enjoy access to the royal courts.
17 'Magna Carta: Treasures in Full', British Library. http://www.bl.uk/treasures/magnacarta/translation/mc_trans.html (accessed 26 October 2010).
18 Miller, 'Background of Magna Carta', 74.
19 Painter, *King John*, 212.
20 Ibid., 212 and 214.
21 Figures from Carpenter, *Struggle for Mastery*, 271.
22 Holt, *Northerners*, 34.
23 Turner, *King John*, 169 and 170.
24 *Rymer's Foedera*, quoted in Turner, *King John*, 170.
25 Turner, *King John*, 172.
26 Danziger and Gillingham, *1215*, 180.
27 Bradbury, 'Philip Augustus and King John in King John', in Church (ed.), *New Interpretations*, 353.
28 Tyerman, *Who's Who*, 305.
29 Coggeshall quoted in Vincent, *Peter des Roches*, 89.
30 Warren, *King John*, 225. Vincent, *Peter des Roches*, 89–113.
31 Miller, *Background of Magna Carta*, 75.
32 Quoted in Warren, *King John*, 231.
33 Holt, *King John*, 23.
34 Turner, *King John*, 189.
35 Quoted in Turner, *King John*, 189.
36 Quoted in Holt, *Magna Carta and the Idea of Liberty*, 114.
37 Hindley, *Brief History of Magna Carta*, 289.
38 Gillingham and Danziger, *1215*, 262.

39 King Stephen (r. 1135–1154). For much of his reign he was at war with his cousin Matilda. The Anglo-Saxon Chronicle averred that during these years 'men said openly that Christ and his angels slept'.

40 For perhaps the first espousal of the interpretation that Magna Carta is a document of feudal reaction see C. Petit-Dutaillis, *Studies Supplementary to Stubbs*, I, 127ff.

41 Quoted in Warren, *King John*, 232.

42 M. Strickland, *Oxford DNB* entry on Robert Fitz Walter http://www.oxforddnb.com/view/article/9648?docPos=1 (accessed 26 October 2010).

10. Civil War Renewed, 1215–1216

1 Carpenter, *Struggle for Mastery*, 297.

2 Cheney and Semple (eds), *Selected Letters*, 215–16.

3 Powicke quoted in Turner, *King John*, 190.

4 Warren, *King John*, 242.

5 Quoted in Warren, *King John*, 242.

6 Quoted in ibid., 191.

7 'Innocent's letter to the bishop of Winchester', in Cheney and Semple (eds), *Selected Letters*, 208.

8 Painter, *King John*, 349.

9 Ibid., 352.

10 Annals of Waverley.

11 Painter, *King John*, 363.

12 Quoted in Warren, *King John*, 247.

13 Wendover, *Flowers of History*, 351.

14 Warren, *King John*, 251.

15 Quoted in Warren, *King John*, 253.

16 Warren, *King John*, 256.

17 Turner says that this epithet is 'assumed today to derive from [John's] loss of Normandy, 1202–4. In fact, Gervase of Canterbury states that it was first applied in 1200 by John's detractors, hostile to the peace of Le Goulet. Gervase himself thought the king had been wise in preferring peace to war'. Turner, 'King John's Military Reputation Reconsidered', 173.

18 Turner, 'King John's Military Reputation Reconsidered', 183.

19 Quoted in ibid., 173.

20 Wendover, *Flowers of History*, 207.

21 Quoted in Bradbury, *Philip Augustus*, 149.

22 M. Powicke, 'England: Richard and John', in Tanner, Previte-Orton, Brooke (eds), *Cambridge Medieval History*, vol. 6, 219.

23 Warren, *King John*, 99 and 248.

24 Gillingham, *Angevin Empire*, 80.

25 McLynn, *Lionheart and Lackland*, 473.

26 Poole, *Domesday Book to Magna Carta*, 480.

27 McLynn, *Lionheart and Lackland*, 444. Wendover, *Flowers of History*, 352.

28 Appleby, *John King of England*, 137.

29 Bradbury, *Philip Augustus*, 282.

30 Turner, 'King John's Military Reputation Reconsidered', 171.

31 Quoted in ibid., 175.
32 Brown, *Rochester Castle*, 10–11.
33 Norgate, *John Lackland*, 96. J. R. Green (*Short History of the English People*) usually presented as a supporter of Stubbs' view of John, believed that John's scheme for relieving Chateau-Gailliard 'proved the king's military ability'.
34 Barnwell Chronicler quoted in Holt, *King John*, 24–5.

11. Conclusion: Will the Real King John Please Stand Up?

1 Stubbs 'The Historical Collections of Walter of Coventry', in Hassal (ed.), *Historical Introductions to Rolls Series*, 443. Holt, *King John*, 14.
2 Hollister, 'King John and the Historians', 16.
3 Poole, *Domesday to Magna Carta*, 424.
4 Holt, *King John*, 26.
5 Warren, 'What was wrong with King John?', 806.
6 Stenton, *English Society in the Middle Ages*, 46.
7 Wendover, *Flowers*, 336.

BIBLIOGRAPHY

Appleby, J. T. *England without Richard*. London: G. Bell, 1965.

Aurell, M. *The Plantagenet Empire 1154–1224*, trans. D. Crouch. Harlow: Pearson Longman, 2007.

Bachrach, B. S. 'The Idea of the Angevin Empire'. *Albion* 10 (1978): 294–9.

Baldwin, J. W. *The Government of Philip Augustus*. Berkeley: University of California Press, 1986.

_____. 'Persona et Gesta: The Image and Deeds of the Thirteenth-Century Capetians: The Case of Philip Augustus'. *Viator* 19 (1988): 195–207.

Barber, R. *Henry Plantagenet*. Totowa: Rowman and Littlefield, 1964.

Barlow, F. B. *The Feudal Kingdom of England 1042–1216*. 5th ed. London and New York: Longman, 1999.

Barraclough, G. *The Medieval Papacy*. London: Thames and Hudson, 1968.

Barratt, N. 'The Revenue of King John'. *English Historical Review* 111 (1996): 835–55.

_____. 'Lackland: The loss of Normandy in 1215'. *History Today* 54, Issue 3 (2004).

Bates, D. 'Normandy and England after 1066'. *English Historical Review* 104 (1989): 851–80.

Bartlett, R. *England Under the Norman and Angevin Kings 1075–1225*. New York: Oxford University Press, 2000.

Bates, D and A. Curry (eds). *England and Normandy in the Middle Ages*. London: The Hambledon Press, 1994.

Benjamin, R. 'Angevin Empire'. *History Today* 36, Issue 2 (1986).

Bossy, J. and P. Jupp (eds). *Essays Presented to Michael Roberts*. Belfast: Blackstaff Press, 1976.

Bradbury, J. *Philip Augustus, King of France 1180–1223*. London: Longman, 1998.

Britnell, R., R. Frame and M. Prestwich (eds). *Thirteenth Century England VI: Proceedings of the Durham Conference of 1995*. Woodbridge: Boydell and Brewer, 1997.

Brown, R. Allen. *Rochester Castle*. London: English Heritage, 1986.

Carpenter, D. A. *The Minority of Henry III*. Berkeley: University of California Press, 1990.

_____. 'Abbot Ralph of Coggeshall's Account of the Last Years of King Richard and the First Years of King John'. *English Historical Review* 113 (1998): 1210–30.

_____. *The Struggle for Mastery: The Penguin History of Britain 1066–1284*. London: Penguin, 2003.

Cheney, C. R. 'King John's Reaction to the Interdict on England'. *Transactions of the Royal Historical Society* 31 (1949): 129–50.

_____. *From Becket to Langton English Church Government 1170–1213*. Manchester: Manchester University Press, 1956.

_____. *Innocent III and England*. Stuttgart: Hiersemann, 1976.

_____. *The Papacy and England 12th–14th Centuries*. London: Variorum Reprints, 1982.

Cheney, C. R. and W. H. Semple (eds). *Selected Letters of Pope Innocent III*. London and New York: Thomas Nelson and Sons Ltd, 1953.

Chibnall, Marjorie (trans.), *The Ecclesiastical History of Orderic Vitalis*, vol. 6. Oxford: Clarendon Press, 1968–80.

Church, S. D. 'The Rewards of Royal Service in the Household of King John: A Dissenting Opinion'. *English Historical Review* 110 (1995): 277–302.

_____. 'The 1210 campaign in Ireland: Evidence for a military revolution.' *Anglo-Norman Studies* 20 (1998): 51.

_____(ed.) *King John New Interpretations*. Woodbridge: Boydell and Brewer, 1999.

_____. 'Aspects of the English royal succession, 1066–1199: The death of the king'. *Anglo-Norman Studies* 29 (2007): 17–34.

Chrimes S. B., 'An Introduction to the Administrative History of Mediaeval England', in *Studies in Medieval History*, vol. 7, ed. G. Barraclough. Oxford: Blackwell, 1952.

Clanchy, M. T. *England and its rulers 1066–1272*. 2nd ed. Oxford and Malden, MA: Blackwell, 1998.

Cosgrove, A. (ed.) *A New History of Ireland: Volume II Medieval Ireland 1169–1534*. Oxford and New York: Oxford University Press, 2008.

Crouch, D. *William Marshal*. London: Longman, 1990.

Curtis, E. *A History of Medieval Ireland from 1086 to 1513*. London: Methuen, 1938.

Danziger, D. and J. Gillingham. *1215: The Year of the Magna Carta*. London: Hodder and Stroughton, 2004.

Davies, R. R. (ed.) *The British Isles 1100–1500*. Edinburgh: John Donald Publishers Ltd, 1988.

_____. *Domination and Conquest: The Experience of Ireland, Scotland and Wales, 1100–1300*. Cambridge, New York, Port Chester, Melbourne and Sydney: Cambridge University Press, 1990.

_____. *Age of Conquest*. Oxford and New York: Oxford University Press, 2000.

_____. *The First English Empire: Power and Identities in British Isles 1093–1334*. Oxford and New York: Oxford University Press, 2000.

Devizes, Richard of. *The Chronicle of Richard Devizes of the Time of Richard*, ed. J. T. Appleby. London and New York: Thomas Nelson and Sons Ltd, 1963.

Douglas, D. and G. W. Greenaway (eds). *English Historical Documents 1042–1189, vol. 2*. London and New York: Evre Methuen Ltd, 1953.

Duby, G. *The Legend of Bouvines, War, Religion and Culture in the Middle Ages*, trans. C. Tihanyi. Berkeley: University of California Press, 1990.

_____. *France in the Middle Ages 987–1460*, trans. J. Vale. Oxford: Oxford University Press, 1991.

Duffy, S. 'King John's Expedition to Ireland, 1210: The Evidence Reconsidered '. *Irish Historical Studies* 30 (1996): 1–24.

Dunbabin, J. *France in the Making 843–1180*. Oxford and New York: Oxford University Press, 2000.

Eysench, H. J. *Decline and Fall of the Freudian Empire*. New Brunswick: Transaction Publishers, 2004.

Fawtier, R. *The Capetian Kings of France: Monarchy and Nation, 987–1328*, trans. L. Butler and R. J. Adam. London: Macmillan, 1960.

Flower, C. T. *Introduction to the curia Regis rolls 1199–1230*. Publications of the Seldon Society 62. London: B. Quaritch, 1944.

Fryde, N. F. *Why Magna Carta? Angevin England Revisited*. London and New Brunswick: Transaction Publishers, 2001.

Galbraith, V. H. *Roger Wendover and Matthew Paris*. Glasgow: University of Glasgow: 1944.

———. 'Good kings and bad kings in medieval English History'. *History* 30 (1945): 119–32.

Gillingham, J. *Richard the Lionhart*. London: Book Club Associates, 1978.

———. 'The Fall of the Angevin Empire'. *History Today* 36, Issue 4 (1986).

———. *The Angevin Empire*. London: Hodder Arnold, 2001.

———. *Richard I*. New Haven and London: Yale University Press, 2002.

Gillingham, J. and J. Holt (eds). *War and Government in the Middle Ages: Essays in Honour of J. O. Prestwich*. Woodbridge: Boydell, 1984.

Given- Wilson, C. *Chronicles: The Writing of History in Medieval England*. Hambledon and London: Continuum International Publishing Group, 2004.

Gransden, A. *Historical Writing in England 550c.–1307*, vol 1. London: Routledge and Kegan Paul, 1974.

Green, J. A. *The Aristocracy of Norman England*. Cambridge, New York, Melbourne, Madrid and Cape Town: Cambridge University Press, 1997.

———.'Unity and Disunity in Anglo-Norman State'. *Historical Research* 62 (1989): 115–34.

Green, J. R. *Short History of the English People*. London: Folio Society, 1992.

Hallam, E. (ed.) *The Plantagenet Chronicles*. London: Guild Publishing Ltd, 1986.

Hallam E. and J. Everard. *Capetian France 987–1328*. 2nd ed. New York: Longman, 2001.

Hardy, T. D. (ed.) *Rotuli Litterarum Patentium 1201–1216*. London: Record Commission, 1835.

Harper-Bill, C. and N. Vincent (eds). *Henry II: New Interpretations*. Woodbridge: Boydell & Brewer, 2007.

Harvey, J. *The Plantagenets*. London: Severn House Publishers Ltd, 1948.

Harvey, P. D. A. 'The English Inflation of 1180–1220'. *Past and Present* 61 (1973): 3–30.

Hassall, A. (ed.) *Historical Introductions to Rolls Series*. London: Longmans, Green, and Co., 1902.

Hemholz, R. H. 'Review of Cheney "The Papacy and England 12th –14th Centuries"'. *American Journal of Legal History* 28 (1984): 90–91.

Hindley, G. *A Brief History of Magna Carta*. Philadelphia, New York and London: Running Press, 2008.

Holden, B. W. 'King John, the Braoses and the Celtic Fringe, 1207–1216'. *Albion* 33 (2001): 1–23.

Holden, J. A. (ed.) *History of William the Marshal*, vols 1–3, trans. S. Gregory with notes by D. Crouch. London: Anglo-Norman Text Society, 2004.

Hollister, C. W. 'King John and the Historians'. *Journal of British Studies* 1 (1961): 1–19.

———. 'The Anglo-Norman Civil War'. *English Historical Review* 88 (1973): 315–33.

———. 'Normandy, France and the Anglo-Norman Regnum'. *Speculum* 51 (1976): 202–42.

———. *Monarchy Magnates and Institutions in the Anglo-Norman World*. London: Hambledon Press, 1986.

Hollister C. W. and T. K. Keefe 'The Making of the Angevin Empire'. *Journal of British Studies* 12 (1973): 1–25.

Holt, J. C. 'The Barons and the Great Charter'. *English Historical Review* 274 (1955): 1–24.

_____. *The Northerners: A Study in the Reign of King John.* Oxford: Oxford University Press, 1961.

_____. *King John.* London: Historical Association, 1963.

_____. *Magna Carta and the Idea of Liberty.* New York: John Wiley and Sons, 1972.

_____. 'The End of the Anglo-Norman Realm'. *Proceedings of the British Academy* 61 (1975): 223–265.

_____. *Magna Carta and Medieval Government.* London: Hambledon Press, 1985.

_____.'Alienor d'Aquitaine, Jean san Terre et la succession de 1199'. *Cahiers de Civilisation Medievale* 29 (1986): 95–100.

_____. *Magna Carta.* 2nd ed. Cambridge and New York: Cambridge University Press, 1992.

_____. 'King John and Arthur of Brittany'. *Nottingham Medieval Studies* 44 (2000): 82–103.

Howden, Roger of. *The Annals of Roger de Hoveden,* trans. H. T. Riley. London: Bohn, 1853.

_____. *Chronica,* ed. W. Stubbs, 4 vols, Rolls Series, 1861–1871.

Jolliffe, J. E. A. *Angevin Kingship.* London: Black, 1963.

Jones, J. A. P. *King John and Magna Carta.* London: Longman, 1971.

Jones, W. L. 'Latin Chroniclers from the Eleventh to the Thirteenth Centuries', in *The Cambridge History of English and American Literature,* vol. 1, ed. A. W. Ward and A. R. Waller. Cambridge: Cambridge University Press, 1901–1921.

Jones, M. and M. Vale (eds). *England and her Neighbours, 1066–1453: Essays in Honour of P. Chaplais.* London: The Hambledon Press, 1989.

Keefe, T. K. 'Geoffrey Plantagenet's Will and the Angevin Succession'. *Albion* 6 (1974): 266–74.

_____. *Feudal Assessments and the Political Community under Henry II and His Sons.* Berkeley: University of California Press, 1983.

King, E. B. *Law in Medieval Life and Thought.* Sewanee: University of the South Press, 1990.

Knowles, M. D. 'The Canterbury Election of 1205–1206'. *English Historical Review* 53 (1938): 211–20.

Le Patourel, J. 'The Plantagenet Dominions'. *History* 50 (1965): 289–308.

_____. *Normandy and England 1066–1144.* Reading: University of Reading, 1970.

_____. *The Norman Empire.* Oxford: Oxford University Press, 1976.

_____. *Feudal Empires, Norman and Plantagenet.* London: The Hambledon Press, 1984.

_____. 'Angevin Successions and the Angevin Empire'. *Nottingham Medieval Studies* 44 (2000): 82–103.

Levin, C. 'A Good Prince: King John and Early Tudor Propaganda'. *Sixteenth Century Journal* 11 (1980): 23–32.

_____. *Propaganda in the English Reformation: Heroic and Villainous Images of King John.* Lewiston, New York: Edwin Mellen Press, 1988.

Little, A. G. 'Review of *John Lackland* by K. Norgate'. *English Historical Review* 18 (1903): 349–50.

Lloyd, A. *King John.* Newton Abbot: David and Charles, 1973.

Loengard, J. S. *Magna Carta and the England of King John.* Woodbridge: Boydell and Brewer, 2010.

Lydon, J. F. *The Lordship of Ireland in the Middle Ages.* Dublin: Gill and Macmillan, 1972.

_____(ed.) *England and Ireland in the Later Middle Ages: Essays in Honour of Jocelyn Otway-Ruthven.* Dublin: Irish Academic Press, 1981.

Lyon, B. *A Constitutional and Legal History of Medieval England.* New York: Norton, 1960.

Markowski, M. 'Richard Lionheart: Bad king, bad crusader?' *Journal of Modern History* 23 (1997): 351–65.

McGlynn, S. 'King John and the Barons' Revolt'. *BBC History Magazine,* June 2010.

McLynn, F. *Lionheart and Lackland: King Richard, King John and the Wars of Conquest.* London: Vintage Books, 2007.

Miller, E. 'The background of Magna Carta'. *Past and Present* 23 (1962): 72–83.

Montefiore, S. S. *Monsters: History's most Evil Men and Women.* London: Quercus Publishing, 2008.

Mortimer, R. *Angevin England 1154–1258.* Oxford, UK and Cambridge, MA: Blackwell, 1994.

Newburgh, W. *History.* Medieval Sourcebook.

Norgate, K. *England under the Angevin Kings,* 2 vols. London and New York: Macmillan, 1887.

_____. 'The Alleged Condemnation of King John by the Court of France in 1202'. *Transactions of the Royal Historical Society* 14 (1900): 53–67.

_____. *John Lackland.* London and New York: Macmillan, 1902.

Ormrod, W. M., R. Bonney and M. Bonney (eds). *Crises, Revolutions and Self-Sustained. Growth: Essays in European Fiscal History 1130–1830.* Stamford: Shaun Tyas, 1999.

Otway-Ruthven, A. J. *A History of Medieval Ireland.* London: Ernest Benn Ltd, 1968.

Painter, S. *The Reign of King John.* Baltimore: Johns Hopkins University Press, 1949.

_____. 'The Houses of Lusignans and Chatellerault 1150–1250'. *Speculum* 30 (1955): 374–84.

_____. 'Castellans of the Plain of Poitou in the Eleventh and Twelfth Centuries'. *Speculum* 31 (1956): 243–57.

_____. *William Marshal Knight-Errant, Baron and Regent of England.* New York: Barnes and Noble, 1995.

Petit-Dutaillis, C. *Studies and Notes Supplementary to Stubbs' Constitutional History; Down to the Great Charter.* Manchester: Manchester University Press, 1908.

_____. *The Feudal Monarchy in France and England from the Tenth to the Thirteenth Century,* trans. E. D. Hunt. New York: Harper and Row, 1964.

Poole, A. L. *The Obligations of Society in the 12th and 13th Centuries: The Ford Lectures Delivered in the University of Oxford in Michaelmas Term 1944.* Oxford: Oxford University Press, 1946.

_____. *Domesday to Magna Carta 1087–1216.* Oxford: Oxford University Press, 1955.

Power, D. 'What did the frontier of Angevin Normany Comprise?' *Anglo-Norman Studies* 17 (1994): 181–201.

_____. *The Norman Frontier in the Twelfth and Thirteenth Centuries.* Cambridge, New York, Port Chester, Melbourne and Sydney: Cambridge University Press, 2004.

Powicke, F. M. 'The Angevin Administration of Normandy'. *English Historical Review* 21 (1906): 625–49.

_____. 'King John and Arthur of Brittany'. *English Historical Review* 24 (1909): 659–74.

_____. *The Loss of Normandy 1189–1204.* Manchester: Manchester University Press, 1999.

Ramsey, J. H. *The Angevin Empire.* London: S. Sonnenschein & Co., 1903.

Reynolds, S. *Fiefs and Vassals.* Oxford and New York: Oxford University Press, 1994.

Richardson H. G. 'Review of Boussard, Le Governement d'Henri II'. *English Historical Review* 73 (1958): 659–63.

Richardson H. G. and G. O Sayles. *The Governance of Medieval England from the Conquest to Magna Carta.* Edinburgh: Edinburgh University Press, 1963.

Rothwell, H. (ed.) *English Historical Documents 1189–1327.* Oxford and New York: Oxford University Press, 1975.

Saul, N. *A Companion to Medieval England 1066–1485*. Stroud: Tempus, 2005.

Sayers, J. *Innocent III: Leader of Europe 1198–1216*. London: Longman, 1994.

Shakespeare, W. *King John*. London and New York: Penguin, 1974.

Southern, R. W. *Medieval Humanism and Other Studies*. New York: Harper and Row, 1970.

Stenton, D. M. *English Society in the Early Middle Ages, 1066–1307*. London: Penguin, 1951.

———. *English Justice between the Norman Conquest and the Great Charter, 1066–1215*. Philadelphia: The American Philosophical Society, 1964.

Strevett, N. 'The Anglo-Norman Civil War of 1101 Reconsidered'. *Anglo-Norman Studies* 24 (2004): 159–65.

Stubbs, W. *Constitutional History of England*, 3 vols. Oxford: Clarendon Press, 1897.

———. 'The historical collections of Walter of Coventry', in *Historical Introductions to the Rolls Series*, ed. A. Hassall. New York: Haskell House Publishers Ltd, 1902.

Swanton, M. (ed.) *The Anglo-Saxon Chronicles*. London: Pheonix Press, 2000.

Tabuteau, E. 'The Role of Law in the Succession to Normandy and England 1087'. *Haskins Society Journal* 3 (1991): 141–69.

Tanner, J. R., C. W. Previte-Orton and Z. N Brooke. *The Cambridge Medieval History*, vol. 6, *Victory of the Papacy*. Cambridge: Cambridge University Press, 1936.

Turner, R. V. 'King John in his context: A comparison with his contemporaries'. *Haskins Society* 3 (1991): 183–95.

———. 'King John's Military Reputation Reconsidered'. *Journal of Medieval History* 19 (1993): 171–200.

———. 'The Problem of Survival for the Angevin Empire'. *American Historical Review* 100 (1995): 78–96.

———. 'Richard Lionheart and English Episcopal Elections'. *Albion* 29 (1997): 1–13.

———. *King John England's Evil King?* Stroud: Tempus, 2005.

Turner, R. V. and R. H. Heiser. *The Reign of Richard the Lionheart: Ruler of the Angevin Empire 1189–1199*. Harlow: Longman, 2000.

Tyerman, C. J. *Who's Who in Early Medieval England*. London: Shepheard-Walwyn, 1996.

Ullmann, W. *A Short History of the Papacy in the Middle Ages*. London: Methuen & Co. Ltd, 1972.

Vaughan, R. *Matthew Paris*. London: Cambridge University Press, 1958.

Vincent, N. *Peter des Roches, An Alien in English Politics 1205–1238*. London: Cambridge University Press, 1996.

Wales, Gerald of. *Concerning the Instruction of Princes*, trans. J. Stevenson in *English Historical Documents II*. London: Seeley, 1858. Facsimile reprint by J. M. F. Books (Felinfach, 1991).

Warren, W. L. 'The Historian as "Private Eye"'. *Historical Studies* 9 (1974): 1–18.

———. *The Governance of Norman and Angevin England 1086–1271*. London: Edward Arnold, 1987.

———. 'Painter's King John: Forty Years On. An address to the *Haskins Society Conference*'. *Haskins Society Journal* 1 (1989): 1–9.

———. *King John*. New Haven: Yale University Press, 1997.

———. *Henry II*. New Haven: Yale University Press, 2000.

Weir, A. *Eleanor of Aquitaine*. London: Jonathan Cape, 1999.

Wendover, R. *Flowers of History*, trans. J. A. Giles, 2 vols. London: Bohn, 1869.

Westminster, Matthew of. *Flowers of History*, trans. C. D. Yonge, 2 vols. London: Bohn, 1853.

FURTHER READING

Source Material and Commentaries

Carpenter, D. A. 'Abbot Ralph of Coggeshall's Account of the Last Years of King Richard and the First Years of King John'. *English Historical Review* 113 (1998): 1210–30.

Cheney, C. R. and W. H. Semple (eds). *Selected Letters of Pope Innocent III*. London and New York: Thomas Nelson and Sons Ltd, 1953.

Chibnall, Marjorie (trans.), *The Ecclesiastical History of Orderic Vitalis*, vol. 6. Oxford: Clarendon Press, 1968–1980.

Devizes, Richard of. *The Chronicle of Richard Devizes of the Time of Richard*, ed. J. T. Appleby. London and New York: Thomas Nelson and Sons Ltd, 1963.

Douglas, D. and G. W. Greenaway (eds). *English Historical Documents 1042–1189, vol. 2*. London and New York: Evre Methuen Ltd, 1953.

Flower, C. T. *Introduction to the curia Regis rolls 1199–1230*. Publications of the Seldon Society 62. London: B. Quaritch, 1944.

Galbraith, V. H. *Roger Wendover and Matthew Paris*. Glasgow: University of Glasgow, 1944.

Given-Wilson, C. *Chronicles: The Writing of History in Medieval England*. Hambledon and London: Continuum International Publishing Group, 2004.

Gransden, A. *Historical Writing in England 550c.–1307*, vol 1. London: Routledge and Kegan Paul, 1974.

Hallam, E. (ed.) *The Plantagenet Chronicles*. London: Guild Publishing Ltd, 1986.

Hardy, T. D. (ed.) *Rotuli Litterarum Patentium 1201–1216*. London: Record Commission, 1835.

Hassal, A. (ed.) *Historical Introductions to Rolls Series*. London: Longmans, Green, and Co., 1902.

Holden, J. A. (ed.) *History of William the Marshal*, vols 1–3, trans. S. Gregory with notes by D. Crouch. London: Anglo-Norman Text Society, 2004.

Howden, Roger of. *The Annals of Roger de Hoveden*, trans. H. T. Riley. London: Bohn, 1853.

Jones, W. Lewis. 'Latin Chroniclers from the Eleventh to the Thirteenth Centuries', in *The Cambridge History of English and American Literature*, vol. 1, ed. A. W. Ward and A. R. Waller. Cambridge: Cambridge University Press, 1901–1921.

Newburgh, W. *History*. Medieval Sourcebook.

Rothwell, H. (ed.) *English Historical Documents 1189–1327*. Oxford and New York: Oxford University Press, 1975.

Shakespeare, W. *King John*. London and New York: Penguin, 1974.

Stubbs, W. 'The historical collections of Walter of Coventry', in *Historical Introductions to the Rolls Series*, ed. A. Hassall. New York: Haskell House Publishers Ltd, 1902.

Swanton, M. (ed.) *The Anglo-Saxon Chronicles*. London: Pheonix Press, 2000.

Vaughan, R. *Matthew Paris*. London: Cambridge University Press, 1958.

Wales, Gerald of. *Concerning the Instruction of Princes*, trans. J. Stevenson in *English Historical Documents II*. London: Seeley, 1858. Facsimile reprint by J. M. F. Books (Felinfach, 1991).

Wendover, R. *Flowers of History*, trans. J. A. Giles. 2 vols. London: Bohn, 1869.

Westminster, Matthew of. *Flowers of History*, trans. C. D. Yonge, 2 vols. London: Bohn, 1853.

General Histories

Appleby, J. T. *England without Richard*. London: 1965.

Barlow, F. B. *The Feudal Kingdom of England 1042–1216*. 5th ed. London and New York: Longman, 1999.

Bartlett, R. *England under the Norman and Angevin Kings 1075–1225*. New York: Oxford University Press, 2000.

Bossy, J. and P. Jupp (eds). *Essays Presented to Michael Roberts*. Belfast: Blackstaff Press, 1976.

Britnell, R., R. Frame and M. Prestwich (eds). *Thirteenth Century England VI: Proceedings of the Durham Conference of 1995*. Woodbridge: Boydell and Brewer, 1997.

Carpenter, D. A. *The Struggle for Mastery: The Penguin History of Britain 1066–1284*. London: Penguin, 2003.

Church, S. D. (ed.) *King John New Interpretations*. Woodbridge: Boydell and Brewer, 1999.

Clanchy, M. T. *England and Its Rulers 1066–1272*. 2nd ed. Oxford and Malden, MA: Blackwell, 1998.

Crouch, D. *William Marshal*. London: Longman, 1990.

Galbraith, V. H. 'Good kings and bad kings in medieval English history'. *History* 30 (1945): 119–32.

Green, J. R. *Short History of the English People*. London: Folio Society, 1992.

Harvey, J. *The Plantagenets*. London: Severn House Publishers Ltd, 1948.

Huscroft, R. *Ruling England 1042–1217*. London: Longman, 2005.

Mortimer, R. *Angevin England 1154–1258*. Oxford and Cambridge, MA: Blackwell, 1994.

Montefiore, S. S. *Monsters: History's Most Evil Men and Women*. London: Quercus Publishing, 2008.

Norgate, K. *England under the Angevin Kings*, 2 vols. London and New York: Macmillan, 1887.

Petit-Dutaillis, C. *The Feudal Monarchy in France and England from the Tenth to the Thirteenth Century*, trans. E. D. Hunt. New York: Harper and Row, 1964.

Poole, A. L. *Domesday to Magna Carta 1087–1216*. Oxford: Oxford University Press, 1955.

Saul, N. *A Companion to Medieval England 1066–1485*. Stroud: Tempus, 2005.

Stenton, D. M. *English Society in the Early Middle Ages, 1066–1307*. London: Penguin, 1951.

Tanner, J. R., C. W. Previte-Orton and Z. N Brooke. *The Cambridge Medieval History*, vol. 6, *Victory of the Papacy*. Cambridge: Cambridge University Press, 1936.

Turner, R. V. and R. H. Heiser. *The Reign of Richard the Lionheart: Ruler of the Angevin Empire 1189–1199*. Harlow: Longman, 2000.

Tyerman, C. J. *Who's Who in Early Medieval England*. London: Shepheard-Walwyn, 1996.

Leading Personalities

Baldwin, J. W. *The Government of Philip Augustus*. Berkeley: University of California Press, 1986.

Barber, R. *Henry Plantagenet*. Totowa: Rowman and Littlefield, 1964.

Bradbury, J. *Philip Augustus, King of France 1180–1223*. London: Longman, 1998.

Carpenter, D. A. *The Minority of Henry III*. Berkeley: University of California Press, 1990.

Cheney, C. R. *Innocent III and England*. Stuttgart: Hiersemann, 1976.

Crouch, D. *William Marshal*. London: Longman, 1990.

Gillingham, J. *Richard the Lionhart*. London: Book Club Associates, 1978.

_____. *Richard I*. New Haven and London: Yale University Press, 2002.

Harper-Bill, C. and N. Vincent (eds). *Henry II: New Interpretations*. Woodbridge: Boydell & Brewer, 2007.

Hollister, C. W. 'King John and the Historians'. *Journal of British Studies* 1 (1961): 1–19.

Holt, J. C. *King John*. London: Historical Association, 1963.

Jones, J. A. P. *King John and Magna Carta*. London: Longman, 1971.

Levin, C. 'A Good Prince: King John and Early Tudor Propaganda'. *Sixteenth Century Journal* 11 (1980): 23–32.

_____. *Propaganda in the English Reformation: Heroic and Villainous Images of King John*. Lewiston, New York: Edwin Mellen Press, 1988.

Little, A. G. 'Review of John Lackland by K. Norgate'. *English Historical Review* 18 (1903): 349–50.

Lloyd, A. *King John*. Newton Abbot: David and Charles, 1973.

Markowski, M. 'Richard Lionheart: Bad king, bad crusader?' *Journal of Modern History* 23 (1997): 351–65.

McLynn, F. *Lionheart and Lackland: King Richard, King John and the Wars of Conquest*. London: Vintage Books, 2007.

Norgate, K. *John Lackland*. London and New York: Macmillan, 1902.

Painter, S. *The Reign of King John*. Baltimore: Johns Hopkins University Press, 1949.

_____. *William Marshal Knight-Errant, Baron and Regent of England*. New York: Barnes and Noble, 1995.

Sayers, J. *Innocent III Leader of Europe 1198–1216*. London: Longman, 1994.

Turner, R. V. 'King John in his context: A comparison with his contemporaries'. *Haskins Society* 3 (1991): 183–195.

_____. 'King John's Military Reputation Reconsidered'. *Journal of Medieval History* 19 (1993): 171–200.

_____. 'Richard Lionheart and English Episcopal Elections'. *Albion* 29 (1997): 1–13.

_____. *King John England's Evil King?* Stroud: Tempus, 2005.

Warren, W. L. 'What was wrong with King John?' *History Today* 7 (1957).

_____. 'The Historian as "Private Eye"'. *Historical Studies* 9 (1974): 1–18.

_____. 'Painter's King John: Forty Years On. An address to the Haskins Society Conference'. *Haskins Society Journal* 1 (1989): 1–9.

_____. *King John*. New Haven: Yale University Press, 1997.

_____. *Henry II*. New Haven: Yale University Press, 2000.

Weir, A. *Eleanor of Aquitaine*. London: Jonathan Cape, 1999.

Angevin Empire

Aurell, M. *The Plantagenet Empire 1154–1224*, trans. D. Crouch. Harlow: Pearson Longman, 2007.

Bachrach, B. S. 'The Idea of the Angevin Empire'. *Albion* 10 (1978): 294–9.

Barratt, N. 'Lackland: The loss of Normandy in 1215'. *History Today* 54, Issue 3 (2004).

Bates, D. 'Normandy and England after 1066'. *English Historical Review* 104 (1989): 851–880.

Bates, D. and A. Curry (eds). *England and Normandy in the Middle Ages*. London: The Hambledon Press, 1994.

Benjamin, R. 'Angevin Empire'. *History Today* 36, Issue 2 (1986).

Davies, R. R. *The First English Empire: Power and Identities in British Isles 1093–1334*. Oxford and New York: Oxford University Press, 2000.

Gillingham, J. 'The Fall of the Angevin Empire'. *History Today* 36, Issue 4 (1986).

_____. *The Angevin Empire*. London: Hodder Arnold, 2001.

Green, J. A. 'Unity and Disunity in Anglo-Norman State'. *Historical Research* 62 (1989): 115–34.

_____. *The Aristocracy of Norman England*. Cambridge, New York, Melbourne, Madrid and Cape Town: Cambridge University Press, 1997.

Hollister, C. W. 'The Anglo-Norman Civil War'. *English Historical Review* 88 (1973): 315–333.

_____. 'Normandy, France and the Anglo-Norman Regnum'. *Speculum* 51 (1976): 202–42.

Hollister C. W. and T. K. Keefe 'The Making of the Angevin Empire'. *Journal of British Studies* 12 (1973): 1–25.

Holt, J. C. 'The end of the Anglo-Norman Realm'. *Proceedings of the British Academy* 61 (1975): 223–65.

_____. 'Alienor d'Aquitaine, Jean san Terre et la succession de 1199'. *Cahiers de Civilisation Medievale* 29 (1986): 95–100.

_____. 'King John and Arthur of Brittany'. *Nottingham Medieval Studies* 44 (2000): 82–103.

Jones, M. and M. Vale (eds). *England and her Neighbours, 1066–1453: Essays in Honour of P. Chaplais*. London: The Hambledon Press, 1989.

Keefe, T. K. 'Geoffrey Plantagenet's Will and the Angevin Succession'. *Albion* 6 (1974): 266–74.

Le Patourel, J. 'The Plantagenet Dominions'. *History* 50 (1965): 289–308.

_____. *Normandy and England 1066–1144*. Reading: University of Reading, 1970.

_____. *The Norman Empire*. Oxford: Oxford University Press, 1976.

_____. *Feudal Empires, Norman and Plantagenet*. London: The Hambledon Press, 1984.

_____. 'Angevin Successions and the Angevin Empire'. *Nottingham Medieval Studies* 44 (2000): 82–103.

Norgate, K. 'The Alleged Condemnation of King John by the Court of France in 1202'. *Transactions of the Royal Historical Society* 14 (1900): 53–67.

Painter, S. 'Castellans of the Plain of Poitou in the Eleventh and Twelfth Centuries'. *Speculum* 31 (1956): 243–57.

_____. 'The Houses of Lusignans and Chatellerault 1150–1250'. *Speculum* 30 (1955): 374–84.

Power, D. 'What did the frontier of Angevin Normany Comprise?' *Anglo-Norman Studies* 17 (1994): 181–201.

_____. *The Norman Frontier in the Twelfth and Thirteenth Centuries*. Cambridge, New York, Port Chester, Melbourne and Sydney: Cambridge University Press, 2004.

Powicke, F. M. 'The Angevin Administration of Normandy'. *English Historical Review* 21 (1906): 625–49.

_____. 'King John and Arthur of Brittany'. *English Historical Review* 24 (1909): 659–74.

_____. 'The Angevin Administration of Normandy'. *English Historical Review* 21 (1906): 625–49.

Ramsey, J. H. *The Angevin Empire*. London: S. Sonnenschein & Co., 1903.

Turner, R. V. 'The Problem of Survival for the Angevin Empire'. *American Historical Review* 100 (1995): 78–96.

The Church

Barraclough, G. *The Medieval Papacy*. London: Thames and Hudson, 1968.

Cheney, C. R. 'King John's Reaction to the Interdict on England'. *Transactions of the Royal Historical Society* 31 (1949): 129–150.

_____. *From Becket to Langton English Church Government 1170–1213*. Manchester: Manchester University Press, 1956.

_____. *The Papacy and England 12th–14th Centuries*. London: Variorum Reprints, 1982.

Hemholz, R. H. 'Review of Cheney *The Papacy and England 12th–14th Centuries*'. *Merican Journal of Legal History* 28 (1984): 90–1.

Knowles, M. D. 'The Canterbury Election of 1205–1206'. *English Historical Review* 53 (1938): 211–20.

Ullmann, W. *A Short History of the Papacy in the Middle Ages*. London: Methuen & Co. Ltd, 1972.

Britain

Church, S. D. 'The 1210 campaign in Ireland: Evidence for a military revolution?' *Anglo-Norman Studies* 20 (1998): 51.

Cosgrove, A. (ed.) *A New History of Ireland: Volume II Medieval Ireland 1169–1534*. Oxford and New York: Oxford University Press, 2008.

Curtis, E. *A History of Medieval Ireland from 1086 to 1513*. London: Methuen, 1938.

Davies, R. R. (ed.) *The British Isles 1100–1500*. Edinburgh: John Donald Publishers Ltd, 1988.

_____. *Domination and Conquest: The Experience of Ireland, Scotland and Wales, 1100–1300*. Cambridge, New York, Port Chester, Melbourne and Sydney: Cambridge University Press, 1990.

_____. *Age of Conquest*. Oxford and New York: Oxford University Press, 2000.

Duffy, S. 'King John's Expedition to Ireland, 1210: The Evidence Reconsidered'. *Irish Historical Studies* 30 (1996): 1–24.

Holden, B. W. 'King John, the Braoses and the Celtic Fringe, 1207–1216'. *Albion* 33 (2001): 1–23.

Lydon, J. F. *The Lordship of Ireland in the Middle Ages*. Dublin: Gill and Macmillan, 1972.

_____. (ed.) *England and Ireland in the Later Middle Ages: Essays in Honour of Jocelyn Otway-Ruthven*. Dublin: Irish Academic Press, 1981.

Otway-Ruthven, A. J. *A History of Medieval Ireland*. London: Ernest Benn Ltd, 1968.

France

Baldwin, J. W. 'Persona et Gesta: The Image and Deeds of the Thirteenth-Century Capetians: The Case of Philip Augustus'. *Viator* 19 (1988): 195–207.

Duby, G. *The Legend of Bouvines, War, Religion and Culture in the Middle Ages*, trans. C. Tihanyi. Berkeley: University of California Press, 1990.

Dunbabin, J. *France in the Making 843–1180*. Oxford and New York: Oxford University Press, 2000.

Fawtier, R. *The Capetian Kings of France: Monarchy and Nation, 987–1328*. trans. L. Butler and R. J. Adam. London: Macmillan, 1960.

Hallam E. and J. Everard. *Capetian France 987–1328*. 2nd ed. New York: Longman, 2001.

Governance and Economy

Barratt, N. 'The Revenue of King John'. *English Historical Review* 111 (1996): 835–55.

Chrimes S. B., 'An Introduction to the Administrative History of Mediaeval England', in *Studies in Medieval History*, vol. 7, ed. G. Barraclough. Oxford: Blackwell, 1952.

Church, S. D. 'The rewards of royal service in the household of King John: A dissenting opinion'. *English Historical Review* 110 (1995): 277–302.

———. 'Aspects of the English royal succession, 1066–1199: The death of the king'. *Anglo-Norman Studies* 29 (2007): 17–34.

Harvey, P. D. A. 'The English Inflation of 1180–1220'. *Past and Present* 61 (1973): 3–30.

Jolliffe, J. E. A. *Angevin Kingship*. London: Black, 1963.

Keefe, T. K. *Feudal Assessments and the Political Community under Henry II and His Sons*. Berkeley: University of California Press, 1983.

King, E. B. *Law in Medieval Life and Thought*. Sewanee: University of the South Press, 1990.

Lyon, B. *A Constitutional and Legal History of Medieval England*. New York: Norton, 1960.

Ormrod, W. M., R. Bonney and M. Bonney (eds). *Crises, Revolutions and Self-Sustained. Growth: Essays in European Fiscal History 1130–1830*. Stamford: Shaun Tyas, 1999.

Petit-Dutaillis, C. *The Feudal Monarchy in France and England from the Tenth to the Thirteenth century*, trans. E. D. Hunt. New York: Harper and Row, 1964.

Poole, A. L. *The Obligations of Society in the 12th and 13th Centuries: The Ford Lectures Delivered in the University of Oxford in Michaelmas Term 1944*. Oxford: Oxford University Press, 1946.

Prestwich, J. O, J. C. Holt and J. Gillingham (eds). *War and Government in the Middle Ages: Essays in Honour of J. O. Prestwich*. Woodbridge: Boydell, 1984.

Reynolds, S. *Fiefs and Vassals*. Oxford and New York: Oxford University Press, 1994.

Richardson H. G. and G. O. Sayles. *The Governance of Medieval England from the Conquest to Magna Carta*. Edinburgh: Edinburgh University Press, 1963.

Southern, R. W. *Medieval Humanism and Other Studies*. New York: Harper and Row, 1970.

Stenton, D. M. *English Justice between the Norman Conquest and the Great Charter, 1066–1215*. Philadelphia: The American Philosophical Society, 1964.

Stubbs, W. *Constitutional History of England*, 3 vols. Oxford: Clarendon Press, 1897.

Warren, W. L. *The Governance of Norman and Angevin England 1086–1271*. London: Edward Arnold, 1987.

Magna Carta and Civil War

Danziger, D. and J. Gillingham. *1215: The Year of the Magna Carta*. London: Hodder and Stroughton, 2004.

Fryde, N. F. *Why Magna Carta? Angevin England Revisited*. London and New Brunswick: Transaction Publishers, 2001.

Hindley, G. *A Brief History of Magna Carta*. Philadelphia, New York and London: Running Press, 2008.

Hollister, C. W. *Monarchy Magnates and Institutions in the Anglo-Norman World*. London: Hambledon Press, 1986.

Holt, J. C. 'The Barons and the Great Charter'. *English Historical Review* 274 (1955): 1–24.

———. *The Northerners: A Study in the Reign of King John*. Oxford: Oxford University Press, 1961.

———. *Magna Carta and the Idea of Liberty*. New York: John Wiley and Sons, 1972.

———. *Magna Carta and Medieval Government*. London: Hambledon Press, 1985.

———. *Magna Carta*. 2nd ed. Cambridge and New York: Cambridge University Press, 1992.

Loengard, J. S. *Magna Carta and the England of King John*. Woodbridge: Boydell and Brewer, 2010.

McGlynn, S. 'King John and the Barons Revolt'. *BBC History Magazine*, June 2010, 25–9.

Miller, E. 'The background of Magna Carta'. *Past and Present* 23 (1962): 72–83.

QUESTIONS

Chapter 1

1) Outline the arguments and processes used by historians seeking to redeem King John from his malign reputation.

Chapter 2

1) 'Rivalry with his brothers and awareness of their resentment over his father's schemes to find land for him must have influenced John's character.' R. V. Turner. What were these 'schemes' and in what ways, and to what extent, do you think they may have affected the young John?
2) For what reasons had William of Newburgh judged John to be 'Nature's Enemy'? To what extent do you agree with Newburgh's judgement?

Chapter 3

1) What do you understand by the term 'Angevin empire'?
2) In what ways was the 'empire' inherited by John naturally fissiparous, disposed to split apart?

Chapter 4

1) Outline the main phases in John's relations with Philip Augustus, 1199–1204.
2) In what ways did John gain more than he conceded according to the Treaty of Le Goulet in 1200?
3) How far do you agree that the main reason John lost Normandy was because of what Wendover called his 'incorrigible idleness'?

Chapter 5

1) 'Energetic but misjudged and misguided.' How far do you agree with this interpretation of the schemes devised by John to win back the lost continental territories, 1205–1214?
2) Consider how the remainder of John's reign may have developed if his forces had won at Bouvines.

Chapter 6

1) 'John's British achievement was significant and lasting.' To what extent do you agree?
2) 'The destruction of the House of Briouze is one of the most important events of King John's reign.' To what extent do you agree with this judgement?

Chapter 7

1) What were the origins of John's struggle with the papacy and why did this conflict last so long?
2) Assess the view that the conflict between John and Pope Innocent III was a conflict more about personalities than principles.

Chapter 8

1) In what ways does the so-called record evidence contradict the impression of John presented in the chronicle material? In what ways, and why, is it possible to trust the record evidence more than the chronicle material?
2) How able a ruler was John in domestic policy areas?

Chapter 9

1) 'Not forward-thinking visionaries seeking a great assertion of principle, but feudal reactionaries hankering after office and privilege.' To what extent do you agree with this view of the barons who participated in the formulation of Magna Carta?
2) How far do you agree that Magna Carta is first and foremost a complaint about Angevin despotism in general rather than a particular lament about the actions of King John?

Chapter 10

1) Assess the view that the civil war of 1215–16 was more the result of baronial actions than John's own actions.

2) To what extent does John deserve the epithet 'Softsword'?

INDEX

Page numbers in boldface refer to figures. Numbers in italics refer to chronicle and record material documents.

24379097R00144

Printed in Great Britain
by Amazon